W9-BYL-868

791.4334 VIS
Vischer, Phil.
Me, myself, & Bob :

w714   JUN   2007

3   w
·/10 7/16

WITHDRAWN

Me, Myself & Bob

PROPERTY OF CLPL

Me, Myself & Bob

A True Story about God, Dreams, and Talking Vegetables

Phil Vischer

NELSON BOOKS
A Division of Thomas Nelson Publishers
Since 1798

www.thomasnelson.com

© 2006 Phil Vischer. All rights reserved. No portion of this book may be reproduced, stored in a retrieval system, or transmitted in any form or by any means—electronic, mechanical, photocopy, recording, or any other—except for brief quotation in printed reviews, without the prior permission of the publisher.

Nelson Books may be purchased in bulk for educational, business, fund-raising, or sales promotional use. For information, please e-mail SpecialMarkets@ThomasNelson.com.

Published by W Publishing Group, a Division of Thomas Nelson, Inc., P.O. Box 141000, Nashville, Tennessee 37214.

All Scripture quotations, unless otherwise indicated, are taken from *The Holy Bible,* New International Version (NIV). Copyright © 1973, 1978, 1984, International Bible Society. Used by permission of Zondervan.

Library of Congress Cataloging-in-Publication Data

Vischer, Phil.
   Me, myself, and Bob : a grown-up book about God, dreams, and talking vegetables / Phil Vischer.
     p. cm.
   ISBN-13: 978-0-7852-2207-1 (hbk.)
   ISBN-10: 0-7852-2207-3
   1. Vischer, Phil. 2. Motion picture producers and directors—United States—Biography. 3. Animators—United States—Biography. 4. Big Idea Productions. I. Title.
PN1998.3.V566A3 2007
791.43'34092—dc22
[B]   2006032315

Printed in the United States of America
07 08 09 10 QW 5 4 3 2

Contents

Introduction

T echnically, the cucumber came first.

By that I mean he was created first. The cucumber. Larry. But he was alone, and it was not good. So I gave him a sidekick. A tomato. Named Bob. Larry was the loveable goofball—the guy who would entertain your kids at a birthday party. But Bob had ambition. The first words that ever came out of his mouth were, in fact, "I have a dream . . . ." Bob was a dreamer. Bob wanted to change the world. Like me.

Have you ever had a dream?

If you responded, "Sure, I was at my high school reunion—in my underwear," well, that's not what I mean. Unlike, say, *walrus* or *taco*, *dream* is a word with more than one meaning. According to Webster, in fact, it has four.

Dream (*n.*):

1. A series of thoughts, images, or emotions occurring during sleep.
2. An experience of waking life having the characteristics of a dream.

3. Something notable for its beauty, excellence, or enjoyable quality.

4. A strongly desired goal or purpose.

That whole "high school reunion/underwear" thing was a "type 1" dream. (At least I hope it was. If not, you may need to look at Webster's definition of *therapy*.) What I am referring to is a "type 4" dream: "a strongly desired goal or purpose," or, to put it another way, a deep longing.

I had a dream. I wanted my stories to make the world a better place. I wanted to build the next Disney. Be the next Disney. And as of September 26, 2002, everything appeared to be working perfectly. I had led the team that created and launched VeggieTales, the most successful direct-to-video series in history. I had built the largest animation studio between the coasts. And that night found me standing in front of a cheering throng at the premier of our first animated feature film, choking back tears as I stared out at the happy faces of hundreds of friends and coworkers.

They weren't tears of joy.

Unlike most of the artists and animators in the room that night, I knew just how deceiving appearances can be. I knew that more than half of them would lose their jobs the very next day. I knew that the company and ministry I had built in 12 years of often exasperating work was on the verge of disintegrating—collapsing right before my eyes. Most perplexingly, I knew that God knew it, too. He knew about the financial crisis and the impending layoff of so many good people. He knew about the looming death of this work that had benefited so many families around the world—that had inspired hundreds of young Christian filmmakers and earned kudos from skeptics of Christian art like *Time Magazine* and the *New York Times*. He knew how hard we had worked. He knew how far we had come. And it appeared, from where I sat, that he was going to do nothing to help us.

Have you ever had a dream? Give me a few hours to tell you my story, a story that begs to be told from the beginning, where a young boy in Iowa dreams of doing God's work—with a movie camera.

It goes something like this.

1

Muscatine and Me

E velyn Schauland was a fancy woman.

I always liked stories that start with a really great line, like "It was the best of times, it was the worst of times," or "They call me Ishmael." So I wrestled around a bit and came up with "Evelyn Schauland was a fancy woman." Not bad, eh? I mean, maybe it isn't "In the beginning, God created the heavens and the earth," but it's got some rhythm. And the best part is, it's true.

But first, let me go back to the very beginning. I was born in Muscatine, Iowa, a town of about 25,000 people on the banks of the Mississippi River. If you're like most folks, you've probably never heard of Muscatine, Iowa. If you aren't from the Midwest, you may not even be sure which one is Iowa and which one is Ohio. We get that a lot. For the record, Iowa is the one with all the corn, right across the Mississippi from Illinois. (And that's a silent s in Illinois. Same with Des Moines. Which is in Iowa. But not the same with Des Plaines, which is in Illinois. It has noisy s's. Don't ask me why, because I don't know. I'm pretty sure we can blame the French, though.) As for Muscatine—well, if you look at a map of Iowa, you'll notice that the eastern edge, the one on the

Mississippi, looks sort of like a face. A man's face, to be exact, with a big ol' nose in the middle and a little beard hanging off at the bottom. And if you look at it that way, Muscatine is very easy to find because, well, it's the nostril. I was born in Iowa's nostril.

You might expect growing up in a state's nostril to be an olfactorily intriguing experience, and, in that regard, Muscatine did not disappoint. My childhood memories of Muscatine are dominated by two very strong and not entirely pleasant odors. The first emanated from the Kent Feed plant on the south side of Muscatine, not far from the church we attended. I don't know much about the Kent Feed Company, but I do know that any product whose name implies that its primary purpose is to be eaten should not emit such a foul odor during its manufacture.

The second strong odor resided in the middle of Muscatine, near the house of my grade school years, and arose from a large Heinz ketchup factory. Now, you may be thinking, "Ketchup! Yum!" And having a ketchup factory in the middle of town was *kind* of fun, in particular during harvesttime every year when all the roads leading to the plant were covered with smashed tomatoes. (Insert VeggieTales joke here.) But before you get too jealous, spread some ketchup—Heinz or otherwise—around your kitchen table, let it get nice and warm, and then smell it. It smells terrible. Ketchup is made with vinegar, and that is exactly how the middle of Muscatine smelled when the wind blew past the ketchup plant on a warm day.

If you're paying attention (and I hope you are, because otherwise none of this will make sense when you reach the end), you've probably noticed that Muscatine was not exactly a sleepy little farm community. It was an industrial town. Besides the Kent Feed plant and the Heinz factory, the Muscatine of my youth also hosted the world headquarters of HON Industries, a large office furniture manufacturer, and Bandag, the world's largest retreader of truck tires. As much as I've always liked really cool office furniture (don't ask me why—it's a strange, lifelong fascination), my family connection was with Bandag, the world's largest retreader of truck tires. My grandfather, you see, was the executive vice president of sales and marketing at Bandag, having helped grow the company from almost nothing to an international concern with dealerships in more than a hundred countries. My father was Bandag's vice president of advertising, reporting to his father for the entire fourteen years he worked for the company. This, in hindsight, may not have been the best choice.

But I digress.

Evelyn Schauland was a fancy woman. Yes. That's where I started, and here we are back again. Her dyed blond hair was always freshly styled in one of those amazing 1970s configurations that seemed more architectural than biological. Her pantsuits were immaculate and colorful. As mayor of Muscatine through much of my childhood, she was as close to royalty as we got, and she looked the part.

Which only made it more embarrassing when my father dumped her into the Mississippi River.

Okay, not exactly into the river *itself*, but rather into the mud along the western banks (which, from the point of view of a pantsuit, may actually be worse). And it really wasn't his fault, you see, because she was in a hot air balloon. The Bandag hot air balloon, to be exact. It was a publicity stunt—my dad taking the mayor up in the Bandag hot air balloon. And I'm sure it would have been a huge success if it weren't for the unexpected wind that grabbed the balloon—and the fancy mayor—and sent them swiftly out toward the big river. Fortunately, the quick-thinking pilot was able to set the balloon down before the wind could carry them out over the river and on to Illinois, where, undoubt-edly, the fancy mayor would have been captured and held for ran-som. Given that interstate hostage situations seldom make good press, especially when your company logo is emblazoned all over the interloping vehicle, we believe the best decision was made. Nonetheless, the balloon came down in Mississippi mud, and the mayoral pantsuit was soiled.

This was rather embarrassing for my father. But none of that was on my young mind at the time. None of that was responsible for the nagging ache in my gut. No, what I couldn't stop thinking about was the fact that the entire incident took place on Sunday morning. When my father should have been in church. In all my life I had never known either of my parents to miss church for anything short of hospitalization, and yet here was my father skipping church for a publicity stunt with the mayor. An event with no redeeming spiritual significance whatsoever.

I feared for his soul.

Beginnings

W e were a very religious family. I was in church every Sunday morning, Sunday night, and Wednesday night Awana Clubs. My parents were in church every Sunday morning, Sunday night, and Wednesday night prayer meeting. All my grandparents were in church every Sunday morning, Sunday night. . . . You get the picture. When Pastor Leonard's sermons ran long, my grandmother's pleasantly soft shoulder made them tolerable for an eight-year-old boy who would rather have been home playing with Legos. But my spiritual heritage went back farther than that.

My great-grandfather on my father's side attended A. W. Tozer's church in Toledo and occasionally hosted the now famous pastor-author in his home on Sunday afternoons for dinner and rousing theological discussions.

But wait—it gets better. My great-grandfather on my mother's side was a pioneering radio preacher, the Reverend R. R. Brown of Omaha, Nebraska. As the story goes, when Omaha's Woodman of the World insurance company launched one of middle America's most prominent early radio stations, WOAW, in 1923, they wondered what to air on their first Sunday morning.

5

Commercial radio in the United States had just begun in earnest the year before, and no one was quite sure yet what to do with all the airtime. "Let's have a church service!" someone suggested. My great-grandfather, the young, dynamic pastor of the nearby Omaha Gospel Tabernacle, got the call.

"We'd like you to preach on the radio."

"On the what?"

"The radio. You'll come to our offices and preach into a can."

"A can?"

"Yes. Your voice will go out on the airwaves, and folks will listen on their receivers at home."

"Won't they be in church?"

"Not everyone. It's for the elderly and the homebound."

Pause.

"Okay."

Thus, the new station was launched with a prayer of dedication and a word from the Good Book. A small choir sang, my great-grandfather preached into the can, and the station manager was happy.

In fact, he was so happy that he wondered, "Why not have a church service on the radio *every* Sunday morning? You know— for the elderly and the homebound!" And so was born the World Radio Congregation, a weekly broadcast that, due to the uncluttered airwaves of the '20s and '30s, could be heard in ten different midwestern states and would grow to boast an estimated listening audience of more than 100,000 people. Before Jimmy Bakker, before Pat Robertson, before James Dobson—R. R. Brown.

While still fulfilling his roles as pastor of the Omaha Gospel Tabernacle (now Christ Community Church of Omaha) and founder and director of the Okoboji Lakes Bible and Missionary Conference (still held each August in Arnolds Park, Iowa), my great-grandfather preached to his radio congregation every Sunday from 1923 until his death in 1964. Even without him, the radio show continued until 1978, at which point it was the oldest continuously broadcast radio program in America. Today R. R. Brown's picture is one of the few that hangs in both the National Religious Broadcasters Hall of Fame and the National Broadcasters Hall of Fame.

We were a very religious family. Did I say that already? Well, it's true. My mother was not allowed to work or even swim on Sundays and could not play cards at any time (with the exception of Rook, because, as far as I can tell, it's the card game Jesus's disciples played while waiting for the Holy Spirit to descend on Pentecost). My father could play cards and swim on Sundays but was not allowed to see movies. Ever. When I was about twelve years old, I took my grandfather to the first movie he had seen since his "rebellious" college years: the *Jesus* film. He fell asleep halfway through, though, because he'd already read the book and he knew how it ended. To this day my grandfather will not set foot in a movie theater, though he did make a second exception when our VeggieTales movie *Jonah* came out in theaters in 2002. I'm pretty sure he fell asleep halfway through that one too. He's exceptionally good at falling asleep.

You were more likely to find a little green man from Mars in my parents' homes than a trace of alcohol, tobacco, or cursing. The same had been true of their parents' homes. And *their* parents' homes.

While some kids might have found all the rules of a strict Christian upbringing a bit restraining, I took pride in my heritage. In the fact that my great-grandfather was a famous radio preacher. That my grandfather was always running Sunday school attendance contests and giving the winners rides in the

Bandag jet or the Bandag hot air balloon (with no Mississippi mishaps, fortunately). That my parents were always up in front, leading choir, singing, even preaching sometimes. Heck, they even had their own Christian folk band for a few years in the late 1960s—The Free Folk—touring local churches in a Dodge van with a handful of squeaky-clean college kids from our church. My dad sang and gave a mini-sermon, my mom sang and played the electric bass (even when she was eight months pregnant with my little brother, if you can picture that).

It was against this backdrop of spiritual giants that I entered the world on June 16, 1966—or 6-16-66—a date that would make other very religious folk look at me slightly askew, as if they might need to keep an eye on this one. I was born with a shock of black hair so long I would occasionally grab hold of it and pull until I screamed and screamed and turned blue. My parents made sure I kept a hat on in church and took to calling me "Flip," a nickname that stuck with me until the third grade.

My name is Phillip Roger Vischer. I was the first male grandchild on either side of my family and bear the middle names of both noteworthy great-grandfathers. I grew up in and around churches and Bible conferences. I knew lots of missionaries, and they knew me. (After all, I was one of R. R. Brown's great-grandchildren.) I also knew that overseas missions was the best thing you could possibly do with your life. Pastoring a church or preaching on the radio was pretty good too, but not nearly as good as carrying the gospel to an unreached people group. Preferably one whose language had yet to be reduced to writing. Preferably one that might consider eating you if you looked at them cross-eyed.

I knew this with my whole heart, but I didn't want to do it. I was shy like my father. The thought of traveling internationally—among strangers—was terrifying. I wanted to stay home and draw or build with Legos or make little men out of clay or build dams in the creek that ran behind our house. I liked to build things. One afternoon at my great-grandfather's Bible conference, several kids and I passed the time by building miniature cities out of twigs and clumps of moss around the base of a huge oak tree outside the dining hall. The other kids' cities were cute, but mine was the only one with a functional fire suppression system. On a family vacation in Colorado, the campground manager had to knock on the door of our rented RV to point out to my parents that the small dam I had built in his drainage ditch was, quite effectively, flooding his parking lot.

I loved to build things, and I loved TV. There was nothing better than a Saturday morning with a bowl of Count Chocula and a full two hours of the best kids' shows the big three networks could muster. Shows like *Sigmund and the Sea Monsters*, *Land of the Lost*, and those crazy-weird animated shows starring the Jackson Five, the Osmond Brothers, or the Harlem Globetrotters. Where did these shows come from? I had no idea. But with the enthusiasm most kids reserved for Christmas, I awaited the day each fall when the new Saturday morning season was announced. I also discovered the movies, and, due to my father's strict upbringing, the first movies I ever saw were also some of the first movies he ever saw. Our favorite, by far, was Walt Disney's *The Apple Dumpling Gang*, starring Tim Conway and Don Knotts, two actors who would remain my father's favorites his entire life. This was during the period when the Disney company had apparently completely forgotten how to produce animated films, so we made do with live-action "classics" like *Hot Lead and Cold Feet*, *The North Avenue Irregulars*, *The Shaggy D.A.*, and *Gus* (the field-goal-kicking mule).

Fairly early in my life I noticed my brain was weird. By that I mean that I noticed it had a way of looking at normal things from a slightly twisted angle—just twisted enough that it often made me chuckle. As I got into kindergarten and Sunday school, I tried sharing some of my brain's thoughts that had made me chuckle with the kids around me, and they chuckled too. At this point I discovered something remarkable: I was funny. Or at least the weird thoughts that frequently popped into my brain were considered funny by other kids my age. And so they laughed at my thoughts, and this convinced me that they probably liked me. So I shared more of my brain's weird thoughts, and they laughed more and more until my Sunday school teacher and my first-grade teacher each called my parents in for a "conference." I was being "disruptive" in class, they said. A few days later, my parents sat me down and we had a "talk." This was one of the first times I can remember doing anything that required both my mother and father to have a "talk" with me, and I didn't like it. Apparently I had done something terrible, and this had disappointed them. I hated disappointing my parents, so I decided I would try hard not to do that ever again, even if it meant not sharing my weird thoughts anymore. And so I stopped. I didn't stop *thinking* my weird thoughts, but I stopped sharing them. Already a quiet kid, I became quieter—so quiet that I started to feel invisible. Like no one could see me at all.

I had a few friends as a kid, but not very many, and we rarely did things together after school. I actually remember my surprise in grade school when I learned that other kids were going over to each other's houses after school and playing. *What?* I thought. *How long has this been going on?* I decided I wanted to try this amazing new thing, so one day after school I walked home with a guy I sort of knew and we played at his house for a while. But when it was time for me to head home on my own, I couldn't remember exactly how I had gotten there and ended up wandering around his neighborhood lost and in tears until a man who said he knew my uncle gave me a ride home. After that I didn't walk home with anyone. Too risky.

I know you're probably saying, "That's so sad," but it really didn't bother me much at the time. We had a nice house with three acres of woods and a creek in the backyard, and I spent my time building mud and twig dams, drawing and playing in the tree house my dad and uncle had built in our backyard. Sometimes my brother and I would have acorn wars with the neighbor kids, where we'd pelt each other with acorns and call each other the worst names we could think of, which for them were words I knew I wasn't supposed to say and for me was "fat goose."

One day near the end a particularly frustrating game of recess kickball, a friend of my older sister heard me yell in great exasperation, "For crying out loud!" and told my sister I was a doofus. I never swore as a kid. Honestly. Never. I never smoked a cigarette and I never tasted alcohol until I got to Bible college. I always wanted to follow the rules, and I never wanted to get in trouble, which is why disappointing my parents made me decide I needed to keep my funny thoughts to myself.

But a couple of things made my funny thoughts start to pop out again. The first was when my Grandpa Vischer bought me a hand puppet. It was a cute little brown fuzzy guy he had picked up somewhere, and I quickly discovered that I could bring him to life, and he could say all the funny thoughts that popped into my head while I stayed hidden behind the couch. My parents laughed, and I felt good. A few years later when I was seven or eight, I learned that you could actually make your own animated films. All you needed was a Super8 camera that shot a single frame at a time! This was marvelous news, so I ran to my

Grandpa Vischer and asked if his new Super8 movie camera could shoot single frames. He said it couldn't. Deflated, I got some film leader and tried another technique I had read about where you drew pictures directly on the tiny 8mm frames. It seemed to work, but the process was a bit too laborious for my eight-year-old attention span.

Then something remarkable happened. My dad got a big Christmas bonus and went a little bit nutty. He had always been a provider of creative playthings—model planes and trains and lots and lots of Legos. But the Christmas of my eighth year, he really outdid himself. First, we opened a portable cassette recorder for each member of the family—himself, my mom, me, my older sister, Cristy, and my younger brother, Rob. My mother, sister, and brother all gave a collective "Huh?" My weird little brain, though, said, "Whee!" I grabbed the little microphone and immediately started recording my own voice. But he wasn't finished. He walked into the other room and returned with a big, industrial-looking suitcase locked with heavy metal clasps. Inside was the most amazing thing I had ever seen—an early video camera and recorder! And by "early" I don't mean Betamax. We're talking a black-and-white industrial camera tethered to a reel-to-reel video recorder. Pre-VHS. Pre-Betamax. This was a state-of-the-art, early 1970s industrial video rig—the kind they used in community colleges to teach television production. The rest of my family was dumbstruck. I was in heaven!

I hit the ground running, shooting footage all over the house. I tried to bribe my little brother into acting out dramatic rescue scenes in the snow outside the patio doors. ("Mom! Tell Rob he has to be in my movie!") And though a video camera technically can't record single frames, if you turned it on and off really fast, maybe, just maybe . . . I put my Batmobile on the basement floor and clicked the camera on and off as quickly as I could. I nudged the Batmobile an inch and clicked the camera again. After a few minutes of this, I replayed the tape, and sure enough, the Batmobile was driving! Eureka! I was in business! I made short films with Legos and GI Joes. This was great! But with only one reel of videotape, I was constantly recording over my old films with my new films. And no matter how hard I tried, the camera wiggled every time I flicked the button on and off. My film career had begun, but I desperately needed a real film camera if I was going to go any further.

One day over at my grandfather's house, I opened the case of his Super8 film camera and looked closely. It *did* do single-frame recording! And it recorded sound! And it even had an interval-ometer, allowing single frames to be recorded at preset intervals! This sucker was loaded!

"Grandpa, can I borrow your movie camera?" "Sure, Flip! Give it a try!" He wouldn't see his camera again for ten years, by which time I had worn it out attempting every film trick imaginable.

My childhood was somewhat idyllic, what with the small river town full of potlucks, Sunday dinners with grandparents, Legos, sugared cereal and video cameras. At least, it started out that way. My grandparents lived right around the corner from us in Muscatine—my father and grandfather going to work each day at Bandag, changing the world, one truck tire at a time. My grandfather's office wall was covered with awards and press clip-pings, including a tire industry magazine cover featuring a hand-ful of executives, including my father and grandfather, walking out to the new Bandag jet under the heading "Muscatine's High Fliers." I even got to ride in the jet a few times myself. Cool.

But by my eighth year, something was changing. My parents weren't smiling much any more. My father had always been shy, and thirteen relocations before his high school graduation as his father worked his way up the corporate ladder at Firestone only exacerbated his shyness—to the point where he was voted "Most Serious" by a senior class completely unaware that he was, on the inside, hilariously funny. Early in their marriage, he and my mother talked of full-time ministry as he studied theology at St. Paul Bible College in Minnesota. But after college he found himself joining a new kind of tire company in Muscatine, Iowa, reporting to his larger-than-life father for the next fourteen years. No one could deny that my father is creatively gifted, and he advanced quickly at the growing company. Since each promotion came from *his* father, though, whispers of nepotism abounded. Each day after working with his dad, my father came home to a sometimes equally challenging character—my mother. My mother wasn't moody or ill-tempered, but rather somewhat untouchable. Growing up in the public scrutiny of a ministry-superstar family where she found herself playing the piano on the radio at the age of five, my mother had emerged in a sort of protective shell. The smile was always there, as expected, but it was very, very difficult to get inside—to find the real person. Today my mother acknowledges she remained more or less "locked up" like this until her early forties.

So there was my father, a shy kid with a heart for ministry and a gift for storytelling, conceiving ads for truck tires and feeling increasingly trapped between two very strong personalities in a decade that, post-sexual revolution, had decided no one should ever feel trapped in a marriage. Sociologically speaking, it shouldn't have surprised me when, in my ninth year, my father came downstairs with a suitcase in his hand, kissed me on the forehead, and walked out the door. It shouldn't have surprised me. But it did. I hadn't read the experts who had decided ending a difficult marriage was the best thing for everyone. I hadn't read the books declaring that children of divorce would bounce back resiliently, with little or no long-term impact. My father moved into a nearby motel, then eventually out-of-state with a female coworker. My mother sank into depression. I fell hard, and I didn't bounce back. I landed with a dull thud and the crack of something breaking. Something that would stay broken well into my adult years.

Whatever 'fun' there was in the sexual revolution was squandered entirely on my parents' generation. My generation got the short end of the stick. Sitting around a lunchroom table with eleven other boys in high school, the topic of divorce came up, so we went around the table and were shocked to find that eleven of the twelve boys had watched their parents' marriages collapse— had seen one of their parents walk out the door. Eleven out of twelve. A few years later in Bible college I found myself living in a dorm apartment with four other guys, all from Christian homes. Four out of five of us were children of divorce. A year later it would be five out of five.

Divorce in America—even in the church—has become painfully common. But does that make it less painful? I don't think so, just as I don't believe a random bullet to a sleeping child in a violent, inner city neighborhood will hurt any less or do any less damage than a bullet to an upper-class child in a wealthy suburb. The latter will surely garner more press attention and community outrage, but both kids are equally hurt. My father walked away from his family and his faith that day. The message I internalized, whether I knew it at the time or not, was this: "The people who mean the most to you will leave." That message would impact my friendships, my marriage, even my company, for years to come and in ways I could never imagine. Fear that those I valued most would abandon me, coupled with an overwhelming desire to fill the hole in my life where my father had been, would become recurring themes in my story for nearly 30 years.

My father's story has a happy ending. He returned to his faith while I was still in high school, just a year or two after my mother had remarried. My dad also remarried shortly thereafter, and has been happily married for the last 20+ years. I got a really fun stepbrother and very complicated family holidays out of the deal. My dad once again leads Bible studies in his home, and even preaches from the pulpit when needed. He and my stepmother pulled together a singing group in their small rural Michigan church that tours other small rural churches, giving overworked pastors a needed rest. My stepmom sings, my dad writes and performs skits and gives short messages. It's a lot like the Free Folk—my parents' folk band from the late sixties—though the squeaky-clean college kids have been replaced by retired friends with bad knees and a soundman with two hearing aids. It's a really cool thing.

Of course, back in 1977, I didn't know how the story would end. I only knew that my dad was gone, and my mother was never completely there. I moved my bed out of the room I shared with my little brother and down into my father's old office in the basement. Over the next few years, I would spend more and more time there and less and less time anywhere else, until an old family friend who was at the time chaplain of Wheaton College outside Chicago told my mother she should consider moving away from Muscatine and starting over somewhere else. For whatever reason, the idea clicked, and just before the end of my eighth-grade year, with the help of my Grandpa Vischer and guys from our church youth group, we packed up a moving van, said goodbye to the woods behind our house and the treehouse my dad had built and moved to a tidy little one-story brick ranch home in

Glen Ellyn, Illinois. After unloading, my grandfather prayed for us and our new life but accidentally said "Hoz and Scottie" (my parents) rather than just "Scottie" (my mother) and broke down in tears. Right in front of the youth group guys.

Life is tricky. God gave us all the freedom to choose, and with that gift comes the freedom to choose poorly. My dad's choices were costly to us, and even more so to him. But as I think you'll see in my story, God has an uncanny ability to redeem our mistakes. To use them for good. I'm not saying God wanted my parents to split—my pain and isolation wasn't his initial plan for me—but I am overwhelmed by his ability to take our hurts and our lousy choices and turn them to gold. To bless us—and others—through our broken lives. And somewhere in the isolation of my basement bedroom, as I thought about movies, read comic books and experimented with my grandfather's Super8 camera while waiting for my dad to show up on visitation weekends, ideas began to germinate that would someday touch more lives than I could possibly imagine.

3

Making Stuff

Swords flashed in the afternoon sunlight as King Arthur drove his worthy opponent to the crest of a small footbridge. Knocking the sword from his enemy's hand with a mighty stroke, Arthur followed with a crushing right hook that sent the scoundrel tumbling off the footbridge into the muddy creek bank below, where he lay motionless—thoroughly beaten. Arthur held his sword aloft, then, with epic drama, dropped it blade first into the mud next to his vanquished foe. It stuck fast and straight. The villain winced.

Wait—he wasn't supposed to wince. I took my eye away from the camera and stared at the scene. It was a perfect take—the climax of the film my youth group friends Mark Mayer and John Klem were making for a class project. Mark and his brother Pete attended Wheaton Central High School, the school best known for famous alumni Red Grange and John and Jim Belushi. Unlike my high school in neighboring Glen Ellyn, Wheaton Central had cool electives like filmmaking, and this was Mark's senior film project. His masterpiece. Most of our youth group had been enlisted in the project and, due either to my shyness or the fact that I too was a filmmaker, I had been elected cinematographer. So I was the one looking through the lens, and I was the one who knew this had been a perfect take, except for the fact that the villain, lying in the mud and supposedly unconscious, had visibly winced.

"Cut!" I yelled. The guy playing the villain slowly stood to his feet, and we knew immediately why he had winced. The sword had gone through his leg.

The idea had been simple: Mark, playing the title role in his own modern-day Arthurian adaptation, would drop the sword from about four feet above the creek bed. It was supposed to stick dramatically into the mud, next to his fallen enemy. But Mark missed. Or rather, Mark hit.

The guy playing the villain looked at us, eyes wide. With two hands he held the sword on either side of his leg. "What do I do?" he asked. "Pull it out!" someone yelled back. We were all frozen in horror. Grimacing, he slowly pulled the sword out of his leg and fell back onto the ground. We scooped up our fallen comrade and carried him back to John Klem's house where, for lack of a better plan, we called my mother, the only parent we could think of with a nursing degree.

"There's been an injury."

"How bad?"

"It has a point of entry and a point of exit."

Long pause.

"I'll be right there."

My mother swooped to the rescue and cleaned and disinfected the wound in a manner that would have made any Army medic proud. The skewered actor showed up at church a few days later hobbling on crutches but clearly on the mend. Fortunately, he was a missionary kid and, as such, had a pain threshold at least twice that of the average American teen.

My high school years in Glen Ellyn, Illinois, were filled with filmmaking. The year before, Mark's younger brother, Pete, and I had created our own Star Wars film, a stop-motion animated epic using Star Wars action figures, spaceships, Legos, and lots and lots of firecrackers. We had filmed in my basement, on a snow fort built in my backyard (the "Ice Planet"), and in the broken down swimming pool in Pete's backyard (the "Swamp Planet").

The next year, for his own senior-year film project at Wheaton Central, Pete conceived a sort of Christianized sequel to *Raiders of the Lost Ark*, called *Raiders of the Ark of the New Covenant*. Pete played Indiana Jones and enlisted a bunch of Cambodian refugees his family had befriended to dress up like natives and chase him through a local forest preserve. Pete asked me to provide the "special visual effects."

"Special visual effects" was the term given at some point in the history of filmmaking to any sort of effects work in a movie that didn't happen on the set as the film was being shot, but rather that was added afterward through a variety of mysterious and semi-magical processes. Blowing up a car was not a "special visual effect." Blowing up a planet while the lead actor escaped in a rocket ship through laser blasts from a pursuing alien battle cruiser was.

I had always enjoyed figuring out how things worked. I liked rocket ships and fighter planes and little electric motors. I liked anything with wires. I wondered how they made the professor's car fly in Walt Disney's *The Absent-Minded Professor*, and how they made Gus the mule appear to kick a football so darn far in *Gus*. On one of our last family trips before my parents split up, we visited Disneyland in California. I loved all the rides, but the highlight for me was sitting in a little boat and floating through The Pirates of the Caribbean attraction, eyes wide, mouth hanging open. I had to know how they did that, so my dad bought me a book from the gift shop on the making of the ride, and I took it home and studied it.

I started making my own sketches for a small robotic pirate ride of my own, which I never actually got around to building.

But all this was just an appetizer for the movie that would change everything, the movie that would inspire a whole generation of future filmmakers like me—*Star Wars*. I saw *Star Wars* five times in the theater, and I couldn't take my eyes off it. I had to know how they did everything. Shortly thereafter I discovered *Starlog* magazine, a strange little magazine targeting boys my age who loved sci-fi movies. More important, I discovered the books you could buy out of the back pages of the magazine between the ads for x-ray vision glasses that "really worked" and kits for building your own hovercraft—books about stop-motion animation and making your own "special visual effects" at home. Whoa. Cool! So by the time my friend Pete Mayer asked me to create the "special visual effects" for his Indiana Jones film, I had already experimented with numerous animation techniques and had built an animation stand in my mom's basement out of two-by-fours I had carried home from the lumberyard on my ten-speed bike.

The dramatic climax of the real *Raiders of the Lost Ark* movie was full of special visual effects—swirling light and wispy, ethereal vapor spinning around characters and such—and that's what Pete wanted for the climax of his film. So I bought a huge piece of black fabric from a local fabric store and hung it in our basement. I filmed Pete in his leather jacket and fedora in front of the black cloth, spinning around and reacting to all the "special visual effects" I would add later. I built a light table, consisting of a Super8 projector shining images into a mirror that reflected them up onto the backside of a translucent drawing surface. Then, frame by frame, I drew beams of light flying through the frames, wrapping around Indiana Pete, lighting up his eyes and leaving a glowing cross on his chest. (It was, after all, a Christian film.) Since all these drawings were black pencil lead on white paper, I photographed each drawing with high contrast 35mm negative film and had each negative image mounted in a slide. Pete also wanted a cloud of some sort (representing the Holy Spirit, I think) to come streaming out of a small wooden box (the Ark of the New Covenant). I grabbed my brother's aquarium, filled it with water, and then poured milk into it while the Super8 camera ran. If the resulting film was played upside down through colored gels and positioned just right, a "cloud" would emerge right from the "Ark." Play the film backward and the cloud would be sucked back inside. Cool!

Then came the tricky part: putting it all together. In moviemaking, up until computers took over the world, that is, multiple strips of film were combined using large, expensive pieces of equipment called "optical printers." I didn't have access to one of those, so I decided to make my own, which I did (more or less), using several cannibalized Super8 projectors, a 35mm slide projector, and parts from the *Edmund Scientific* catalog. I loved the *Edmund Scientific* catalog. (That bit of information right there should tell you it was a mistake to go out for tackle football in the seventh grade.) The process worked like this: My original footage of Indiana Pete went on one film projector. The black and white slides—which now had clear white animated "light streaks" on solid black backgrounds—went into a 35mm slide projector. Both projectors shone into different axes of a special "partially silverized" or "beam-splitting" mirror, which combined them into one image and rear-projected that image onto a small screen set up in front of my grandpa's Super8 camera. By inserting colored gels into the slide projector, I could change the color of the "light beams" wrapping around Indiana Pete. (Which is how I quickly discovered, for example, that glowing red eyes did not make it seem as if Pete had just been filled with the Holy Spirit.)

Some high school kids attended football games on fall weekends. Others partied or just "hung" with friends. Not me. I spent several entire weekends in our basement with all the lights out and the small, high windows masked, tediously advancing film through a projector and changing 35mm slides by hand. I would get everything lined up, then walk over and click off one frame on my grandpa's camera. One frame at a time. Twenty-four times for each second of screen time. Over and over. For hours and hours. And hours. The final images were muddy and soft, but technically speaking, the system worked. My homemade, two-headed beam-splitting optical printer worked! Operating it, however, was as tedious as mowing your lawn with a nasal hair trimmer. "Are you *sure* this is what you want to do for a living?" my mother asked when I complained about the tedium of my optical printing operation. "Sure, I'm sure!" I responded without hesitation. It wasn't that I particularly enjoyed mind-numbingly tedious tasks, but rather that I was already conceiving an improved process. As I was clicking off the frames, I was becoming more and more convinced that there was a way to automate the entire process—if only I could figure out how to hook up my new optical printer to the device sitting in the next room that was now competing with my grandpa's Super8 camera for my attention—my brand-new Atari 400 personal computer.

I don't know when I first became aware of computers, but I distinctly remember my enchantment at a fairly early age with a book about two grade school kids who had a computer to help them with their homework. It was a fictitious scenario at that point in the early seventies, but I was smitten with the idea. Electronic calculators were just beginning to appear at the time, and I remember daydreaming about saving up enough money to buy one, then encasing it in a much larger, more impressive wooden box, and giving it to my dad as his very own "computer" to help him with his work. Like everything else I was interested in, I learned what I could about computers from magazines (mostly bought by my father on visitation weekends) and then saved up my dollars and quarters until I could buy my very own. I believe it was my junior year of high school—late 1982—when I plunked down my hard-earned cash for an Atari 400 with 8 kilobytes of memory, a flat "membrane" keyboard, and an audiocassette tape drive for storing data. By that time I had taken some programming courses in high school (on Radio Shack TRS-80 personal computers), so I knew a little of the BASIC and COBOL programming languages. I hooked up my little Atari to the old TV in the basement and started pecking away at the flat keyboard. What fun! Who needed football games and parties when you had one of *these* sweet babies?

I immensely enjoyed the logic of computer programming—the beauty of the "if . . . then" statement. I loved the fact that once I had figured out the language for a simple operation, the computer could repeat it flawlessly—ad nauseam. Computers, I discovered, were infinitely reliable. Unlike, for example, oh, let's see . . . people. A piece of code that accomplished a certain task would continue accomplishing that task forever. Install that code on one hundred more computers, and they all would accomplish that task with equal aplomb. Forever.

Cool.

I was still awfully fond of animation and filmmaking though, which seemed like a very different track from all this logic-driven computer stuff. Until, that is, I noticed in physics class that many motions, say, a bouncing ball, for example, could be reduced to mathematical equations. Oh my. *That was* interesting. I ran home, cracked my physics textbook open in front of my trusty Atari 400, and worked several equations into a few lines of code. A few minutes later, voila! A ball bounced across the TV screen, drawing perfect little parabolas and accelerating and decelerating through its arcs with delightful believability. Eureka! Motion could be reduced to math! And math was what computers did best! I wrote a simple video game that used physics equations to fire cannonballs at randomly placed hot air balloons. Whee! I was providing the math, and the computer was doing all the "grunt work" of repositioning objects frame by frame. The computer was animating! Or was I animating, using math and a computer? I wasn't sure who was doing the animating, but pictures were moving and I wasn't having to draw every one, which was way cool. Still, though, computer graphics were so blocky and dull looking. The Death Star schematic scene from *Star Wars* was innovative, with its high-tech computer-drawn wireframe images (created not far from my house at the University of Illinois at Chicago), but you could never make a whole film that way. At least not a film that anyone would want to see.

Enter *Tron*, the second film that, for me, changed everything. If you aren't old enough to remember or are too old to have noticed at the time, *Tron* was an immensely innovative film produced by the Walt Disney Studios in 1982, based on the premise of real people being "sucked" into a video game. It didn't have much going for it by way of story or acting, even though the sight of Jeff Bridges running around in tights painted with glowing circuit board patterns may have been worth the price of admission in and of itself. But the scenes inside the video game were like nothing I'd ever seen in a movie. Virtually everyone who was "anyone" in the very early days of computer graphics helped out with the film, and the resulting imagery was breathtaking. Far from the simple wireframe graphics of the Death Star schematic sequence in *Star Wars*, *Tron*'s computer-generated images were fully shaded and rendered at full film resolution. They looked *real*. I had no idea you could do that with a computer. Suddenly my interest in computers and my interest in filmmaking didn't seem like separate tracks at all. I had seen the future, and it was *Tron*. Much to my displeasure, the Academy of Motion Picture Arts and Sciences had not yet seen the future and gave the Oscar for Best Visual Effects that year to the traditionally generated work of the forgettable *Altered States*. Boy, did they miss that boat.

The following year the Oscar for best visual effects (the only category I really cared about) went to George Lucas's third Star Wars film, *Return of the Jedi*. It was an astonishing achievement in terms of visual effects complexity, but it struck me as the "swan song" of the traditional special visual effects movement. I remember predicting as I walked out of the theater that no one in particular that no film would exceed *Jedi*'s effects complexity until visual effects were accomplished digitally. I was convinced that *Return of the Jedi* would go down as the ultimate achievement of the "old school" and would never be surpassed until visual effects moved from optical printers and photochemical processes to computer workstations and lines of code. I was just a seventeen-year-old kid living in suburban America, a thousand miles from Hollywood, but I was right. It would be fifteen years before films like James Cameron's *Titanic* and the Wachowski brothers' *The Matrix* would rival *Return of the Jedi*'s complexity, with nary an optical printer in sight. The future was digital.

Of course, *Tron* wasn't the only thing pointing in this direction. I was equally enraptured with a brand-new entertainment form that was now being streamed twenty-four hours a day through a little box that sat on top of our television, a new entertainment form that would prove even more influential, perhaps, than Star Wars. It was a brand-new cable network called MTV, and, in very different ways, it would influence both the style and the content of everything I would do thereafter.

4

"I Want My MTV"

MTV changed the world. That may seem like an extreme statement, but I really don't think it is. Remember television advertising before MTV? It was full of pithy little statements like "No more ring around the collar!" and "You got your peanut butter in my chocolate!" It was full of "jingles." Remember jingles? They were the catchy and chipper little songs—for example, "You deserve a break today"—that promoted a product. After MTV, a more typical statement in a TV commercial would be "Yo, dude! This rocks!" or Pop-Tarts' remarkable bit of word craft, "So cool, it's hot! So hot, it's cool!" Television advertising copy today is light on logic, heavy on exclamation points. And jingles? Forget it. All those cute little selling songs of the past have been replaced by distortion guitar and licensed pop tunes. Want to sell a car? Try Aerosmith. Mouthwash? Let's see . . . Twisted Sister? MTV even affected children's programming, as the crossover between children's culture and youth culture began to blur and shows targeting older children "aged up" with quick cuts and lots and lots of distortion guitar. Heck, churches even MTV'd themselves, adding "quicker cuts" and distortion guitar to services that targeted the "MTV Generation."

Technically speaking, I think I am the MTV Generation. MTV was born August 1, 1981, with the ceremonial and highly symbolic airing of the Buggles music video *Video Killed the Radio Star*. The following year our neighborhood in Glen Ellyn was wired for cable, and MTV came pouring into our old RCA console television through a little brown set-top box. I was a sophomore in high school at the time and, as such, was squarely in MTV's target demographic. Up until this point, TV had always been considered relatively benign by my parents, so I don't think my mother or new stepfather spent much time wondering whether this new intrusion was a good or bad thing. It just was. And in our house, it was on a lot. Especially after school before my mother came home from work and throughout the summers when I often found myself sitting around the house with nothing to do. Thus I got an eyeful of what was arguably the most significant cultural influence of the latter part of the twentieth century.

The first few years of MTV were exciting to watch and evoked two very strong emotions in me. The first emotion was, "This is so cool!" The voracious appetite of this new twenty-four-hour network for music videos—which were basically short films—generated tremendous opportunities for artsy filmmakers wanting to try new things on someone else's dime. For me, MTV represented an explosion of new filmmaking techniques. Groundbreaking videos like Dire Straits' *Money for Nothing*, A-ha's *Take on Me*, and Peter Gabriel's *Sledgehammer* brought highly innovative animation techniques to television. The premiers of Michael Jackson's big-budget *Beat It* and *Thriller* videos became "must-see TV" for the entire nation. Watching MTV in its early years was akin to attending a twenty-four-hour-a-day film festival, and I was eating it up.

I was thrilled about the technical and creative implications of what I was seeing on MTV. But the more I watched and the older I got, the more I became concerned about the *moral* implications. MTV was the visual embodiment of rock-and-roll culture, and rock-and-roll culture has never been a bastion of Christian values. While the major broadcast networks had for the most part taken a "parental" tone with their youth-targeted programming—using experts and advisers to create after-school specials that gave kids and young adults what they *needed*—MTV was clearly in the business of giving kids what they *wanted*. And if anyone needs proof that we are a fallen people living in a fallen world, look no further than the painful truth that the images and ideas our kids and young adults *want* are very seldom the images and ideas our kids and young adults *need*. In many cases, they are the exact opposite. Youthful rebellion has always found its voice in rock music, and MTV created the platform for rock stars young and old to turn their messages into visuals—to bring their rebellion to life. While in some cases the results were beautiful and compelling, quite often the videos turned out as meaningless and crass as the lives of the artists behind them. I could always picture in my head the scene in the offices of a big record label somewhere as a young, hot, newly signed artist is given a budget for his first music video and shown a stack of photographs of attractive models from which to choose his fictitious "romantic interest."

"You mean I can pick any one of these girls, and she'll be my girlfriend in the video?"

"Yep."

"Can I say she has to kiss me?"

"Sure."

"And wear something kinda skimpy?"

"You bet. It's your video."

"Heh-heh. Cool."

Newly hatched rock stars barely out of their teens—not to mention genuine rock legends in their forties and fifties but with the libidos and emotional maturity of teens—became movie stars, directors, and screenwriters all at the same time and began playing out their juvenile fantasies on the screen with MTV, always the willing accomplice, piping the results through little brown set-top boxes into RCA console television sets all across America. From sea to shining sea.

It worried me.

It isn't that I was a prude or anything—the "babes" on MTV appealed to me as much as to any other red-blooded American male. But I had always possessed a strong sense of right and wrong, based on my religious upbringing as well as my own convictions about what was healthy and beneficial and what clearly wasn't. And much of what I saw on MTV clearly wasn't. And then it dawned on me: I was supposed to do something about that. I knew how to tell stories. I was pretty good at making people laugh. And technology came easily to me. I figured if I got my hands on the tools they used to create these videos, I could get the hang of it pretty quickly. I knew God hadn't given me my passion for storytelling, for technology, and for doing what was "right" by accident. I was supposed to use them—and now I knew what for.

The term *calling* is bandied about often in Christian circles. By the time I was eighteen I had sat through countless services where we "youngsters" were asked to consider whether God might be "calling" us to world missions. I knew folks who had been "called" to Africa, "called" to Sweden, "called" to the inner city. Sitting through those services, though, I didn't feel called to any of those places. But here I was, sitting on the couch in front of our old RCA console television, watching Madonna gyrate her way through "Like a Virgin" on the front of a Venetian gondola, thinking to myself, "Oh, Lord, someone has to do something about this." And suddenly I knew that someone was me. I had to do something about it. I wasn't supposed to picket the record label or spray paint Bible references on Madonna's garage door or don a choir robe and chain myself to the axle of her tour bus. I was supposed to actually *do* something about it.

Fred Rogers describes the shock of his initial exposure to commercial television as his parents fired up their first TV set in the early 1950s like this: "They were throwing *pies* at each other." The sight of grown adults using this amazing new medium to showcase something as juvenile and pedestrian as a pie fight unsettled young Fred so deeply that he decided to spend the rest of his life showing the world how television could be *good* for you. And that is exactly what he did. By the time I was in high school, though, a pie fight would have been a welcomed respite from the drivel Hollywood was cramming through America's set-top boxes on an increasing basis. And this was my calling. To do something about it. To use my God-given creativity in combination with Hollywood's technology to make—hmm, to make what?—*to make a difference.*

So there it was. The work I would do for Christ. I had been making films since age eight, and had been convinced since fourteen that filmmaking would be my occupation. But now it was clear that it would be much more than just my occupation—it would be my ministry.

Okay, so how would I start?

5

Off to School We Go

I am not a "Type-A" personality. I am not a born leader. I do not look, taste, or smell like an "alpha dog." I was a shy kid who did not need to be taught the term "stranger danger." When strangers approached, I hid behind my mother. I don't know how much my parents' divorce affected my shyness, but I can't imagine it helped any. Other than church youth group events, I spent most of my later high school years watching MTV, making films in the basement, and waiting for my father to show up on visitation weekends. I was a teenage recluse. I hadn't gotten to the point of wearing Kleenex boxes on my feet, but that may not have been far off.

One weekend night during my senior year, two girls who sat near me in my honors English class knocked on my door and invited me to come to a party. Nervously, I agreed. The party wasn't anything crazy—it was the honors English crowd, after all—just a bunch of kids sitting or standing around someone's house talking and listening to Michael Jackson's *Thriller*. I couldn't quite find the handle on the experience, but I tried to play along. Evidently, though, I didn't give off whatever party vibe I was supposed to give off, because I was never invited back. Tricky stuff, parties.

Not nearly as tricky, though, as college. I was shy. Have I mentioned that? The thought of packing up my stuff and getting deposited in a strange place filled with *nothing but strangers* was, suffice it to say, less than appealing. But grown-ups kept asking me what college I planned on attending, so I had to come up with an answer. All the filmmakers went to school in California, but that was too terrifying even to consider. Not only would I be a million miles from home, but I'd also be up to my *NIV Study Bible* in people my grandfather would never approve of. Hippies and liberals and union backers, oh my.

I applied to the University of Michigan—partly because they had a small film program and partly because the campus in Ann Arbor was just forty-five minutes from my dad's house. That could work, I thought. But then they accepted me, and I got to thinking about how many strangers there were at a large state school. A school whose football stadium seated more than a 100,000 people. Maybe not. There had to be another choice—one that didn't seem so much like making a choice at all. My sister had spent a year at St. Paul Bible College in Minnesota, as had my father. It was the closest of the three schools affiliated with our family denomination, the Christian and Missionary Alliance. There was actually a small scholarship at the school in my family's name. That felt safer somehow. I thought, *I'll just go where my sister went—just for a year. I'll get a Bible certificate, then I'll figure out what to do next.* I'm not sure if it was a decision or a lack of decision, but in the fall of 1984, my mother packed all my earthly belongings into the back of our little yellow Datsun station wagon—the same station wagon she had bought in Muscatine right after the divorce—and drove me a half hour past Minneapolis to the tiny town of St. Bonifacius, Minnesota.

Up until this point in my life, I had never even gone to camp, so this was a big step. I felt numb. It was a defense mechanism I had used a lot since my dad had left, and I was now pretty good at it. I figured no feeling was better than a bad one. My mother helped me unload all my stuff into the small dorm room with my name and the name of some Italian kid on the door. They had put me in a room with a stranger. One from whom I could not get away. Yikes. The look on my mother's face told me that the look on my face wasn't very comforting. She looked as if she was beginning to rethink this whole college thing. She pulled herself together, though, said good-bye, and headed back to Chicago. I sat on my bed and waited for the Italian kid to show up. I looked around. No basement. Rats.

I didn't realize it at the time, but this was actually a major turning point in my life. The Italian kid walked in, and I noticed he, too, had a slightly frightened, numb look on his face. His mother helped him unload his stuff and then left us there together. We both gulped and then started talking. His name was Tony. He was funny. His parents were divorced, too. It was about time for dinner, so we headed down for our first collegiate meal. The dining hall was packed with strangers, but I wasn't alone. I was with Tony. And we clicked. Tony told me about his mom and his "Tom," and I told him about my mom and my "Bob." Over the next few weeks, we became good friends, and I slowly started letting more and more of my brain's "weird thoughts" out. Tony thought they were pretty funny. I got a little rambunctious. One day at lunch the men's dean caught me throwing an olive at someone across the dining hall and made me scrub the room's baseboards that night as penance. After noticing that nowhere in the student handbook was the throwing of food explicitly banned, I rebelled, but not as you might expect. I first gave a speech in my speech class about the injustice of punishing students for violations of unwritten, unknown rules, describing my crime as "the liberation of an olive from the bonds of gravity." Then Tony and I formed a secret society we called OLO— the Olive Liberation Organization—to commit acts of civil disobedience. We snuck out of our room after curfew and scrawled "OLO" and our logo, an olive on a toothpick, on the corners of various signs and banners throughout the school. We drew a giant Mickey Mouse head with a toothpick and olive hanging out of his mouth and hung it from the chapel balcony the night before an all-school chapel service. I was pretty sure we were breaking some rules, which was very new for me. It was kinda fun. Most amazingly, I wasn't homesick. At all. Then things got really crazy, because I tried out for the puppet team.

First, let me explain: St. Paul Bible College required that each student participate in some service ministry. For example, you could join the street-witnessing team or the team that visited the elderly. Being a shy fellow, the thought of engaging strangers in spiritually meaningful conversations didn't appeal very much, so I kept reading further down the list. Puppet team. They had a puppet team. I could do that. I showed up for tryouts on the specified date, along with five or six others. We were called one at a time into an empty classroom, handed a homemade puppet that had clearly spent too much time under the backseat of a church bus, and asked to lip sync our way through the classic Christian kids' song, "Bullfrogs and Butterflies." No sweat. I was on the team. The next two candidates passed me as I left the room—one very tall and thin, the other shorter and more roundish. The short one's name was Eric. The tall one's name was Mike. They both hailed from Aurora, Colorado, and had come to school more or less together. Eric's parents had divorced several years earlier, and Mike's parents would divorce in about fifteen months.

My excitement about making the team was slightly tempered by the fact that *everyone* who auditioned had made the team. Including several people who really had no business hoisting a puppet aloft in the name of ministry. Including one kid named Don who had some unidentified mental and emotional issues and who, beyond his complete lack of puppetry skills, would provide the team with lighthearted moments such as the time he intended to rebuke Satan but accidentally rebuked Jesus in a preshow prayer, and the time he, without the school or the team leader's knowledge, began booking churches for a puppet team tour of Montana over the summer after our freshman year. You can imagine Don's disappointment when he was required to call the churches back and tell them we wouldn't be touring Montana over the summer. Overall, though, the puppet team was a blast. We played conservative Baptist churches where the walls were covered in giant dispensational charts, and homes for mentally handicapped kids where the puppet stage was repeatedly rushed and puppets pulled from our hands midshow. The adult leader of the team taught us improv games and encouraged us to write our own scripts, which I did with relish. (The short segment "The Forgive-O-Matic" from the VeggieTales video *God Wants Me to Forgive Them?!?* was actually a puppet script written during this period.)

But most of all, I noticed that I really clicked with this tall kid from Colorado. Our senses of humor were almost identical, and his mind was blazingly quick. We stayed up late writing puppet scripts. We snuck out of our rooms after curfew and hid behind walls with puppets to terrorize the night watchmen. We snuck down to the phone booth in the "professional lobby" to place collect calls to televangelist Benny Hinn at 2:00 in the morning. (We never got through.) One night there was a tornado warning in the area, requiring the entire student population to dutifully hustle downstairs and take their assigned positions along the interior lower level walls. Everyone except Mike and I, that is. We were outside in the storm, racing around the school grounds with rolls of toilet paper and garbage bags in our hands—my pith helmet on my head. (What? You didn't bring your pith helmet to college?) We had a simple plan: throw the toilet paper into the air to locate the torna-does, then catch them in our garbage bags. We were "tornado hunters." We even composed a theme song for the occasion, which we sang over and over while hunting. (After all, anything worth doing really should be done to the accompaniment of a theme song.)

I was having fun. So much fun that, when the year was up, I decided I wanted to come back for a second year. I switched from the one-year Bible certificate program to a two-year associate of arts track.

As a wise man once said, though, "All good things must come to an end." Halfway through the first semester of our second year, personalities started to clash within our little group. Feelings were hurt. A new guy had entered the mix, and the tone darkened. Suddenly I wasn't having as much fun anymore. So when the dean of men pointed out that I had failed chapel two semesters in a row (attendance was required), and that failing chapel two consecutive semesters disqualified a student from returning the following semester, I declined his offer to sign a paper stating the chapel attendance records were "wrong" and opted instead to end my time in Minnesota after three semes-ters. Mike, too, had failed chapel, and went home to Colorado. He was headed for medical school, hoping to eventually become a missionary pediatrician. He liked kids. He liked God. It seemed like a good match. We briefly talked about moving to California together to pursue, respectively, medicine and film school. But something strangely providential happened when I returned to the suburbs of Chicago that would change both of our lives.

I got a job.

6

Work

Women's clothes. All I could see were women's clothes. Everywhere. I had dozed off, and when I opened my eyes, my entire field of view was filled with women's clothes. As I regained my senses, I realized that my peculiar perspective was due to the fact that I had been, in fact, sleeping beneath a rack of women's clothes in a Montgomery Ward store. And I was being paid by the hour.

Now, most stories involving an hourly employee falling asleep beneath a rack of women's clothes at a department store usually end with the words "You're fired!" Mine is different. I was doing my job—sort of. We were shooting a training video for Montgomery Ward in one of their stores in suburban Chicago. This sort of shooting happens after hours, of course, and is called a "lock-in." Most big department stores, you see, are locked and alarmed via computer from faraway cities, so a "lock-in" shoot requires having all your personnel and equipment inside the store by 11:00 p.m., at which point no one can leave without triggering alarms and summoning the police until 7:00 a.m. So there we were, somewhere around 4:00 a.m.—the shoot dragging on and me feeling a wee bit sleepy. Since I didn't have anything specific to do at that moment, I just sort of crawled off to the side to rest my eyes and woke up an undetermined amount of time later with a faceful of women's clothes.

So what was the shoot? Um . . . that's a bit touchy. Prior training videos for Montgomery Ward had instructed salespeople in the art of selling stereo gear and other "hard goods." But this one—well, this one was different. So different that the president of the video production company—a strong Christian who ran the company on behalf of the Christian media ministry that had funded it—wondered aloud if he would need to turn down the job. The subject? Bra- and girdle-fitting techniques. I'm not kidding. In the end, the need to keep the new company solvent overcame any moral squeamishness about the subject matter. He accepted the assignment, with the one unique instruction that we not mention it to anyone at the parent company. So four or five Christian guys loaded up a van and headed to the store to be locked away for the night with a handful of models and a big box of bras and girdles. Jeepers. As a nineteen-year-old intern fresh out of Bible college, I was beside myself to discover that not only was I assigned to the shoot, but even more that my primary role would be to focus a fan on the models to keep them from sweating. Part of me was saying, "Gee—I think I need to ask my mom about this" and part was saying, "Showbiz! Rock on!"

In reality, the affair was significantly less tawdry than one might have expected, as the combination of the late hour, unflattering fluorescent lights, and bras and girdles designed primarily with your grandmother in mind left me, well, asleep under a rack of women's clothes. But I was finally making movies!

My career in show business started inauspiciously enough the summer after my freshman year of Bible college. A friend

from church knew someone who worked at a Christian video production company. That company had lined up an intern for the
summer, but something had happened and the intern had
dropped out. I threw my hat in the ring and, through some divine
intervention, got the gig. The president led me around the small
facility, filled to the brim with nearly a million dollars worth of
high-end video gear, circa 1985. I had never seen nor touched any
of it before in my life, a fact the president knew. "You may not be
able to learn much this summer . . . we'll see," he said, and headed
back to his office, leaving me to focus on the assembly of an artificial tree he had purchased both as a prop and an office decoration. Later he returned and handed me a book on video
production. "Here," he said, "see what you can get out of this." I
took the book home and devoured it, as I had devoured so many
issues of *Starlog* magazine.

A few days later, he handed me the operator's manual for the
Chyron VP2, an electronic text-generating device. (If you were
watching the news in the '70s, '80s, or '90s and saw someone's
name appear along the bottom of the screen under their face, you
were likely seeing the output of a device manufactured by the
Chyron corporation.) I took the manual home and read it cover to
cover. It all seemed fairly logical—no big deal. Reading through
the manual that night brought to mind some ideas that weren't
covered in the material, though—ideas that might work if one
used some of the built-in tools in a slightly different way. The
next day I couldn't wait to give it a shot. I sat down at the VP2
and created a new page, using punctuation marks as design elements behind an otherwise dull page of text. Just then the president walked by the doorway and paused. "Hmm," he said, "I've
never seen anyone do anything like *that* on a VP2." I learned a
great deal that summer—setting up lights, wrapping cables, even

some basic video editing—but the things that got me noticed were my neat tricks on the VP2. I headed back to college in the fall, more intrigued then ever about the possibilities of electronic video production. My only regret was that I hadn't been able to learn my way around more of the company's toys. My chance would come—sooner than I could have expected.

Kicked out of Bible college. Oh, the shame. Actually, it didn't bother me that much, since I'd only planned on attending for a year anyway. But returning to Glen Ellyn, Illinois, at Christmastime in 1985, I now needed a real job. I gave my old friends at the video production house a call to see if they had anything available. As it turned out, they all remembered me and had been using my VP2 tricks in some of the shows they were editing. In fact, there was a job for me at the company, created in part by a hot new device over-taking America's living rooms: the VHS deck. Everybody and their brother was buying VHS decks by the mid-1980s, and, as a result, video production houses were stocking up on VHS duplicators to crank out copies of every new program. Just that fall, my friends had installed about one hundred VHS recorders along a wall and were ready to begin cranking out thousands of cassettes for various clients. What they were missing was someone to run all those VHS decks. On the graveyard shift.

In the world of entertainment, it sounds like the bottom of the barrel—duplicating VHS cassettes on the graveyard shift—but for me, it was perfect. Every night I came in at 11:00 p.m., loaded up one hundred VHS decks, started a big one-inch reel with the master program, and hit "record." Then, for the duration of the show (up to two hours), I was free to do whatever I wanted. Some of this time was filled with labeling and boxing videocassettes, of course, and I got a kick out of watching an investment training series we duplicated called Wealth Unlimited, which ultimately led to my losing $2,000 trading silver futures, but during the majority of the time, I read manuals. All the manuals. I was the only one in the facility, which, given my introverted personality, was perfectly fine with me. I had found an old lab coat in a closet, so I'd crank up the radio, put on the lab coat, and read manuals. Over the winter of 1986, I became familiar with almost every piece of equipment in the shop. One-inch recorders, high-end cameras, proc amps, CMX editors—you name it, I read about it. In the wee hours of the morning, I tinkered about the shop in my lab coat like a mad scientist. I taught myself enough to attempt my own small editing project in the one-inch CMX editing suite—a daunting undertaking for a novice. I was having fun. When the president of the company heard a rumor that I was teaching myself how to edit, he gave me a pet project of his to work on in my spare time.

As a result of all my late-night tinkering, several weeks later when the fourth-string editor walked out for a cigarette before an edit session and never came back, I was hastily dubbed "new fourth-string editor" and thrown into a session with a client. Gulp.

The year 1986 was also the epoch of the first wave of computer animation companies. Often closely related to or located around pioneering computer graphics research universities like Ohio State, NYU, the University of Utah, and Stanford, early pioneers like Pacific Data Images, Digital Pictures, Abel & Associates, and Cranston/Csuri were winning awards and earning reams of press for their cutting-edge TV commercials and network promotional pieces. Some were even dabbling with character animation, as in Dire Straits' *Money for Nothing* music video, produced with a Bosch FGS-4000, the first commercially available computer animation system. As much as I enjoyed learning video editing and shooting, my heart was still with animation and computers. *Tron* still echoed in my brain, and I wondered how I would transition from *Bra- and Girdle-Fitting Techniques* to the world of computer animation. That all changed one day when the president of our production company walked up to me with an announcement. He was buying a Bosch FGS-4000. At that time there was only one FGS-4000 in the Chicago area, and he thought the purchase could catapult his company into the big leagues. And he wanted me to be the artist. Whee!

So it was a strange confluence of events, trends, and my peculiar fondness for technical manuals that led to me finding myself in Salt Lake City in the fall of 1986 for two weeks of intensive Bosch FGS-4000 training at the tender age of twenty. The company president sent me off with $200 cash in hand for meals and was shocked when I returned two weeks later with more than $100 left. "Did you eat?" he asked. Ninety dollars will buy you a whole lot of Arby's roast beef sandwiches. The world of Bosch animating was laborious but intriguing. Flying logos and bar charts were relatively simple and represented the bulk of the work (especially for our corporate/industrial clientele), but it was hard to tell a story with a bar chart. I tried to build a simple, limbed character. Bringing him to life, on the Bosch, at least, was a nightmare. The software simply wasn't set up for that sort of work. My foot was in the door, but I still couldn't see exactly how I would be able to tell my own stories. Unless they involved bar charts, that is.

About this time, my friend Mike Nawrocki had had enough of Colorado. His parents' marriage was falling apart, and he felt caught in the middle. Since it was now clear I wouldn't be heading to California for film school anytime soon, he decided to pursue pre-med in Illinois, with me. Mike moved into our basement in Glen Ellyn and applied to the University of Illinois at Chicago. After a brief stint selling magazine subscriptions for the Illinois State Troopers, he landed a job with me at the video production house duplicating videocassettes and helping out on shoots and in edit sessions. Life in my mother's small ranch house in Glen Ellyn was fun, though a little cramped. We now had so many cars in the driveway and spilling onto the grass that one of our neighbors called the cops to complain. Glen Ellyn was an "upscale" community, the officer informed us, and cars hanging off the sides of a driveway didn't quite cut it. No matter, though, since the president of the production company had just made an announcement that would significantly impact both Mike's and my lives and the state of my parents' driveway: he was moving the company downtown, forty-five minutes east into the heart of Chicago. Mike and I resolved that we would head downtown too; and after a bit of searching about, we found a decent little apartment in one of Chicago's famous graystone buildings on the north side. We invited a new work buddy, Joe, to join us. We had jobs, an apartment, bus passes, and memberships at the nearest Bally's health club. We were ready for anything.

7

Life in the Big City

Besides the muggings (two), home invasion (one), car break-ins (three), and chronic lack of parking, life in Chicago was fun. There were improv clubs and bizarre little theater troupes like the one that would attempt to stage thirty plays in sixty minutes every Friday and Saturday night in a small space over a funeral home. (The ticket price for that show was set for each attendee by the role of one six-sided die.) Mike and I ate up the creative atmosphere. I was also thrilled by the creative opportunities at the now-expanded production company, whose recent acquisitions included some of the key technologies that had enabled the music videos I found so alluring on MTV just a few years earlier. Eager to experiment with all this new gear, Mike, Joe and I made a series of short "weekend films" (dubbed "weekend films" because I figured if we didn't start and finish them in one weekend, they'd probably never get done at all). Each project took me a little deeper into the new editing and effects gear. One film in particular was a strange harbinger of things to come. Called "A Day at the Beach," the two-minute short featured me and Mike in sunglasses, shorts, and beach towels, driving a banana car through a cartoon world to a cartoon beach where we surfed on a bagel until a giant vacuum cleaner appeared over the horizon and sucked us up. As bizarre as the content may have been, the production so impressed the company president that he began using the film to show off the company's technical capabilities. Swap out Phil and Mike for Bob and Larry, and you were probably looking at the first VeggieTales film.

At this point I discovered I really did not enjoy being an employee. I liked having access to all that gear, and it was fun working with other creative types, but I didn't like my limited role as simply a provider of one service within a larger service-oriented company. I liked the big picture—marketing strategies, finance and business decisions, the whole enchilada. Running a creative business seemed relatively simple and looked like a whole lot of fun. Create a brand, market the brand, get clients, do great work, get more clients, do even better work—rinse, and repeat. I had a small group of clients that I figured would work with me whether I was inside a larger company or out on my own, and the thrill of building a business was, for some reason, immensely alluring. So in February 1989, after three years inside a production company and at the tender age of twenty-two, I left my relatively safe job and hung out my own shingle, founding the company that would eventually become Big Idea Productions. I called my company "GRAFx Studios," a name I chose primarily because, well, I thought it sounded cool. I designed a logo and had an artist lay out business cards and letterhead. Mike and I were still roommates, but he stayed behind at the production company and kept working toward medical school.

There are certain seasons in life that make starting your own business easier or harder—more terrifying or less terrifying. Being married with a mortgage and high school–age kids headed for college is a particularly terrifying time to start a business. Being twenty-two with roommates sharing the rent and no kids, no mortgage, and very low expenses is a wonderfully easy time to start a company.

Of course, it begs saying that the "low-risk" opportunities of youth come hand-in-hand with the youth's inexperience, blind optimism, and naïveté. In other words, those who can most afford to risk everything on a new business idea are also those with the least experience and the least preparedness for just such an outing. Not knowing what I didn't know, and with an unflappable "How hard could it be?" attitude, I strode forth into the world of business ownership. If I had known how hard it would in fact be for a shy kid like me to build a service business dependent entirely on client relationships and networking, or how resistant Chicago's ad agencies were at the time to working with solo artists who didn't have the resources of giant production houses behind them, I would have thought twice about striking out on my own. If Steve Jobs and Steve Wozniak had known what they were up against right from the beginning, we probably wouldn't have Apple Computer. The same could be said for Hewlett Packard, Yahoo, Google, and countless other companies founded by bright-eyed kids who didn't know how much they didn't know. Without the irrational exuberance of youth, we wouldn't have any of those companies. And, most likely, we wouldn't have VeggieTales either.

GRAFx Studios got off to a decent start. Unable to afford my own gear, I struck a deal with another Chicago production house to buy time on their equipment in the evenings, after their editor and graphic artist had gone home. So I'd meet with my clients during the day at their offices, work out the details of the animation or graphics project, then execute the work that night in peace and quiet. I bought the time at a wholesale rate, marked it up to my clients, and lived off the margin. It wasn't a bad gig. I wasn't making a lot of money, but I wasn't starving. As long as I had roommates to help with the rent and no family to feed, that is.

But there was this girl I had met the year before at my great-grandfather's Bible conference in Iowa. This cute blond from the

suburbs of Minneapolis. She had walked into the evening conference meeting and sat down in the row in front of Mike and me,
bumping her head on my foot, which I had propped up on the
back of her chair. She turned and said something sarcastic. I was
intrigued. Most Bible conference girls aren't familiar with sarcasm.
We hung out. She was funny. We made up songs on the dock at the
lake. Turns out she was a singer, headed for the Conservatory of
Music at Wheaton College. In Illinois. Just a few blocks from my
mom's house in Glen Ellyn. Very interesting.

That year we talked on the phone for hours—often while I
worked into the night at the production house. Her parents had
split when she was twelve, due to her father's rapidly declining mental health. That at least partly explained the sarcasm and why we
clicked so well. Things progressed quickly, and it soon became clear
that my days of splitting the rent with roommates were numbered.

I could write volumes about Lisa, her life, her own woundedness, how we came together, and the often excruciating work we
did over the first decade of our marriage to unpack our pains and
to slowly see ourselves succeed where our own parents had failed.
As I write this, we are just a few months from our sixteenth wedding anniversary—the last anniversary my parents celebrated
together. I can't tell you how much emotion I feel about passing
that milestone—about building a marriage that has outlasted
those of both our parents—in the face of statistics that show kids
of divorce are more likely to divorce themselves. As is typically the
case, our sarcasm masked shells of hurt—shells that had to be
chipped away slowly over years and years of sometimes wonderful,
sometimes horrible interactions. But each day we managed to keep
our woundedness from wounding each other was a victory. Each
victory convinced us more and more that we could do this—that we
weren't "doomed" to repeat the mistakes of our parents—that our

kids would not experience what we had experienced. Looking back, this work has been our biggest achievement. Much bigger than that talking vegetable thing. A marriage that grows and lasts in a culture that sneers and spits on the very idea of lifelong commitment. That is a big deal. But that's material for a different book. One, perhaps, for when our kids are a little older.

A year after founding GRAFx Studios, I found myself married. Not only that, we were expecting a child. Almost overnight, it seems, that whole "roommates share the rent while I work day and night" idea sort of flew out the window. On top of that, though, I knew I couldn't develop my own storytelling ideas when I had to buy equipment time by the hour. I hadn't forgotten the call I had felt to spread God's truth through filmmaking. I just couldn't figure out how to do it. The animation system I was using now was from a company called Symbolics, and while the software was much more versatile than the old Bosch FGS-4000, the computer itself (also manufactured by Symbolics) was discouragingly slow. My sole attempt at creating a character produced a simple dancing stop-light for my demo reel, which, though cute, was laboriously tedious to animate, taking several days for just a few seconds of screen time. I was still convinced that computer animation would be the key to my own storytelling—to my work for God—but the technology of the day wasn't cooperating. It just didn't seem ready yet.

So why not abandon animation? Why not just grab a video camera and start shooting, like the short "weekend films" Mike and I had made a few years earlier? I had actually considered that as I started GRAFx Studios. Given the extreme complexity and expense of computer animation (thirty-second computer-animated TV commercials like the old classic Scrubbing Bubbles ads cost $300,000 to $500,000 at the time), I thought perhaps I should start with something easier. A show for Christian teenagers, maybe. Mike and I could write really wacky stuff, I could host it, Mike could be my Ed McMahon or Paul Schaeffer or something similar, and we could sell it through Christian bookstores on home video. A show like that would be relatively inexpensive to produce. My mother worked at the large Sunday school literature publisher David C. Cook at the time, so I wrote up the idea for *The Phil & Mike Show*, and she set up a lunch for me with one of their creative directors. He listened politely, then pointed out that, at least at that time in history, teenagers didn't buy many videos. Parents bought videos for their little kids. Not for their teenagers. He had a point. I hadn't seen many Christian teenagers walking out of bookstores with videos in their hands. *The Phil & Mike Show* never saw the light of day.

Then something interesting happened. The large Christian ministry Focus on the Family launched into Christian bookstores a new home video series called McGee and Me. The series featured a very high-quality mix of live action and traditional animation, and looked as good as just about any kids' show on TV that year. Most amazingly, my mom had heard through friends at work that the first episode had sold something like 20,000 copies in its first two weeks—unheard of numbers for a video in Christian book-stores. *Hmm*, I thought. *Maybe I'm not supposed to do something simple like* The Phil & Mike Show *as a warm-up. Maybe I'm just sup-posed to go for it—the whole enchilada—a fully computer-animated, half-hour home video for Christian bookstores.* At this point in my career, the longest piece of animation I had ever produced was less than sixty seconds. Not only had I never produced a half-hour computer-animated home video, but as far as I knew, *no one* had ever produced a half-hour computer-animated home video. *But really*, I thought, *how hard could it be?*

Ha. Ha ha. Ha.

8

Technical Mumbo Jumbo

It was not long after my marriage to Lisa in early 1990 that I committed in earnest to the pursuit of a computer-animated kids' show. My plan was simple: do commercial animation for clients by day to pay the bills and pay for my gear, and then in the evenings develop the kids' show. Of course, I didn't have my own gear. What's more, I wasn't sure if any of the currently available animation systems were capable of creating believable characters.

I first attended the SIGGRAPH (Special Interest Group on Graphics and Interactive Techniques) convention, the international computer graphics convention put on by the Association for Computing Machinery, in 1987. Far from the Hollywood-driven George Lucas/Pixar blockbuster carnival that SIGGRAPH attendees know today, the convention in the mid- to late 1980s was a small affair, focused mostly on medical imaging and computer-aided design for the automotive industry. The animated short films featured in the popular "electronic theater" showcases were mostly scientific visualizations and tests of new rendering techniques, interspersed with the occasional attempt by a researcher to do something funny. The big exceptions—and by far the biggest crowd-pleasers in this era—were the experimental short films created by ex-Disney animator John Lasseter at Pixar, the cutting-edge computer animation firm founded by George Lucas but by then owned by ousted Apple cofounder Steve Jobs. Eight years before *Toy Story* would make John Lasseter a household name, he was already becoming a bit of a rock star in this tiny world of engineers and techno-geeks. I'll readily admit that I envied John—the fact that he was paid every day to think up experimental short films, that he never had to cold call agency producers or corporate A/V guys to scrounge up enough boring logo and bar chart work to pay his rent. I watched John's short films *Luxo Jr.* and *Red's Dream*. Pretty impressive stuff. I was there when he premiered *Tin Toy*, the short that inspired *Toy Story*. While clearly an amazing technical achievement, I thought *Tin Toy* was a little clunky creatively—not nearly as fresh and fun as one of John's traditionally animated student films I had seen earlier that year. I wondered if all the technical complexity of a film like *Tin Toy* made it harder to keep the creative on track, and, after attending one of his presentations, approached him and asked him as much. He stared at me for a bit, then said, "I don't know how to answer that," and turned and walked away. It suddenly dawned on me that I had just insulted John Lasseter.

Fourteen years later, while taking a tour of Pixar's mammoth new facility with a friend, I spotted John heading into the cafeteria. It seemed like a perfect opportunity to say hi, but I couldn't decide whether to approach him and say, "Hi, I'm the VeggieTales guy, and I was that kid who insulted you at SIGGRAPH fourteen years ago," approach him and say, "Hi, I'm the VeggieTales guy, and no, we've never met before, but you may have met someone who looked like me a long time ago but it wasn't me," or just watch him walk by. Thoroughly flummoxed, I just watched him walk by.

So John, if you're reading this, I'm sorry I asked you that stupid question about *Tin Toy* and creativity. I was just jealous because your job looked a lot more fun than mine. No wait—come to think of it, that wasn't me at SIGGRAPH in 1989. It was my twin brother, Rudy, who has since been institutionalized. Problem solved.

Up until the mid-1980s, computer animation systems came from companies like Bosch and Symbolics that designed both the software and the accompanying hardware, making the creation of a new animation system a huge undertaking. This started to change mid-decade when Silicon Graphics introduced a line of "visual workstations"—UNIX computers with high-powered graphics systems tailored primarily for medical imaging and industrial design. This new platform inspired the launch of several new animation software packages, most notably one from a Canadian company called Alias (now the number one high-end animation software package, used for thousands of feature films as well as the production of every VeggieTales episode since 2001). With my kids' show in mind, I walked up to the small Alias booth at SIGGRAPH in 1987 and asked what they were doing for character animation. "Nothing," the salesman responded. I had clearly arrived at the party several hours ahead of the caterer. I went back home and waited.

By SIGGRAPH 1989 (the year of my Lasseter faux pas), things were starting to get interesting. Attendance was way up, and there were almost as many kids with spiked hair and leather jackets as there were middle-aged men with pocket protectors. The words *entertainment* and *animation* could be heard at least as frequently as *medical imaging*. More Hollywood films and TV commercials were using computer-generated elements, swinging the content of SIGGRAPH's film showcase further away from scientific visualizations and more toward entertainment.

One TV commercial in particular caught my eye. It had been

produced by Rhythm & Hues, a new CGI (computer-generated imagery) studio founded out of the ashes of pioneering effects shop Robert Abel & Associates. It was a commercial for a Sunbeam toaster oven, and it featured two CGI salt and pepper shakers cavorting with a CGI toaster oven on a CGI yellow ceramic tile kitchen countertop. What amazed me—besides how cheerful a yellow ceramic tile kitchen could be when rendered in 3D—was the behavior of the salt and pepper shakers. They were squishy. Now, this might not seem like a big deal to you, but to me, in 1989, it was a very big deal. Up to that point, you see, computer animation had been, with very few exceptions, rigid—hard, little plastic objects moving around with mathematical precision. Classical, hand-drawn animation is all about the flow of a line and the exaggeration of a shape. A bouncing ball animated by hand was filled with life as it stretched and squashed through its arc. A bouncing ball animated on a computer was mathematically perfect but emotionally sterile—like a metal ball bearing bouncing across a lab table in physics class. Up to this point, most computer animation lacked "squash and stretch," the common term for the exaggeration of shape in traditional animation (think classic Warner Brothers cartoons or Goofy riding a horse). Even Pixar's early shorts featured rigid objects like a metal lamp or a unicycle that moved realistically but without any squash and stretch. But these salt and pepper shakers—they had it. They squashed. They stretched. Even without faces, they came to life like Pepé Le Pew in pursuit of that terminally unlucky cat. Like no computer animation I had ever seen before. I had to know how they did it.

The answer, I discovered, was a brand new technique called "lattice deformation," which radically simplified the process of animating shape changes on computer-generated objects by allowing an animator to modify the shape of a complex object not by moving every point in the object, but instead by placing the object inside a box-like container, or "lattice," and then simply animating the points on the lattice. Whatever you did to the lattice would automatically happen to the object inside. Twist the lattice and the object inside twists. Bend it over and the object bends. The genius of lattice deformation was that even if the object inside was composed of hundreds or even millions of pieces, the animator only had to manipulate the twelve or sixteen points on the lattice. Everything else was calculated automatically.

This was big. Huge. Efficient character animation on the computer now seemed feasible. All I had to do was wait for one of the commercially available software packages to add lattice deformation to their tool kit. But how long would that take?

The answer came that very SIGGRAPH as I wandered into a small booth at the far end of the exhibit hall. It came via a new Canadian company called Softimage, exhibiting at SIGGRAPH for the first time. Their product was animation software created *by* animators *for* animators. They weren't finished writing their code yet, but there on the list of features they planned to add was—gasp!—lattice deformation. Oh boy, oh boy, oh boy. I was onto something, and I knew it.

Amazingly, not many others seemed to notice. For me, lattice deformation opened up a whole new world of character animation possibilities. Most of the rest of the animation community, however, was focused on the one thing lattice deformation couldn't handle: limbed characters. People. Animals. You know, the stuff television shows and movies are made of. Saltshakers might hold your attention for a thirty-second TV commercial, but surely not longer than that. The rest of the industry kept its focus on solving the massive complexities of animating limbed, appendaged characters with hair and clothes. They didn't see the potential in lattice deformation to bring much simpler characters to life, much sooner and much more cheaply. It occurred to me that I could be the first person to produce a half-hour CGI kids' film. All I had to do was come up with compelling yet simple characters—characters that would have to do their acting without arms, legs, hair, or clothes. In a kids' animation world accustomed to talking mice, rabbits, ducks, fairies, bears, monkeys, mermaids, and a million other humanoid creatures, I needed to come up with not just one character, but a whole cast of characters who would be naked, bald, and limbless. And I wanted to sell them in Christian bookstores. As daunting as that challenge appeared, an even more daunting challenge was staring me down first: Where would I get the money to buy the gear?

My mother and stepfather were extraordinarily frugal. Before my mom remarried, we had so little extra money she had us bring our brown paper lunch bags home from school to be used again. Things didn't improve much after she remarried, as my stepfather's electrical business made only modest profits. Some years he was unable to pay himself at all, and my mother's small paycheck had to feed all of us. The thermostat was kept teeth-chatteringly low in the winter, and in the summertime the air conditioner was to be activated only in cases of life-threatening heat. My stepdad bought only used cars and drove them until no amount of duct tape or rubber bands could keep them going. I distinctly remember, while driving high school friends around in our family van, having one of them point inquisitively at a rubber band stretched across the dashboard. "Don't touch that!" I yelled, "It keeps the turn signals working!" So you can imagine my shock when, after returning from SIGGRAPH with my news about the latest developments and the software I was considering, my stepfather said, "Maybe we can help you."

I was flabbergasted. I had negotiated a good deal with Softimage's sales director, who at that time was eager to get their new software in real production settings in the United States, but even so, we were looking at a $25,000 price tag for the software and the Silicon Graphics workstation on which it ran. But that's what my stepdad said—even after I told him the price. "Maybe we can help you." My mother and stepfather were in the process of taking out a second mortgage on our house to support my step-father's business, and here he was, a guy who never bought anything new in his life, offering to help me buy $25,000 worth of computer equipment for a business he didn't understand by borrowing more money against our house.

Wow.

I seriously considered turning down the offer, not wanting to jeopardize, you know, the "family farm." But I carefully thought through my business plan, the clients I had, the advantage I would have as the first Softimage animator in Chicago, and the possibilities lattice deformation brought to character animation. It made sense. I told them I would accept their help, and my step-father and I signed a simple, one-page loan agreement. Several months later, I was sitting in the second bedroom of the loft apartment I had originally rented with Mike but now shared with my pregnant wife, staring at a beautiful new Silicon Graphics Personal Iris workstation with a 280 megabyte hard drive and 16 megabytes of memory. Whoa. I fired it up. The screen came to life, and, after typing a few UNIX commands, I was staring at the Softimage interface. Awesome. Only one problem—the lattice deformation button didn't work. That part of the software wasn't finished yet. No big deal. I still had plenty of work ahead of me learning the rest of the software, and the lack of lattice deforma-tion wouldn't affect the majority of the corporate work I was doing to pay the bills. I devoured the documentation and waited eagerly for my clients to dream up projects that would let me show the world my new capabilities. Unfortunately, as most of my clients were corporate A/V producers, few of them had the budgets or the need for serious animation. They mostly needed logos and bar charts, just as before. So my new workstation and I did a lot of logos and bar charts, which, while it kept my family from starving, were sort of like driving your grandmother to the post office in your new Ferrari. In a school zone. With children present. Whee. It didn't bother me *that* much, though, because my thoughts were still with my theoretical hairless, limbless kids' show and the date on the calendar Softimage said they would deliver the rest of the key features.

In mid-1990, I finally received the software update. The "lattice deformation" button lit up. It worked just as I had hoped. Cool. I decided to test it out on a job I had just picked up from Chicago's power utility, Commonwealth Edison. They wanted a fun open to a show they were producing for grade school kids about safety called *Safety Town*. Perfect. Using lattice deformation, I animated each letter in the title by having it drop down and then do a little dance step. Each letter had its own unique dance step, created relatively easily by animating a few points on the corresponding lattice. The client loved it, and I was jazzed. I had a few days before my next paying job, so I decided to try my hand at my first character. I made a sphere. I gave him two simple eyes, a nose, and a little smile. I put another sphere over him, slightly lower, and then used a lattice to reshape that sphere until it looked like the first sphere was wearing sort of a turtleneck sweater—with very rudimentary feet poking out the bottom. (I was making it up as I went.) Now I put the whole thing inside a lattice that had one extra row of points on each axis for more control, and I tried animating that lattice to make the little guy appear to walk. It worked! He sort of looked like a Nerf ball wearing a sweater, so I called him "Nerf Ball Guy." I showed him to my wife, Lisa. She thought he was cute. I had a couple of concerns though. First, trying to give the impression of two-legged walking with lattice deformation was fairly difficult, and I feared such characters would be too time-consuming for me to single-handedly animate a thirty-minute film. I needed simpler characters. Monopods. Characters that, maybe, hopped. The second issue was faces. Rhythm & Hues' saltshaker didn't have a face, and I hadn't thought much about how I would bring my characters' faces to life. "Nerf Ball Guy" had eyes and a mouth, but I had no ability to make them move. They just sat there—frozen. If I was going to produce a half-hour film starring hairless, limbless, hopping monopods, I decided they'd better have extremely expressive faces. I mean, what else would they have to act with? The eyes, I decided, were absolutely critical.

If you had taken the time back in 1990 to study all the existing computer-generated characters, you would have noticed they all shared one common and distinctly unappealing attribute: rigid eyes. The typical CGI eye at that point was a solid white, perfect sphere, with a perfectly round black dot painted on one side. Eyes had to be perfectly spherical so they could rotate in any direction without breaking through the face around them. Obviously, if the eye was oblong or bean-shaped, rotating it significantly inside the head would look peculiar at best, disturbingly grotesque at worst. Just as with robotics or animatronic pirates at Disneyland, to rotate a ball inside a socket, the ball needed to be perfectly round. But as most artists well know, visually speaking at least, perfect circles are boring. They lack energy. Single-frame your way through any classic Warner Brothers cartoon and look for a perfectly round eye on any character. You'll never find one. Watch Daffy Duck's eyes through a typical six-minute short and you'll be amazed at the variety of shapes they assume—oblong, bean-shaped, triangular slanting in, triangular slanting out. Eyes in classic animation were almost more liquid than solid. And yet in the world of computer animation, as engineers wrestled over hair, limbs, and elbow joints, character after character hit the stage with lifeless, ping-pong ball eyes. Looking at stills from Daffy Duck shorts, I decided my characters' eyes would make or break the show. They had to be squishy, like Daffy's, even to the point where they would squish through each other and sort of "merge" into a single unit—like Daffy's did when he was freaking out and his pupils shrunk to tiny dots and his eyes merged together and became one big "mono-eye" spreading entirely across the top of his bill. That's what I wanted. But how? How could I get my eyes into such extreme positions while still retaining the ability to move the pupils around and, just as important, blink? Simple. Lattices. Lattices could do it.

I built two perfectly round, boring eyes, then enclosed each one within a lattice. Next I grabbed the top row of points from each lattice, pulled them up to make the eyes oblong, then crossed them over each other to push the eyes together at the top. And immediately, they came to life. This profoundly appealing look is a big part of the reason kids immediately respond warmly to VeggieTales characters. Even if they aren't moving—just still images on a page. The eyes of almost every VeggieTales character are exactly the same as the very first eyes I built in my spare bedroom back in 1990. More than any other visual element, this basic eye shape was the key to VeggieTales.

I wasn't sure why no one had thought of it before, but lattices took robotic CGI eyes and made them deliciously cartoony. When I took a simple sphere nose and stuck it under the eyes, making sure it overlapped the eyes "just right" (again using Daffy eye-to-bill relationship as my cue), I now had an enormously appealing face. A face that, I was pretty certain, could engage a kid for at least thirty minutes. Maybe more.

Staring at my new face, the next question was pretty obvious: What do I stick it on?

9

Cue the Vegetables

O ver the years, fans and journalists have proposed all sorts of theories for my choice of vegetables as characters. Some have concluded my goal was the promotion of good nutrition—that I wanted kids to eat more vegetables. Others suggested it was because I wanted kids to eat *fewer* vegetables. (We've heard anecdotal stories supporting both theories—parents who've told us their kids *will* eat any vegetable they have seen in VeggieTales, and parents who have told us their kids *won't* eat any vegetable they have seen in VeggieTales. One mother described in great detail her effort to sneak a cucumber away from her toddler so it could be secretly sliced in the next room without traumatizing the young Larry fan.)

If you've been paying attention (and again, I hope you have, because all this typing is going to give me carpal tunnel syndrome, and my wrists will be bitter if you've been zoning out), you probably realize by now that my choice of vegetables was technological rather than nutritional. It was a case of technological pragmatism. But vegetables weren't my first choice.

Once I finished my face and had put him through a few tests

("Look! He can blink!" "Now he's looking over there! Now he's looking over *there*!"), I wracked my brain for something to put him on. He needed a home. And for whatever the reason, I thought of a candy bar. I needed something sort of tallish and thinnish to make the best use of the lattice (bending over, twisting, and such), and a chocolate bar, standing up, seemed just the right shape. So I whipped up a chocolate bar, then made my face's eyelids and nose brown and stuck them on. Voila! I had a really friendly candy bar. Face attached, I put Mr. Candy Bar in a lattice and made him bend from side to side. Not bad. Just then, something happened that could go down in history as one of those pivotal moments—those providential, existential occurrences that hold within them the potential to change the course of humanity: My wife walked by. She walked by the spare bedroom, looked in, noticed her husband playing with a computer-generated candy bar, and uttered these immortal, life-giving words: "You know, moms are going to be mad if you make their kids fall in love with candy bars."

That's what she said. Divine wisdom had dripped from her lips like honey. She spoke the truth. Then she headed off with the laundry.

"Good heavens," I thought, "she's right!" I couldn't make characters that were unhealthy! That would go against every-thing I was trying to accomplish! I needed something good for kids! I needed something that would make moms rise up and call me blessed! Something that would make them say, "Oh, thank you, Phil Vischer, for making my kids fall in love with ——!"

With what?

The next image that popped into my head was a cucumber.

I kid you not.

Lisa, in her infinite wisdom, had not only pointed out the error of my unhealthy pursuit, but also had turned me around and pointed me down the path of health. The path that ended in vegetables. And it only took her nineteen words to do it.

Quickly I traced the profile of a cucumber on my workstation and instructed the software to rotate it 360 degrees to form a cucumber-shaped dimensional object. I snatched the face off Mr. Unhealthy Candy Bar, the poor bit player whose fifteen minutes of fame came and went in the blink of an eye, and slapped it on Mr. Cucumber. Brown eyelids and a brown nose didn't go real well with Mr. Cucumber's dark green, so I recolored them, choosing a lighter shade of green to make them stand out. He was cute! We were on to something! But alas, he lacked a mouth. How would he speak? I looked deep into his sympathetic, Daffy Duck eyes, and I asked him, "What kind of mouth would you like?" And he answered, "A big grin. And one tooth."

Really. That's how it happened. Perhaps it was because his eyes were so playful, or perhaps I was subconsciously alliterating "kooky" and "cucumber," but for whatever reason, it was clear to me that he wanted a big grin and one tooth.

As I set out to make his mouth, I kept two important facts in mind. First, whatever technique I used to make my characters' mouths needed to be simple enough to apply to lots of characters and easy to animate over an entire half-hour film. By myself. (At this point I was still assuming I'd be making the first film solo. I figured Mike would help in any way he could, but since he wasn't an animator, I assumed I'd be handling all the computer work.) The second thing I kept in mind was that I was not very good at building complex shapes on the computer. I'll admit it—some people have that gift. I do not. For me, the simpler the better. Most other CGI artists working on characters in those days were wrestling with complex sculpted mouths with dimensional lips and chins. They were beautiful, but I had no idea how to model such detail. So I decided to simply cut a hole in his face in the shape of a grin. That was it. There is a technique in computer animation called "texture mapping" that allows a 2D painted or photographed image to be projected (or "mapped") onto a 3D object. I had already used it to give Mr. Cucumber his mottled green skin. So for his mouth, I simply created a solid white image in the shape of a grin, then told the animation software to use the white part of that image as a hole cutter for the middle of his face. For his tooth, I squished a tiny white cube down nearly flat and suspended it just beneath his skin. Now when the "grin mapper" cut the hole in his face, his tooth would show through. What was even better, I could change his mouth shape by creating a simple 2D animation of a frown changing into a smile and rendering that out as a sequence of frames. Now I could point to Mr. Cucumber's face and tell it to cut his mouth using each successive frame from that sequence. Eureka! Now as Mr. Cucumber moved through a sequence of frames, his mouth moved accordingly! (The fact that the mouth animation was driven from a separate sequence of images, combined with the fact that I, partly out of laziness and partly because I'm a weak illustrator, designed all subsequent veggie characters with nearly identical mouths, just scaled or stretched a bit, saved us countless hours when animating things like a crowd of veggies singing the same song. Instead of having to animate each veggie's mouth separately, we were able to animate our generic white mouth singing the song, render out the sequence of images, and then apply them to every veggie that was singing. Want one hundred veggies singing the "Hallelujah Chorus"? No problem! It's done!)

I had my eyes, and now I had my mouths. But how would the little guy get around? How exactly does a cucumber hop? I needed to take him out for a test drive, and for that, I needed a set. Since

I was so fond of that ceramic tile kitchen from the toaster oven commercial, I decided to build my own version. Making the tiles was easy. (Computers are great at cutting and pasting.) I added an electrical outlet on the wall and several Fiestaware canisters and a large Fiestaware bowl. Cheery. I put Mr. Cuke (as I was now calling him) into the bowl and made him scrunch down until he was hidden from view. Then I animated a ten-second scene. The scene that would tell me whether the little guy would come to life—or not. Whether we were in business—or not. Whether it was time to make a show or time to go back to the drawing board. Or not. My virtual camera slowly dollied down the countertop and came to rest in front of the bowl. Pause. A small, green head peeked out, apprehensively at first, then popped a big, one-toothed grin. After another beat the wee fellow leaped from the bowl and hopped up to the camera, leaning his head to the right and smiling.

I tested the animation over and over, but since the computer could only play back a monochromatic wireframe image in real time (long before the graphics cards that now blast out billions of shaded pixels a second), I wouldn't know for sure until the frames were fully rendered and I could see Mr. Cuke in all his green glory. Several hours later the frames were done. Apprehensively, I loaded them into memory for real time playback and sat back to watch Mr. Cuke take his first steps.

It worked.

I mean, it really worked.

He was alive. He wasn't robotic. He didn't really look computer-animated at all, at least by 1990 standards. He looked like a cartoon character. A really fun one at that. The way his eyes and tooth and goofy grin came together, well, you just wanted to hug him. I was euphoric.

It was time to make a show.

But how? I'd have to record audio, make music, add sound effects. I figured the animation would take me at least a few months—four? Five?—I wasn't sure. Ideally, I wanted to focus on this full-time, without the time and energy drain of selling and completing the myriad corporate jobs that were now (sort of) paying the bills. I was pretty sure I needed some money. How much? I didn't know—maybe $20,000 or $30,000? Surely that would be enough. If someone was going to give me money, they'd probably want to know a little more about the show. What would the stories be like? How would they teach? I went over to Mike's apartment to brainstorm. I'd already thought of doing a spoof of *The Grapes of Wrath*, starring a bunch of really cranky grapes. Mike added *Bridge over Pumpkin Pie*, *Lime and Punishment*, and *War and Peaches* to the list. We could spoof classic literature. That'd be funny. (Neither of us seemed to notice at the time that everything on our list featured fruit, not vegetables, or that, botanically speaking, our two lead characters were also, in fact, fruits.) I wrote up a one-page treatment on *The Grapes of Wrath* and added another page describing the basic concept. Fruit, vegetables, and small kitchen appliances singing, dancing, and telling Bible stories. That sort of thing. We needed a name for the show. Mike suggested "VeggieTales." Oooh. That was good.

I pulled together a packet of info and headed out to see my friends at David C. Cook—the guys who steered me away from *The Phil & Mike Show*. I showed them Mr. Cuke's screen test and talked about the concept. They smiled. They liked it. Then they said, "If you make that, we'd be interested in selling it for you." Hmm. No money. Maybe they didn't have any money. I got to thinking about who might have money, and I thought of *McGee and Me*, which by then had sold close to a million copies. Even though the show was owned by Focus on the Family, the videos were distributed by a

Christian publisher, Tyndale House, located not far from my mother's home. I set up a meeting with the executive in charge of *McGee and Me.* This would be perfect. McGee was selling so well, they were bound to have money lying around, ready to invest in a similar project. Especially one starring a cucumber with Daffy Duck eyes. The day came, and I made my pitch.

"See the cucumber? Heh, heh—*The Grapes of Wrath!* Heh— Bible stories. Hoo-boy . . ."

The executive smiled. "Very interesting," he said. Then he continued, "If you make it, we'd be interested in selling it for you."

Right.

But . . . the money. I needed the money.

How was I supposed to make it without the money?

I packed up my cucumber and headed for the car. This wasn't going as well as I'd hoped.

10

Selling the Veggies

The year 1991 was difficult. With all the time and energy I'd invested in VeggieTales, I had sort of taken my eye off the commercial work—the paying jobs. Not yet twenty years old, Lisa now found herself the mother of a baby girl, our daughter Shelby. Our unexpected pregnancy had forced her to drop out of college after only one semester, putting her long-imagined singing career on hold. She hadn't planned on having her first child at nineteen. I hadn't planned on needing to support a family in the midst of launching a business. We had no health insurance. We were several months behind on rent. Our income for the year, after my business costs were deducted, amounted to $13,000. Still, I was convinced God wanted me to keep going. I saw a direct connection between VeggieTales and the call I had felt years earlier while watching MTV. To give up now seemed like walking away from God's call. I couldn't do it.

So I redoubled my efforts both to sell more commercial work and to raise money for VeggieTales. On the commercial side of things, it seemed Chicago's ad agencies and larger corporate producers were reluctant to work with a guy whose animation system was set up in his apartment. Since Chicago's ad agencies were clustered along Michigan Avenue, most major production houses and animation studios set up shop in the same neighborhood. A friend from the Bible study group Lisa and I had recently joined at our north-side church owned a space planning/interior design firm just a block off Michigan Avenue and offered to let me work out of his space for free. I moved my animation system into an empty cubicle next to one of his draftsmen, updated my demo reel with my latest experiments (including a certain smiling cucumber), and started cold calling ad agencies. Boy, did I hate cold calling. Real animation houses had sales reps wining and dining on their behalf—working the parties and industry events the agency folks frequented. And here I was, a shy twenty-four-year-old kid, dialing numbers out of a directory.

On the VeggieTales side, I wasn't doing much better. I had submitted my ten-second cucumber test to Nickelodeon, which was, at that time, looking for ideas as they attempted to launch their first three original animated shows. No luck. (I got a letter back several months later informing me that "Nickelodeon does not produce computer-animated shows." You Nickelodeon historians out there probably know the first three shows they ultimately chose were *Rugrats*, *Doug*, and *Ren & Stimpy*. You probably didn't know that *VeggieTales* was also considered.)

It still didn't make sense to me that Christian publishers wouldn't be interested in VeggieTales, especially Tyndale House, given their success with *McGee and Me*. Maybe they didn't believe I could actually make the show, I thought. Maybe the ten seconds of smiling cucumber wasn't enough. Maybe I needed to show them more. In between commercial jobs, I pulled up "Mr. Cuke" and stared at him. He was alone, and it was not good. He needed a buddy. Since he was tall and thin, I figured he needed a buddy who was short and round. Like Laurel and Hardy or Abbott and Costello. Hmm . . . short, round vegetable . . . hmm . . .

The "creativity experts" will tell you always to throw away your first idea, since it is often the most obvious or clichéd. Set aside your first idea and dig deeper—that's where genius is found. I never had much regard for creativity experts. After abandoning candy bars, my very first idea was a cucumber. I ran with it. And now, looking for a short, round veggie to compliment my tall, skinny guy, the first thought that popped into my head was a tomato. And I ran with it.

I quickly built a tomato on the computer—round, red, little stem and the simplest of leaves (more like a leaf-shaped paper cutout than realistic leaves). I made copies of Mr. Cuke's nose and eyes and stuck them on Mr. Tomato, turning the green parts red. I took Mr. Cuke's mouth, stretched and enlarged it slightly, and positioned it on the tomato. The only significant difference between the two characters' faces was teeth. Whereas the single tooth seemed to fit with Mr. Cuke's goofy persona, it was clear to me that this tomato fella would need to play the straight man— would need to do the "heavy lifting" when it came time to teach a lesson. If Mr. Tomato shared the cucumber's single tooth, we'd have a hillbilly show. *Hee Haw* in a vegetable patch. No, thank you. Mr. Tomato got a full set of teeth.

But what to name them? If it were a typical Christian show, I figured, they'd be Tommy Tomato and Kooky Cucumber. But the last thing in the world I wanted to make was a typical Christian show. I wanted plain names. Practically boring. Names that didn't rhyme, alliterate, or anything. They were just two regular Joe vegetables, and they needed regular Joe names. I immediately thought of my stepdad, the electrician. He was a regular Joe. His name was "Bob." Hmm. "Bob the Tomato." That worked. I wrote down a list of equally plain names for the cucumber, and one just seemed to fit. I think you can guess which one. Mr. Cuke and the Tomato were now Larry and Bob (which I immediately reversed to "Bob and Larry" for rhythmic reasons). All they needed was a short film in which to showcase their talents. Something that would show the Christian publishers I knew what I was doing. That I wasn't just another twenty-four-year-old Bible college dropout with a loony idea asking for a bunch of money.

By early 1992 I had moved yet again, this time into the space of a small production company in a newly renovated warehouse east of Michigan Avenue. I paid them a little rent, and they let me use their pro video deck to output my work to tape. Feeling optimistic about some of my new prospective clients, I had even asked Mike to join me full-time at GRAFx Studios. I told Mike we needed to make a longer demo for VeggieTales and showed him the script I had written. I told him I would voice the tomato and asked him to take a shot at the cucumber. We recorded the script and then listened to it a few times. It was flat. It just wasn't as funny as I had hoped. I threw it out, and we both sat there, late at night in the darkened space, staring at the microphone. I knew I wanted the tomato to try to sell the show, but I couldn't figure out what the cucumber would be doing. Finally, Mike said, "He's looking for his plastic, wind-up lobster."

Perfect. Bob was trying to sell the show, while Larry was running around looking for his plastic, wind-up lobster. In a few minutes, I had written out a new script, focusing on Bob delivering a Martin Luther King Jr.–type "I have a dream" speech about his new kids' show, while Larry hopped around in search of his lobster. It had just the feel I was looking for, showing Bob's immense drive to do something big and wonderfully beneficial, mixed with Larry's carefree, lackadaisical goofiness.

Over the next few weeks, I animated Bob and Larry hopping and smiling and lip-synching along with our voice track. Mike and

I hummed "The Battle Hymn of the Republic" in the background to show the publishers we could handle music, too. The finished two-minute film looked great. Surely this would do the trick! I made the rounds to the local Christian publishers one more time, showing them the new VeggieTales test and then standing back, waiting for their response.

"That looks very interesting," the executives said, "If you go make it, we'd love to sell it for you."

I couldn't believe my ears. They still weren't willing to put any money into my talking vegetables—even after seeing Bob and Larry talk and hearing Mike and me hum "The Battle Hymn of the Republic." What more did they need? I drove back home confused and depressed. To make matters worse, all the time I had put into producing that film was time that hadn't gone into generating any revenue. I didn't have any money to pay Mike, so I told him he should probably start looking for work elsewhere. Several family members advised me to do the same. Mike found a job at another production company, and I found myself working alone once again.

A week or two later, I was sitting at the kitchen table in our small loft apartment assessing our finances. Things looked really bad. Our checking account was overdrawn. We were late on rent. I had no leads on VeggieTales and no leads on new commercial jobs. In my wallet was a ten-dollar bill. That was it. All the money we had in the world.

"We're out of dog food."

"What?" I turned to see who had spoken. It was my wife.

"We're out of dog food," she said again. Oh, great. A twenty-five pound bag of Purina was about ten dollars. I looked at the ten-dollar bill in my wallet and looked at our dog, Max. He looked hungry. Reluctantly, I handed the bill to my wife, who headed for the store, leaving me alone with my thoughts. The apartment was still and dark. Our daughter, Shelby, now eighteen months old, was sleeping in the next room. I couldn't afford to give her health insurance. I couldn't afford to pay her rent. Now I didn't even know how I would feed her.

"You fool," a voice inside me said. "Look at what a mess you've made. No one can rely on you. You can't even take care of your family. And for what? This stupid kids' show dream? This thing you think God told you to do?" My eyes welled up with tears as the doubt grew louder. "What if you were wrong all along? What if all this *wasn't* from God? What if all this was just *your* idea? Just *you*? Man, would that ever make you the fool of the year!"

For the first time, I doubted. For the first time, I wondered if perhaps I had made the whole thing up. My "call"—everything. "God," I called out, "tell me this isn't just me—tell me you're in this, too!"

A friend stopped by. He noticed the desperate look on my face and asked what was wrong. I told him about our state, and he immediately pulled out his wallet and offered me everything he had. "No, thank you," I heard myself say. Something told me this wasn't the answer I needed. My friend left. I turned back to the stack of mail on the table in front of me, looking for something to distract me from the screaming doubt. Bill. Bill. Bill. Wait . . . what's that?

There was a letter tucked among the bills, hand-addressed to us, with no return address. I opened it. Inside was a cashier's check for $400, with a handwritten, unsigned note that simply said, "God laid it on my heart that you might need this."

My heart stopped. Four hundred dollars wasn't necessarily going to turn our lives around, but the message was crystal clear. God was there in the room, at the table, with me. He was with me in my darkest hour, when voices were screaming "Give up! This isn't God, it's just you, fool!" There he was. Sitting beside me at the black laminate table in our loft apartment as my daughter slept in the next room and my wife hunted for dog food with our last ten dollars—God was there, quietly whispering, "I'm with you. Don't give up."

That wasn't the end of our "hard times," of course. We had many more crises to face, and we still do. But since that day, I have never once doubted that God has called me to use my gifts for him, and that he will supply whatever resources I need in his perfect timing.

And I will never give up.

Shortly after the dog-food incident, it occurred to me that I should get a job. Not as a way of "giving up," but rather as part of a new plan to launch VeggieTales. It would work something like this: I would approach a production company and offer to sell them my animation gear and come on board as their in-house CGI artist. But there would be a condition. In my spare time, I would be allowed to use their gear (and my old system) to work on my kids' show, which I would own.

I pitched the idea to one of the post houses I had worked with, and they liked it. Once the papers were signed, I had a decent salary and health insurance. We didn't need to worry about money or our daughter's medical bills anymore. I didn't need to spend my days on the phone trying to sell commercial work anymore. The money they paid for my gear paid off the loan from my parents. Just as vitally, though, I had picked a production company that hadn't done much CGI work in the past, knowing, therefore, they wouldn't have a ton of work for me to do, at least for the first year or so. I figured I would have a lot of downtime, and I would be able to continue work on VeggieTales. I was right. While other employees found their down-time filled with tasks as menial as polishing the apples the company president liked to keep on the reception desk, I was free to work on my veggies. The production house was quite happy, too, since they got to use my demo reel—by now looking pretty good with the dancing stoplights and smiling cucumbers—to attract new clients and sell current clients on their new capabilities.

Sitting in my office at the production company on a slow day, I discovered an interesting bit of software on my workstation I hadn't noticed before. It was a demo copy of the spreadsheet Wingz, a predecessor and short-lived competitor of the now ubiquitous Microsoft Excel. I had never touched a spreadsheet before, and I found it fascinating. Fill the rows with forecasted expenses and revenues, lay a series of months or years out in the columns, and voila! A business model! Though I had never taken a business course or even read a business book, I found myself enchanted with the ability of a spreadsheet to forecast various business models and scenarios. I started to think less and less about simply making a show and handing it off to a publisher and more and more about building a business. Why couldn't I just sell the show myself? Lots of people were selling lots of things through the mail. I forecasted my own salary, equipment expenses, advertising and shipping costs, maybe another person or two to help out once it got going. How many copies could I sell? How fast would it grow? I plugged in numbers and forecasted out three years. I figured I wouldn't sell more than a few hundred copies the first month, but then if those folks really liked it, maybe 50 percent more each month thereafter? The spreadsheet calculated. Whoa. My eyes widened. This could be a business! I could build the Amway of Christian video!

My spare time was now split between financial modeling (a task complicated by the fact that the demo version of Wingz wouldn't allow me to save my work, requiring me to rebuild my model from scratch every time I had to turn off my computer) and further creative development of the show. I met with my mom, who by now had her doctorate in Christian education and was being deployed by David C. Cook as a children's ministry consultant to large churches.

We talked through the teaching angle for VeggieTales. "First rule," she said, taking a somewhat parental tone, "you will not portray Jesus as a vegetable." Good point, I thought, not quite grasping that this guideline would eliminate much of the New Testament as source material for VeggieTales. "Second rule," she continued, "try not to imply that vegetables can have redemptive relationships with God. Don't show vegetables praying unless they're playing the role of a historical or biblical figure." *Yikes*, I thought. *This is going to be tricky.*

"Finally," she continued, "try to communicate to kids how God made each one of them unique and how much he loves them. That's your most important message."

I went home and thought it over. No Jesus-as-a-vegetable. We'd have to avoid the Gospels. Since most of the rest of the New Testament was letters, I concluded we'd be spending most of our time in the Old Testament. Don't imply vegetables can go to heaven. As I wrote the very first script, I took pains to have Bob say, "God loves kids," rather than "God loves us." Focus on the kids, not on the vegetables. And last, but definitely not least, I needed some sort of tagline that would remind kids at the end of each episode how special they are and how much God loves them. Something like, "God made you special, and he loves you very much." Yeah. Grammatically imperfect, but catchy. That would do the trick.

Next, I needed a veggie kid, someone the kids in the audience could relate to. Someone with a family so we could portray family situations. I had already created an asparagus character (later to become Archibald Asparagus), because, well, asparagus have "hair." I decided an asparagus kid could work. I made a short asparagus and gave him a ball cap. I gave him a little off-to-the-side smile to distinguish him from Bob and Larry. I named him Junior because, as usual, it was the first thing that popped into my head. I whipped up a set of vegetable parents. Dad wore a tie, and Mom, a string of pearls. I named them "Mom" and "Dad." Wow. I am a creative genius.

It was now time for the first story. Something about Junior. Something fundamental, like being scared of the dark. Over a few days, I pieced together a story about Junior alone in his room, unable to sleep after watching a Frankencelery movie on TV. Bob and Larry "magically" appear with a lesson about God being bigger than anything Junior could fear. I got out my three-quarter-sized guitar from third-grade guitar lessons and strummed a few chords, plunking out a song about God being "Bigger than the bogeyman." I played it for my wife, the music major, who immediately declared it "too simple to be a real song." I wasn't so sure, though. After watching our daughter and a zillion other kids become enraptured with *Barney*, *Wee Sing*, and a hundred other shows and videos that featured the simplest of public domain songs, I thought really simple songs with witty lyrics might be just what we needed. Besides, I wasn't good enough to write anything more complex. Simple songs would have to suffice.

Back at work, I built Junior's living room and bedroom sets, using as little detail as possible to save on rendering time (the time it takes for a computer to calculate the finished image). With just a few exceptions, almost everything in Junior's house was composed of flattened or reshaped cubes.

I also avoided applying painted textures as texture maps. This reduced render time, gave the sets the simpler, "cartoonier" feel that I liked, and avoided the issue that I'm not much of a painter. Almost everything about the look of VeggieTales is a result of my personal tastes combined with my financial and artistic shortcomings. I am not a brilliant artist, and I did not have much to work with in terms of either time or money. The result: simple, limbless vegetables singing simple songs on simple sets. Suffice it to say, if my father hadn't blessed me with his quirky sense of humor, I'd still be making bar charts for a living and you wouldn't be reading this book.

It was just that quirky sense of humor that led me to find myself crossing the plaza of the Dirksen Federal Building in March of 1993 with a fistful of tax forms, suddenly and inexplicably singing a weird little song about everyone having a water buffalo. I liked the song so much I hummed it on the bus all the way back to work so I wouldn't forget it, and then wondered if perhaps Larry could come out in the middle of the show and sing such ridiculousness. I imagined a dry, British narrator intoning, "And now it's time for Silly Songs with Larry, the part of the show where Larry comes out and sings . . . a silly song." And then Larry could sing the water buffalo song. Yeah. That's the last thing you'd expect in a Christian kids' video (short of full frontal nudity, of course). Perfect.

Things were now moving along swimmingly on all fronts, except, of course, for the money. I was getting busier by the week at the production company as more and more CGI work came in, and I knew there was no way I could produce an entire thirty-minute show in my dwindling downtime. The company's sales rep was having luck with my reel, and in rapid succession I found myself working on two national TV commercials, the first for Pop-Tarts and the second for Miller beer. In the commercial production world, national TV commercials are the top of the heap. The big leagues. This is what I'd been aiming for when I started GRAFx Studios four years earlier, and now I was there. National spots on my reel would no doubt attract more big-time TV work. I had a chance to become a "big shot" animator in the Chicago advertising world, the largest ad production market in the United States after New York. This could be big. But I didn't care. I looked at what these spots had to say—one was selling sugar to kids, the other alcohol to grown-ups.

In the meantime, the characters I'd created to teach kids about God's love were sitting on the shelf waiting. Staring at me. Saying, "Phil, can we start, now? The kids, Phil, the kids!" National spots or no national spots, I was ready to say good-bye to the world of animation-for-hire. I had a business plan. I had a script. I had a really simple song about God and the bogeyman and another one about a water buffalo. All I needed was some money.

Shortly after Lisa and I were married, we had formed a small group at our church with three other couples. As a result, these couples had front-row seats for our vegetable drama. They had prayed with us for financing and direction. They had seen the dancing cucumber and the visionary tomato. They, too, were baffled when the Christian publishers smiled and then showed us the door. Then, in late June of 1993, a year after joining the production company, one of the men in our group took me aside. He was the interior designer who had loaned me office space the year before, and we connected on a creative as well as a spiritual level. "What you are trying to do is too important to not let happen," he said. Then he handed me a check for $80,000 taken from his retirement savings.

I couldn't believe it. I had looked at my friends as spectators and cheerleaders, not participants. But here he was, handing me the largest check I had ever seen in my life and telling me to get started. Lisa and I were elated. Just as when my stepfather had offered to loan the money for my first animation system, though, I stopped and swallowed hard. It's one thing to believe in something enough to risk your own money or money from a large, faceless corporation. It's quite another thing to risk money that belongs to people you really, really like. I thought through my plan one more time. I watched some of the other Christian videos offered for sale in those days. Other than *McGee and Me*, which was selling like hotcakes, they were really, really lame. If I could capture what I saw in my head on videotape and get it in front of people, I was convinced they would like it. I was convinced my plan would work.

I accepted my friend's offer and nervously deposited his check.

It wasn't enough, though. Since I had sold my animation system to the production company, I would need new gear. I would also need audio gear for recording and editing the dialogue and the music. And then, since I was now planning on selling the videos directly, I would need money for ads, phone lines, video duplication, shipping, and so on. I needed more money.

Right around that time, a friend told me about a Christian ministry based in Cyprus that was looking for Christian kids' shows to air on satellite TV in the Middle East. A representative from this ministry would be in town the following week for a fund-raising dinner at the Kraft mansion in Chicago's wealthy north suburbs. Yes, *that* Kraft mansion. He got me an invitation, and I brought along Lisa and Mike for moral support. We met Mrs. Kraft. I thanked her for all the macaroni and cheese. After the presentation, I met with the man from the ministry, who, due to Middle East security concerns, traveled in the United States under an assumed name. It was all very hush-hush. Top secret. I showed him my two-minute veggie test. In a few weeks, we had a deal in place. He would give me $110,000 in exchange for the international rights to the first eleven episodes of VeggieTales—$10,000 per episode. It wasn't very much by TV standards, but considering that I wasn't sure I could make *one* episode of VeggieTales, much less *eleven*, I figured it was the best deal I was likely to see anytime soon. I signed the deal.

And thus, the final piece was in place. After spending two years developing, refining, and then trying to convince people I could make the first ever half-hour, computer-animated kids' show, it was time to put up or shut up.

It was time to make the show.

11

"Have We Got a Show for You"

Every truly worthwhile pursuit, it seems, begins with a "Herculean" effort—a period of almost superhuman work from a small band of committed zealots. Mickey Mouse wasn't Walt Disney's first successful animated character, as every good Disney buff knows. That honor goes to Oswald the Lucky Rabbit. Oswald was a modest hit, but Walt's tiny studio wasn't making much money due to an unfavorable deal with distributor Charles Mintz in New York. Emboldened by Oswald's success, Walt took a train to New York to negotiate a better deal, only to be crushed by the news that Mintz was not only taking Oswald away from him (enabled by a one-sided contract that gave the distributor ultimate ownership of Walt's creation), but also that the distributor had already hired away most of Walt's animators, who would now work directly for Mintz. Walt had been cut out of his own business.

Rather than give up, however, Walt spent the long train ride back across the country sketching out a new character—a mouse. He showed the sketch to his wife, Lilly, saying the little fellow would be named Mortimer. As legend has it, Lilly wrinkled her nose at the name Mortimer and instead suggested Mickey.

But that was the easy part. The hard part came when Walt arrived back in Hollywood. He needed to get a short film starring his new character produced as quickly as possible, but he couldn't use his soon-to-depart animators or, for that matter, even let them or Charles Mintz know the new character existed. So he sequestered his old friend and animation buddy Ub Iwerks in a private office with the task of almost single-handedly animating the first Mickey Mouse cartoon. Working in isolation, Ub turned out as many as seven hundred drawings a day—an unbelievable pace, virtually unequaled in the history of animation. By the time Walt's unfaithful animators departed with Oswald for Charles Mintz's new studio, Walt and Ub had a new cartoon to show the world. Oswald the Lucky Rabbit quickly fell into obscurity, and Walt and Mickey—well, you know the rest of that story. But take away Ub Iwerks and his Herculean effort, and what would have become of Mickey? We can only wonder.

For VeggieTales, the Herculean effort began in late July 1993. I didn't know much about direct sales, or fulfillment, or even long-form animation for that matter. But I knew we should probably have our first video done in time for Christmas, and I knew that didn't leave much time to waste. Once my new $70,000 animation system arrived (Softimage was now too big to offer "sweetheart" deals), I set it up alongside a new rack of audio gear in the spare bedroom of the house Lisa and I were now renting in Andersonville, the historically Swedish neighborhood on Chicago's far north side. Before leaving the production company, Mike and I had set up a microphone in one of their edit rooms to record the dialogue for the first segment. Once again, Mike played Larry against my Bob. For Junior, the other key character, my wife Lisa offered to audition. I initially found this idea fraught with peril and tried to discourage her, given the stress-inducing scenario of critiquing—and potentially rejecting—my own wife. She assured me she was a big girl and could handle the rejection. I gave in. It's a good thing I did, too, because lurking beneath her "gonna be the next Sandy Patti" exterior was the cutest little five-year-old asparagus I ever could have imagined. Lisa tried several other character parts through the years, but nothing else quite worked. At the end of the day, she isn't really an actress. She's just "Junior." And once she slips into that character, she steals your heart.

Once the dialogue track was recorded and edited, it was time to get to work. Every day I animated. Every evening, after his day job at a downtown production house, Mike came in to perform the laborious task of breaking down the dialogue track, listening word by word to determine the frame placement of each syllable so my mouth animation would line up with our vocal performance. Ten days in, I came to two significant conclusions. The first was that I was going to die a miserable death and still not have a show done by Christmas. I was animating ten to fourteen seconds each day—a good figure by animation standards—but not enough to stay on schedule. One person simply could not animate a thirty-minute CGI film in four months. It wasn't going to happen. My second conclusion was more encouraging. Animating these simple characters, using the basic techniques I had developed back in 1990, was relatively easy. *So* easy that I figured I could get someone else up and animating with very little training. My final conclusion was truly unexpected: I needed a staff. In all my plans to create a kids' series and build "the Amway of Christian video," it had somehow never occurred to me that I would need employees. Wow.

But who?

I had met Chris Olsen a few weeks earlier as I was preparing to leave the production company. He came in looking for a job as an animator, having just graduated from the art and technology program at the University of Illinois. He didn't have enough experience for the commercial production world where entry-level jobs (besides apple polishing) are few and far between, but now as I thought about it, he was ideally qualified to help out with VeggieTales. He knew his way around a Silicon Graphics workstation, loved animation, and didn't need much money. Perfect! Chris Olsen became my first employee. About the same time, my lawyer tipped me off to a Christian kid at his church who had just completed the computer graphics courses at the Art Institute of Chicago. I talked to Robert Ellis on the phone and found that he, too, met the profile of knowing his way around a workstation and not needing much by way of compensation. Robert was a big animation fan, having seen Disney's *The Little Mermaid* in a theater near the Art Institute something like thirty times. He also brought some interesting quirks to the company, such as his propensity for self-injury (he once showed up on crutches after stepping in a gopher hole during a badminton game) and his potentially fatal allergy to artificial caramel coloring. ("If I drink a can of Coke," he told us one day, "I'll die." We all made a mental note of that.)

Given my wife's reluctance to have strange men working in our spare bedroom late into the night, it was now clear I needed an office. So production temporarily shut down while Chris Olsen and I moved my gear into a tiny, six-hundred-square-foot storefront on Foster Avenue, a few blocks from our house. The space had just been split off from an identical space next door, which had been rented to a nineteen-year-old kid pursuing the dream of opening his own comic book shop. Here, Chris's summer construction experience proved invaluable, as he and I spent a week completing the dividing wall between the two spaces and hanging shelves and the solid wood door that would transform the weird little cinder block storage room in the back into a crude but functional voice-over booth. We bought a couple of cheap desks and chairs from an office supply store, a small phone system to handle the orders I figured would soon be pouring in, and a Macintosh computer for general office work and the laying out of our ads and video sleeves. The comic book kid opened his shop a few weeks later and placed several large arcade-style video games right up against our common wall, filling our evening hours with a plethora of electronic boops and beeps. The single gas meter for the two spaces was on his side of the wall, with the gas account in his name. This point will become relevant a little later.

By mid-August we were up and running in our new space. Chris took the day shift on the animation system, and Robert, the night. My days were filled with frame-by-frame animation direction for my two animators, plus the business duties of planning our direct sales launch. There were still two holes left on our team, though, and I had precious little money with which to fill them. The first was financial. I'd managed to learn my way around a spreadsheet, but I was clueless when it came to bookkeeping, taxes, and payroll. My good friend Dina Cload, an accountant at the time at a real estate firm, volunteered to come in a few hours each week to help out. The next hole I faced was musical. Sure, I could hum a simple tune and Lisa could tell me what chord I needed to match my melodies, but neither of us was capable of producing the kind of polished music I heard on other kids' videos. We needed a musical person who was good with synthesizers. I sat at church one day mulling over this problem and noticed how good the music sounded. Every week. Ours was a contemporary church, and each service featured at least one elaborately arranged solo or ensemble number produced with a live band by the church's music director, Kurt Heinecke. We had gotten to know Kurt through my wife's involvement in the music ministry, and after church one Sunday, I asked if he might be interested in helping with the music for a kids' video. He acknowledged he'd never done anything quite like that but was up for the challenge. Having a film composer who had never composed for film before didn't bother me any more than having two animators who had never animated or a company president who had no experience managing a company (that being me). We were all making it up as we went, which was fine by me. In fact, I kind of liked it that way.

And so, a new company was born. Technically, I didn't need to start a *new* company, since I still owned GRAFx Studios, Inc. But I needed a new name. "GRAFx" was a clear reference to the computer graphics work I used to do, but it didn't fit a company that produced children's videos. I asked Lisa and Mike if they had any ideas. Lisa suggested "101 Salvations." Mike pitched in with "Squeaky Pigs." I thanked them for their input and kept thinking. The best things I had written had always started with some key, central idea—some little bit of inspiration that drove everything else. If I attempted to write something without first developing that key, motivating idea, the end result was usually flat and lifeless. My first attempt at a script for the two-minute VeggieTales promotional film was flat until Mike said, "Larry is looking for his plastic, wind-up lobster." Then the whole thing came to life. Mike's suggestion was the key idea. The "big idea," if you will.

Hmm. "Big Idea." "Life's too short to work on little ideas." I liked it. It smacked of bigger things to come.

On August 6, 1993, I formally changed my company's name from GRAFx Studios, Inc., to Big Idea Productions, Inc. I scrawled the new name on a sheet of paper, drew electricity arcing over it between two tesla coils, and taped it to our front door. Our first logo.

We hit the ground running. Dina was setting up accounts with the credit card companies so we could process orders. Chris and Robert were animating away, following my notes that detailed each character's movements down to individual eye blinks. I was jumping between directing the animation and planning out our ads and our ad buys. I also pitched in and animated whenever I had a chance. Mike continued to stop by in the evenings to help with dialogue breakdown and cowrote the theme song with Lisa. Driving to church one Sunday morning, Lisa and I came up with a cute little ditty we thought would make a perfect "wrap-up the show" song. Lisa hummed it through the entire service to keep from forgetting the tune, and, once back home, we added some lyrics. "And so what we have learned applies to our lives today—and God has a lot to say in his book. . ." It was the perfect little song to "come out of nowhere" at the end of a kids' show and set up the lesson. I decided its relentless, automated intrusion would bug the heck out of control-freak Bob. I'm not exactly sure why. It just struck me as funny.

Before long, Chris and Robert were nearing the end of that first segment. Egads. They needed more! I picked *Daniel and the Lion's Den* as a companion piece and quickly wrote a new script, complete with four or five new songs. Mike and Lisa pitched in with some musical and lyrical ideas. We recorded the dialogue in our weird little sound closet, I built the sets, and Mike broke down the new dialogue tracks. While we did that, I set Chris to work bringing "The Water Buffalo Song" to life. Chris designed and built the sets and directed and animated the entire piece himself. I was impressed. I'd hired an animator who could do more than just animate! Cool!

August passed, and then September. As the animation continued, I realized that, since we were already double-shifting on our single workstation, we wouldn't have enough available computer time to render the film's 54,000 images. I begged Softimage for help, and they agreed to sell me a used demo system at a greatly reduced price. While Chris and Robert animated on our primary workstation, I kept the second system rendering twenty-four hours a day on finished shots. I could only afford a single 2-gigabyte hard drive for storage (a $2,000 purchase at the time), so every couple of days I had to back up that drive to a DAT tape, delete everything, and start filling it again with newly rendered images. If any of those tapes failed, I realized, we were pretty much toast. There really wasn't much time to worry about that though, as our attention was firmly focused on the finished frames counting off on one hand and the days until Christmas counting off on the other.

Then October hit, and things started to get wacky. I had placed a single-page "teaser" ad in the September issues of several Christian magazines, giving no ordering information, but simply showing a selection of the characters peering in around the edges of a "coming soon" message. (The character lineup at this point included a talking toaster—a cute fellow who proved too cumbersome to animate and never made it into an actual video.) Following up on that first ad, readers of the October/November issues were accosted by a huge, two-page spread with the first real VeggieTales cast "beauty shot," lots of information about the new series and the new production technology that enabled it, and an order form and 800 number in the corner. And now, just as I had hoped, the phone started ringing.

This was a good thing and a bad thing. Good, because, obviously, this is how we would generate revenue. Bad, because, well, I didn't have anyone to answer the phone. It wasn't part of the budget. So we set up the phone next to the primary animation system, and whoever happened to be animating when the phone rang was the order taker. So, chances are, if you ordered a video during the day, you talked to Chris Olsen. If you ordered at night, you talked to Robert Ellis. (Imagine calling Pixar to order a video and getting John Lasseter on the phone. "Hello, this is John. May I take your order?") It really was as loopy as it sounds. We printed up small order pads, and every time the phone rang, the animator stopped animating, picked up the phone and a pad and wrote down someone's name, address, and credit card number. Then once or twice a week, Dina would come in and process the orders. Today companies talk about removing the distance between their customers and the people who actually make the products. Let me just say, we were way out in front of that trend.

Then things got even wackier, because we came in one morning and the heat wasn't working. It turned out that the comic book guy on the other side of the wall was a little short of cash and decided to save money by not paying the gas bill. When the gas utility turned off his heat, ours, of course, went with it. Through a cold Chicago November and early December. Picture this scene, if you will: I walk into the office late in the evening to find Robert Ellis, alone on his shift, animating diligently in his parka with a blanket on his lap and a small space heater under the blanket. He's sitting at a $75,000 work station, but we don't have the cash to pay our neighbor's gas bill and get the heat turned back on. In the midst of this, of course, Robert is also answering the phone and writing down people's credit card numbers.

What most amazes me about all of this is that Chris and Robert never complained. They just kept on working—animating, answering phones, whatever it took. They believed in what we were doing, and they were willing to do anything to see it happen.

And this was true for everyone. Dina came in week after week, processing credit card orders, updating the database, handling payroll. I honestly can't remember if we were able to pay her or not, but if we did, I'm sure it wasn't much. When we decided Larry should play the tuba in the theme song, Kurt said, "Hey—I think I could play a *real* tuba!" Turns out Kurt had been an elementary school band instructor at one time, and, as such, had a basic working knowledge of every brass instrument. He called around and found an old elementary school tuba we could borrow, then locked himself away in our tiny sound closet and "blatted" his brains out laying down take after take, slowly reacquainting himself with his inner "tubist." (The tuba you hear on every VeggieTales video ever released is still that original recording of Kurt and his borrowed, beat-up elementary school tuba blatting away in our little cinder block storage room.)

By Thanksgiving, the renders were entering the home stretch. But all those finished frames were scattered across dozens of DAT tapes. Our music and voice tracks were on digital audiotapes in the next room. Our sound effects were still sleeping peacefully on their CDs in our new sound-effects library. We still had to put it all together. It was time to make the show.

As you remember, editing video circa 1986 was a complex affair involving racks and racks of equipment and giant tape machines. By 1992, all that was changing. A small company called Avid was revolutionizing the world of production with their new, computer-based nonlinear edit systems. For the first time, you could load video and audio clips onto a computer and move them around to your heart's content. Assembling complex shows with thousands of elements was now an order of magnitude easier than it had been a few short years earlier. Thinking of VeggieTales, I figured this technology would be vital if I was to produce the show on my own, without the aid of a large, expensive production company. The only problem was the price tag. Avid systems cost in the neighborhood of $80,000. My VeggieTales budget couldn't even afford to *rent* one. As we headed into 1993, though, a new company had caught my eye. Positioning itself as an "Avid killer," Media 100 was about to launch a Mac-based editor with most of Avid's capabilities at one-third the price. I knew I still couldn't afford to buy one outright, but if I could find one to rent, that might just do the trick. In the fall of 1993, as we headed into production on VeggieTales, the first Media 100 in the state of Illinois was delivered to a Chicago area rental house. We were one of the first companies in line to rent it.

Late November 1993. To make our promised Christmas delivery date, we needed to deliver a finished show to our video duplicator in about eighteen days. The rental company dropped off the Media 100 editing system. We excitedly set it up. Great. Now we just had to figure out how to get 54,000 frames from a huge stack of DAT tapes back through our UNIX-based animation system and over to the Mac-based Media 100, import all our music and sound files, lay in sound effects for every hop, squeak, and plop in the entire show, line it all up, set the audio levels on every element, lay it off to a master video tape, and get it to our duplicator. We had the Media 100 reserved for two weeks. Great. How hard could it be?

Very hard, we discovered rather quickly. Sharing files across different platforms (Mac and UNIX in this case) in those days was far from simple, but we had found a piece of software that promised to do the trick. We set up our network, loaded the software, and futzed with it until, sure enough, we could see the contents of the UNIX workstation's hard drive from the Mac. Now all we had to do was tell it to grab all the rendered frames and drag them over. There was only one problem: it would only take about 30 frames at a time. We opened the window, highlighted 30 rendered picture files, then tapped a button and waited as each one came over the network . . . click . . . click . . . click. . . . For some reason, the software wouldn't allow us to grab more than 30 files at a time. So we grabbed the first 30 images, then sat for thirty to forty seconds as they came over. Click . . . click . . . click. . . . Okay, 53,970 frames to go.

It was a nightmare. We had 54,000 frames to import and the only software that could do the job required us to import them manually, 30 at a time! Click . . . click . . . click. . . . This new task made the chore of breaking down dialogue tracks seem positively engrossing! Unable to concoct a better plan, we quickly set up a three-man rotation, with Robert, Chris, and myself triple-shifting around the clock to keep the frames clicking across the network. Click . . . click . . . click. . . . By the end of the first week we had enough frames loaded onto the editing system for Mike to come in and begin pulling the elements together. Click . . . click . . . click—the first half of the show slowly started to take shape. The good news was that, as the elements came together, the show seemed to work. It really worked, just as I'd seen it in my head two years earlier. The bad news was that as we neared the end of our two-week rental, only about 60 percent of the show was finished. I called the rental company.

"We need more time, please!" I said.

"Sorry—someone else has the system right after you."

"You don't understand. It's a matter of life and death! Our company could fail if we can't get more time! *More time, please!*"

"Uh huh. Someone else needs it. Our guy will be there to pick it up tomorrow. Have the hard drives cleaned off by noon."

Click.

My stomach dropped. This was very bad. Our unfinished show was in pieces all over this edit system, which was going to be picked up and carried away in just twenty-four hours. We scrambled to rent a video deck to lay off all our elements from the editing system. By noon the next day, the Media 100 was driving away in the back of a truck, and the first episode of VeggieTales lay half on a video tape, and half in pieces spread across multiple DAT tapes, audio tapes, and computer hard drives. It was Thursday, December 16, 1993—nine days before Christmas. If we didn't get a master to our duplicator within a couple of days, our delivery date was shot. Not only would I have sorely disappointed my first batch of customers, but I'm pretty sure I'd be guilty of mail fraud to boot. It was time to split up and call in favors.

Thursday morning: Mike calls in a favor from an independent producer friend who has recently purchased his own Avid. He's willing to help. Mike moves into his office and begins tediously loading all the elements from our videotape onto the Avid and rebuilding the show as it had been on the Media 100. Once all the video elements are reassembled, Mike will be able to continue adding sound effects and music.

Meanwhile, I call in a favor from the production house that bought my old equipment. I bring in my new system with the remaining DAT tapes, and Chris and I continue the task of reloading and laying off the rest of the rendered frames. We work through Thursday night and through much of the day Friday. We're still not done, though.

Friday afternoon we go home and sleep for about four hours so the production house can use their gear, then return to work through Friday night.

Saturday morning comes and we're still working—Mike assembling sound effects, Chris and I clicking off frames.

Saturday night we're still working.

Sunday morning: Still working. Click . . . click . . . hop, hop here, squeak, squeak there.

Sunday evening: Mike is done with sound effects and is now beginning to adjust final levels on all the audio elements. Chris and I are laying off the final frames of Bob and Larry on the kitchen countertop.

Monday morning: still working. We're all together now, marrying the countertop scenes Chris and I have completed at the production house with the elements Mike has finished on the Avid across town.

Monday evening, 7:00 p.m.: The last edit is made. The show is complete. It's time to make two copies of the master, one for the duplicator and one for safety. Mike, Chris, and I sit back in the edit suite and watch the entire show roll by for the first time. I know each of the 54,000 frames by heart, yet I've never seen them like this. The veggies talk. They "boing" when they hop. Kurt's music plays.

I like it.

We label the tapes, then ride the elevator down to Mike's Jeep. No one says a word all the way home.

We've been working without sleep since Friday afternoon at 4:00 p.m. It is now 9:00 p.m. on Monday. Seventy-seven hours straight. Not counting the four-hour nap on Friday afternoon, we have worked continuously for 100 hours. I look over at Chris in the backseat of Mike's Jeep. He's fast asleep.

We drop off a master at the duplication company, then Mike drops me off at home. I stumble upstairs and fall into bed. My wife looks at me, her eyes asking the obvious question.

"We did it," I mumble. "It's done."

12

Baby Steps

Mickey Mouse was very nearly an overnight success, though, ironically, not due to the film Ub Iwerks had single-handedly animated. Technologically speaking, Walt Disney was what we now refer to as an "early adopter." Rather than fear new technology, he jumped in with both feet. As Ub was locked away furiously drawing *Plane Crazy*, the first Mickey Mouse short film, Walt had an eye on a new technology that was rocking Hollywood to its core. Sound. Al Jolsen's *The Jazz Singer*, released in 1927, had let the genie out of the bottle, and Hollywood was reeling from the implications. Suddenly silent pictures seemed "old-fashioned." "Talkies" were the rage. As of mid-1928, only one attempt had been made at a synchronized sound cartoon—a half-hearted effort by one of Walt's New York competitors. After a screening of the just completed *Plane Crazy* at a local theater proved less than overwhelming, Walt wondered if the addition of sound might get an audience more excited. But he didn't just want to add a few lines of dialogue and sound effects to *Plane Crazy*—he wanted to create a short from scratch to show the world the potential he saw in this new technology.

Plane Crazy—Ub's amazing accomplishment—and a partially completed second silent Mickey short were set on the shelf. Ub and Walt went back to work on a third short, this one designed from the ground up to be driven by music, dialogue, and sound effects synchronized to the onscreen visuals in a way far beyond the reach of any live-action director. This third short, *Steamboat Willy*, premiered at the Colony Theater in New York City on November 18, 1928. Within twelve months, Mickey Mouse was a national craze.

Walt didn't invent the animated film or synchronized sound, but he envisioned a combination of the two technologies—married to a likable character and a serviceable story—that audiences found intoxicating.

Bob and Larry, by contrast and contrary to popular opinion, were not an overnight success. By the week before Christmas we had taken five hundred orders for *Where's God When I'm S-scared?*—not even enough to pay for our magazine ads, much less cover our production cost. Forever the optimist, I thought back to my initial forecasts of sales growing 50 percent each month as people told their friends how much they liked the show. (Assuming, of course, they would like it.) So 500 copies in December, I figured, would translate into 750 copies in January and 1,100 in February. That was still a little on the low side, but if I could hang on long enough, I was sure my small, inexpensive crew would become financially sustainable within four or five months.

Three days before Christmas we picked up five hundred dubs from our duplicator and met at the office to stuff envelopes. We put a small flyer in each video sleeve that I had laid out rather crudely on our Mac. The cover said, "Welcome to the world of Big Idea." Not "Welcome to the world of VeggieTales," but "Welcome to the world of Big Idea." From the very beginning I wanted to focus our audience not simply on a kids' property or group of characters, but rather on the people *behind* the characters and the mission of doing something significant in the world of media. There was a direct connection between the fire I'd felt five years earlier watching MTV and the words I poured into that flyer. I talked about the problem of media saturation. About the loss of family interaction. About the sexualization of our kids. I said we wanted to do something about it—that, for starters, we wanted to make videos that weren't just good "for Christian videos," but were good for *any* videos. I closed by promising that Big Idea would be part of the solution, not just another part of the problem. My goal in that cheap little flyer, looking back, was to make Christian families excited not just about VeggieTales, but more importantly, about the company behind it. It would be a theme I would repeat over and over for the next decade. VeggieTales was just the beginning—just my first idea. If fans got excited about Big Idea, I figured, they'd be there for my next idea, too, just as I had waited for each new Disney movie as a kid. Even a dog like *Gus* (the field-goal kicking mule), which we saw not because we were big supporters of mules in sports per se, but rather because the name Disney meant, to us at the time anyway, "You're going to like this." That's what I wanted for Big Idea.

First, though, we had to get VeggieTales going. When I had calculated my projected monthly sales growth, I hadn't considered that the first month would be December—Christmas. Rather than growing our sales in month two, January saw sales plummet to fewer than two hundred videos. On the bright side, we started getting fan letters almost as soon as those first five hundred copies were popped into VCRs. People really liked the show, it seemed. That was good. On the dimmer side, very little of my original capital was left, and selling two hundred copies per month wasn't going to get us through the winter. This leads us to a valuable business lesson about word of mouth.

Valuable business lesson #1: Word of mouth is a very cool thing, in that your customers become your advertising. A million happy fans talking about your product gives an amazing boost. If, however, your mother is the only one who knows about your product, the impact of word of mouth is somewhat limited. A million fans + word of mouth = good. Your mother + word of mouth = less good.

Not that my mother didn't help—actually all of our families jumped in at this point, talking up VeggieTales and buying a few extra copies themselves to pass around their neighborhoods. Chris Olsen's grandmother managed to sell a dozen copies of *Where's God When I'm S-scared?* to fellow residents of her nursing home. My Grandpa Vischer—he who bought me my first puppet and provided me with his Super8 camera for my childhood films—earned a place in history as the first person ever to buy a VeggieTales video, having mailed in a check and an order for two copies as soon as we started production. He went on to buy more than a hundred copies of that first video, passing them out to friends and relatives all over rural Michigan.

In addition to the formidable sales efforts of our collective grandparents, though, those first five hundred copies had a deeper impact than might have been expected, as several of them went to major Christian publishers. Tyndale House, the folks who had said, "If you make it, we'd be glad to sell it for you," was the first to order, followed by Word Records, one of the three big Christian music companies in Nashville. The order from Word came from a fellow named Wayne Zeitner, recently hired as director of Everland Entertainment, Word's brand-new kids' label. He got his copy of the first video, watched it, and liked it a lot. He showed the video to his boss, Loren Balmen, who liked it so much he gave Wayne a hug. Imagine that. Two grown businessmen hugging because of our video. Within a few hours, Wayne had tracked me down via phone and was offering to fly me and my wife to Nashville to talk more about VeggieTales. We found a sitter for our daughter and hopped a plane to Nashville, where Wayne was waiting at the airport. Word paid for the plane tickets, a nice hotel room, and a yummy dinner. They wanted to help us with VeggieTales. Really. A lot. Lisa and I were pinching ourselves. Just a few months earlier, it seemed, we were digging through our change jar to buy baby formula. Now here we were being "wined and dined" (sans wine, of course) by a big company that wanted to help. Wayne offered a deal to take three VeggieTales videos into Christian bookstores. We talked about the business details, and then Lisa and I flew back to Chicago, excited by the prospect of seeing VeggieTales in hundreds of stores. With that whole "build the Amway of Christian video" angle not panning out very well, retail sales seemed like the answer. Especially with a promised $40,000 advance against each video, which, at this point, I desperately needed to keep my guys working on our second video, *God Wants Me to Forgive Them?!?* Just a few more weeks and a deal would be in place.

Five months later we were still waiting.

It took Wayne and me about sixty days to negotiate the deal, which then had to be approved by Roland Lundy, Word's president. Roland watched the first tape and said, "Three videos? These are good! Let's ask for seven!" We renegotiated a seven-video deal. But Word had just been bought by Bible publisher Thomas Nelson, and now the seven-video deal was too big for Roland to approve. The deal and the first tape went up to Nelson's colorful CEO, Sam Moore. He watched the tape and liked what he saw. "Seven videos? These are good! Let's ask for eleven!" Once again we renegotiated.

By the time the deal was done, it had been five months since our trip to Nashville and forty-five days since I had last been able to give paychecks to Chris, Robert, and myself. We were broke. Amazingly, Chris and Robert continued diligently animating the second video without pay, borrowing money from their parents to cover their bills. Mike, who was still at this point working full-time at a Chicago production house, had pitched in some cash he'd advanced from a credit card in exchange for an ownership stake in the company. He became Big Idea's second shareholder.

In May of 1994, our distribution deal with Word was finally ready to be signed. Mike followed me down to my lawyer's office in Chicago's Loop and videotaped me signing—and faxing—the papers. I made an off-the-cuff remark about "the course of Western civilization changing" that day. The deal was done, and the first $40,000 advance for the first video arrived a few days later. I gave Chris and Robert their back pay and paid our other overdue bills. A big chunk of the money was already gone, and the second video wasn't half done yet.

Hmm. This was going to be trickier than I thought.

Word took orders for 50,000 copies of the first two videos, which were set to arrive in about 750 Christian bookstores in August of 1994, alongside a cardboard floor display of the characters. That was to be the extent of our marketing budget for the launch of VeggieTales. The floor display. No ads. No radio. No PR. No celebrity tie-ins. No TV. No stunts in Time Square. No banners on the sides of buses. No product placement on the Super Bowl. Just a cardboard cutout of some vegetables in the corner of several hundred Christian bookstores. We sent copies of *Where's God When I'm S-scared?* to Christian magazines for review, though, and the response was stellar. "A new standard for Christian videos!" That sort of thing. Cool.

By the summer of 1994, we had received two $40,000 advances. I finally had the money to bring Mike in full-time to do audio and video editing, mouth animation, and writing. A guy named Lesly Benodin, whom I'd met at church, volunteered to come in and help out in any way he could—for free. He didn't need money, he said; it just looked like fun. He started writing simple software to track production and took over the management of shot rendering. We hired a third animator, a recent graduate from Chicago's Columbia College named Heather Jones. Overflowing our tiny storefront, we rented the front offices of a nearby screw manufacturing plant that sported lime green linoleum floors and the perpetual—and occasionally overwhelming—smell of machine oil. (Business partners commented about the whiff of oily air that greeted them upon opening our overnight envelopes.) We also bought our very own Media 100 edit system to avoid another end-of-production fiasco like we had with the first film.

The production of the second video went moderately better than the first, though we still ended up pulling multiple all-nighters over the last few weeks to meet Word's delivery dead-line. When the master finally went out the door at about 3:00 a.m. the morning of our deadline, Mike, Chris, Robert, Lesly, and I staggered down the street to an all-night Mexican restaurant to celebrate. We all felt the second video looked and sounded better than the first. The camaraderie was palpable. We all felt proud of what we were accomplishing, and I was having more fun than I'd had at any time since Bible college. We were building something from nothing—something that existed solely to do good. The stress of the hours was visible in our faces, though, and in the parking lot outside the restaurant, Mike asked me if we could "please never have to work that hard again." I tried to remember where I'd put that knob—the one that controls how hard you'll have to work to start something new. Fifteen years later, I still haven't found it.

In Mike's defense, early productions were extraordinarily stressful. In fact, after only one more show, Lesly Benodin declared the whole affair too stressful for him and went off to become a fireman. (I'm not kidding.) We were doing things that only a handful of much larger, much better-funded studios in the world had ever attempted, and every day seemed to present new challenges. VeggieTales, in the end, wasn't the first half-hour CGI show. That honor most likely went to the *Crash Test Dummies* special produced by Lamb & Company, a much larger animation studio in Minneapolis, and aired on U.S. television a few months before the completion of *Where's God When I'm S-scared?* A French studio had produced a series of three-minute CGI shorts that had aired on European TV a year or two before VeggieTales. But VeggieTales was, as far as I know, the world's first CGI home video series and the first CGI series of any kind produced in the United States. By the middle of 1994, we had probably produced more minutes of CGI character animation than any other studio in North America, if not the world. Our real innovation, though, was in the combination of character design and animation technique that allowed us to make the shows so inexpensively. A consultant working for Nickelodeon concluded in 1995 that no one in the world could produce a half hour of animation as inexpensively as Big Idea. That same year, a visiting team from Warner Brothers Feature Animation was amazed at the shot tracking software Lesly Benodin and Ken Greene had developed in-house, commenting that they knew of no other studio with such a promising tracking system.

The only way things could have been going any better was if people had actually been buying our videos.

Fifty thousand copies of the first two videos hit Christian bookstores in August of 1994, alongside our little cardboard display. They did almost nothing. "What?" you say, "People didn't like them?" No, it wasn't that they didn't *like* them, it was that they didn't *try* them. The early to mid-1990s were the peak of popularity for family psychologist Dr. James Dobson and his über-ministry, Focus on the Family. Christian parents trusted no one more than they trusted Dr. Dobson, and, as a result, when Focus on the Family started producing their own high-quality kids' videos (beginning with *McGee and Me*), the response was overwhelmingly positive. As VeggieTales entered the market, the video sales charts in Christian bookstores were dominated with Focus on the Family productions, each one stamped with Dr. Dobson's seal of approval. So for the first six months or so, the scenario in Christian bookstores played out like this:

"Hmm. Vegetables telling Bible stories."

Long pause.

"Let's see what Dobson has."

The problem was, if you hadn't actually *seen* a VeggieTales video, the concept sounded like the most ridiculous thing imaginable. To see Bob and Larry was to love Bob and Larry, but very few people had seen Bob and Larry, and a cardboard cutout in the corner of the store wasn't doing the trick. Every two weeks I called Word for a sales report and carefully entered the numbers into my spreadsheet to see whether I'd have enough money to finish the next video. It was clear that the $40,000 advances were not enough to fund production and that Word's slow sales rate wasn't going to recoup those advances quickly enough to get us any additional cash before the next video was due. At one point, things looked so bad that I considered selling Big Idea to a new Christian entertainment company that had just been founded by a Christian billionaire. I figured maybe I'd get a couple hundred thousand dollars for my share, plus a steady job making more videos. Not bad, really, considering Bob and Larry weren't exactly setting the world on fire. We had several meetings, then the billionaire got cold feet and walked away, leaving me confused and sorely in need of cash.

At this point, my lawyer, a great Christian guy who had helped me set up GRAFx Studios, stepped in and offered to help by investing $50,000 in exchange for 25 percent of the company. The only problem—he didn't have $50,000. His friend did, though. His friend would put up $25,000 for each of them, and they'd each own 12.5 percent. I was a little concerned by the fact that his friend wasn't a Christian, but my lawyer assured me he would be a "silent partner." We signed the deal, and paychecks flowed once more. Since "Mr. Silent" owned his own two-hundred-person company and we were, at that time, without any real accounting or banking services, he offered to handle our accounts receivable and accounts payable through his accounting team and even to let us dip into his line of credit if necessary. While these gestures were helpful, his daily access to our finances ultimately led to "Mr. Silent" being somewhat less than, well, "Mr. Silent." Within about six months, he became "Mr. Noisy." *Hmm,* I thought. *Should have seen that one coming.*

Nevertheless, the influx of cash and the access to a small line of credit got the next two shows (*Are You My Neighbor?* and *Dave and the Giant Pickle*) out the door. Our third show, *Are You My Neighbor?*, was significant in that it marked the return of Silly Songs with Larry, this time with Mike at the helm. As ludicrous as it may now seem, when I put "The Water Buffalo Song" into show one, I had no intention of making Silly Songs with Larry a recurring VeggieTales feature. The second video, in fact, filled the Silly Song slot with a short called *The Forgive-O-Matic*, based on that puppet script I had written in Bible college. But no sooner had show two hit the shelves than people started complaining. "Where's the Silly Song with Larry?" "We want more Silly Songs with Larry!" Silly Songs with Larry had apparently struck a chord.

Up until this point, Mike hadn't contributed much to the writing of VeggieTales other than the theme song (cowritten with my wife) and a few lines from the wisemen's song in *Daniel in the Lion's Den*. I mentioned to Mike that folks wanted more Silly Songs, and a few days later he walked in with a doozy. He was taking a shower, he reported to me one morning, and couldn't find his razor. Being the playful fellow he is, he immediately began singing, "Oh, where is my razor? Oh, where is my razor? Oh, where, oh, where . . ." It was catchy. It was silly. I was excited that Mike was writing on his own. But there was a little problem.

"Mike, I don't think we want kids running around their houses looking for razor blades."

"Oh," he replied, "Moms won't let their kids play with razor blades!"

Mike did not yet have children.

"I know. But let's not introduce the idea. What else could Larry be looking for?"

Mike returned to my office a few hours later.

"A hairbrush!"

Mike jotted down an extremely silly song about Larry searching for his hairbrush, punctuated by the intrusion of several characters who, besides being "shocked and slightly embarrassed at the sight of Larry in a towel," each present a key bit of information to help unravel the mystery. In the end, of course, we discover that

Bob the Tomato has given the hairbrush to The Peach, because "he's got hair." Originally, Mike intended all the interjecting dialogue to be spoken. Kurt Heinecke composed suitable piano accompaniment, vamping in between Larry's choruses to make time for the spoken parts. But then my wife, Lisa, got into the sound booth to record Junior's spoken part, and instead of speaking "Why do you need a hairbrush—you don't have any hair?" sung it to the tempo and melody of Kurt's vamped piano filler. Kurt and Mike were laughing so hard they couldn't continue. The session was stopped, and the decision was made to attempt to sing every spoken line to the tune and tempo of Kurt's already composed piano underscore. The serendipitous result became VeggieTales' defining Silly Song, "The Hairbrush Song."

With Silly Songs with Larry in Mike's hands and the stories in mine, VeggieTales hit its stride. Kurt was growing as a composer and song producer. My stories were getting stronger and better organized. Chris Olsen was shining as an animation director, modeler, and color stylist. (I designed all the sets, props, and characters for the first six shows, with Chris taking over set construction and color styling after show two.) New animators Tom Danen and Ron Smith were adding subtlety to the performance of the characters that made my attempts at animation look pathetic. Hired right out of art school, Ron Smith first contributed to "The Hairbrush Song" but really got our attention with his hilarious, belly-shaking Jerry Gourd dance during "I Can Be Your Friend." Two years later he would knock me out completely as I watched dailies for *The Toy That Saved Christmas*.

"Wait a minute—did Mr. Nezzer just *shrug his shoulders?*"

Ron smiled. "Yep."

"He doesn't *have* shoulders! How did you *do* that?"

Ron just kept smiling.

Ron would go on to make key contributions till the very end, not the least of which was his stint as director and primary creative visionary for Big Idea's follow-up series, 3-2-1 Penguins. (He also contributed numerous voices to the series, including everyone's favorite Liverpoolian penguin, Kevin.)

Tom Danen would become our resident expert in coaxing subtle, nuanced emotion out of our simple characters—especially Junior. If there was a scene where Junior stole your heart, chances are Tom was responsible.

The team was coming together. Each of the first six shows broke new ground and raised the quality bar a little higher. Every day we'd run into each other's offices to see a new piece of animation or shot management code that promised to make future shows either better looking or less painful to complete on time. The door outside my office was slowly disappearing under a growing mass of stellar reviews and fan mail. No one was making much money—our average salary at the time was less than $30,000 a year—but we were having a blast.

Finances were still tight. Sales were increasing, but painfully slowly. We repeatedly had to dip into "Mr. Silent's" line of credit to cover payroll, which made him even noisier. He complained about the new people I'd hired. He complained about the Big Idea sweatshirts we handed out to the crew for our third anniversary. I was beginning to wonder if "silent partners" perhaps weren't all they were cracked up to be.

In late 1994 we won our first award, a Christian TV award from the Southern Baptists. I flew down to Dallas to accept the trophy in a televised presentation, then, not wanting to spend money on a hotel room, drove back and spent the night napping at the Dallas–Fort Worth airport until my 6:00 a.m. flight home. In the middle of the night, my computer bag, forced into duty as a makeshift pillow, slipped off the bench, breaking the trophy inside. Upon seeing the broken trophy—a thick glass piece engraved with the image of a child's hand holding on to an adult finger, Mike glibly dubbed it the "Pull My Finger Award." We won several more "Pull My Finger Awards," and Mike repeated his funny joke every time.

By early 1995 I was beginning to wonder if VeggieTales would ever be able to sustain us. I started conversations with Focus on the Family and Tyndale House—the team that had made McGee and Me such a huge hit—about developing a new CGI series with them. Tyndale was interested, but Focus decided instead to develop all new concepts in-house with their own creative team. I came back from the meeting with nothing to hang our hopes on but VeggieTales.

Which turned out to be a pretty good thing, because VeggieTales was about to explode.

13

Going Up

Whatever makes something "go big"? From Mickey Mouse to the Beatles, Precious Moments to Pokemon, modern history is filled with stories of unexpected cultural phenomena and surprise smash hits. In his book *The Tipping Point*—itself a bit of a "smash hit"—Malcolm Gladwell theorizes that most cultural phenomena spread not unlike epidemic diseases—from person to person, through social contact. He compares Baltimore's syphilis epidemic in the 1980s to the surprise resurgence of Hush Puppy shoes among New York's fashionistas a decade later. He believes that in both cases the rapid expansion of these "epidemics" was not merely due to the fact that a certain number of people had become "infected" and therefore could spread the word (or the virus), but rather that certain *types* of people had become infected—people who traveled in broad circles and exerted significant social influence. According to Gladwell's theories, it isn't just that people start talking about a product, it's that the *right* people start talking about a product.

So who would be the "right people" in the case of VeggieTales? One would immediately assume moms—the mothers of young children, who would then tell other moms in their churches and neighborhoods. And that would be a good theory, but I believe it to be wrong. Why? Because young moms were too busy taking care of their kids and driving to soccer practice to try every new video that showed up in a Christian bookstore. They bought Dobson videos because they knew Dobson and they trusted him. *But this vegetable thing?* they thought. *Who has time to give it a try? It's probably stupid and cheap, like so many other non-Dobson videos.*

So who do I believe got VeggieTales going? College kids and young, single adults. More specifically, college kids and young, single adults who worked in Christian bookstores. In the early 1990s, most Christian bookstores were small independents that often filled out their staffs with college kids and young singles working part-time. Particularly in less vital areas of the store, like, say, children's products. By 1994, with the home video boom in full swing, just about every Christian bookstore had a TV and a VCR in the back, most often in the kids' department where some Christian kids' video invariably looped away all day long, making the young staff member assigned to that area a little, well, loopy. When VeggieTales came along, it was at least worth a look. So these college kids and young adults would open a VeggieTales video and pop it in just to check it out.

And they loved it. The Monty Python references, the severe tongue-in-cheekiness, "The Hairbrush Song." It was exactly what college kids and young single adults had never seen before in a Christian kids' video: something *they* would actually enjoy watching. We first discovered this dynamic in early 1994, when a woman sent us a copy of an invitation she had created for a VeggieTales party. "Cool," I thought, "a VeggieTales party for her kids." But on the back of the invitation, she had written, "By the way, this was a party for young adults. No kids were invited."

Huh?

Then, shortly after Halloween that same year, we got a letter with a picture of darling Bob and Larry pumpkins created by a husband and wife. "By the way," they wrote in their letter, "we don't have any kids."

Come again?

We soon started hearing about VeggieTales parties springing up on college campuses. First Christian colleges, as you might expect, then secular universities like Texas A&M and the University of Michigan. Many of these parties had one thing in common: the presence of someone who worked in a Christian bookstore.

So you've just watched your first VeggieTales video, and you're sick to death of the kids' videos you've been playing on the in-store TV every day for the last two years. What do you do? All VeggieTales all the time! Christian bookstores became "VeggieTales theaters." Now when harried mothers walked in looking for new videos, the young clerks responded, "Have you heard of VeggieTales?"

"No—what's that?"

"Look! It's playing right here! In fact, your kids are watching it right now! And they're smiling!"

Ring it up, Bucky.

So, contrary to what might seem logical, mothers of young children were not the earliest adopters or promoters of VeggieTales. College kids took that role.

It's interesting to note that this dynamic never could have happened if we had launched first in the mass market. Why? Because in the world of Wal-Mart, Target, and Toys "R" Us, the store clerks can't touch the VCRs. Wal-Mart knows the value of in-store exposure on their TVs, and they guard that airtime religiously, using it as a bargaining chip with key vendors. If a store clerk had swapped Wal-Mart's in-house reel for a VeggieTales video, that clerk would have found himself or herself slinging fries at McDonald's the next week. Had the clerks in local Christian bookstores not been able to play the videos *they* liked, moms may never have bumped into VeggieTales. Big Idea Productions may have gone out of business before anyone knew we even existed. As it happened, exposure through Christian bookstores was the fuse that college kids had just lit. Bob and Larry were ready to explode.

In 1994 Word shipped 50,000 copies of our two existing videos into Christian bookstores. By the end of 1995, we had shipped 150,000 copies of the first four shows. Not bad, but far from stellar and not enough to cover our growing production costs. (Like Walt, I had the annoying habit of wanting each new production to outdo the one before.) Everything changed in 1996. By the time *The Toy That Saved Christmas* hit stores in November, we had shipped nearly 700,000 copies of our first six videos. A year later, the number would reach 1.8 million.

But long before we sold our millionth video, the world had started to notice VeggieTales. The first call came way back in 1994, less than six months after our inauspicious Christian bookstore launch. The caller was a consultant scouting for new children's properties on behalf of the large, mass-market video distributor GoodTimes Video. Founded by a man whose first business had been selling booze and tobacco to tourists out of the duty-free shops aboard cruise ships, GoodTimes Video was best known for riding Disney's coattails with its own low-budget versions of classic Disney-popularized stories like *Snow White*, *Sleeping Beauty*, *The Little Mermaid* and *Pocahontas*. Highly profitable but harassed by Disney lawsuits, the company was looking to diversify its product mix. The consultant had just watched a VeggieTales episode and liked it a lot—so much so that he thought our little Bible vegetable shows might have a place in the Wal-Marts and Kmarts of the world. I wasn't thrilled with most of GoodTimes' products, but it was at least worth a conversation. It had never been my intent to sell VeggieTales exclusively through Christian bookstores, though many people assumed as much and would later label our entrance into the mass market a "sell out" or a radical change in philosophy. As you now know, my first intent was to sell videos direct to families through the mail. As soon as our first show was done, we also worked to get it in front of executives at PBS to see if TV broadcast was a possibility. I knew God wanted me to tell stories that promoted biblical values, and I wanted to do that through any available means.

GoodTimes promised to place VeggieTales in more than 6,000 stores across the country. My eyes widened. But there was a catch: they felt the videos were a little too "religious" for a mainstream audience and asked us to remove the Bible verse from the end and every reference to God.

Hmm.

I'd love to say I immediately jumped up from the table yelling, "Get thee behind me, Satan!" and ran from the room. But I didn't. I considered it. GoodTimes' offer would have gotten Bob and Larry in front of millions of people. If they fell in love with the characters, sooner or later they'd surely bump into our shows that still had God in them. Sooner or later we'd have a chance to tell them about God, wouldn't we? And the revenue from 6,000 stores would help pay for new shows with God in them, as well as the edited versions.

It was my first moral dilemma. (Well, not the first in my *entire life*. That honor would go to the time I saw Scott Reifert's new squirt gun on a table in his garage. I really wanted a squirt gun. No one was looking. Just me and the squirt gun. I agonized over what to do. I chose poorly.)

In the end, I couldn't do it. I thought about our second video, in which we taught kids that we should forgive others because God is always ready to forgive us. I tried to imagine that lesson without God in it—"Forgive others, because . . . it will 'grease the wheels of society'?" If God wasn't in it, our characters were just flapping their jaws. It was all nonsense. God was the "why" behind everything I wanted to communicate. Take him out, and I might as well go home, sit on the couch, and watch MTV. God was why I had started in the first place. He was why I'd stayed up seventy-seven hours straight to finish the first video. He was everything.

Given that I was struggling to meet payroll at the time, it wasn't an inconsequential decision, but the wrestling process helped reinforce exactly why I was doing what I was doing. Surely there was someone else out there who might not mind theistic vegetables. We'd have to keep looking.

In late 1994 a rather interesting fellow named Chip wandered into our offices. He lived nearby, had somehow heard about us, and wanted to help. He offered to shop VeggieTales around for TV and home video deals in exchange for a commission on any sales he made. "Sure," I thought. "Why not?" He reminded me of John Candy in "Uncle Buck"—sort of gregarious and aggressive in an "I still live with my mother" kind of way. He approached PBS and sent out tapes to several Hollywood studios. Nothing came of his efforts, other than the aforementioned visit by the Warner Brothers honchos, who eyed our green linoleum, sniffed our machine oil, and quickly hustled back to O'Hare. A few weeks after he arrived, Chip melted back into the bungalow-filled side streets of Chicago. But those tapes slowly got passed around, person to person, and by the middle of 1995 the phone was starting to ring more frequently. Some of the callers were inquiring about mass-market home video rights. Others were expressing interest in putting Bob and Larry on hats, T-shirts, or neckties for sale in Christian bookstores. Hmm. VeggieTales T-shirts and neckties. Just like Disney! That sounded pretty darn cool to me. As I had no idea how to go about negotiating all these deals and opportunities, and my lawyer's primary area of expertise was lawsuits between car companies and their dealerships, it appeared I needed help. Business help. My lawyer recommended I talk to a friend of his who had recently ended a thirty-year career at Leo Burnett, the influential Chicago ad agency responsible at that time for giant accounts like McDonald's and United Airlines. A few days later, Bill Haljun walked through my office door.

Bill was—how should I say this?—"unique." In his mid fifties at the time, he walked into my office wearing red pants, a red leather vest, a red sport coat, and a red cowboy hat. Startled, the first words I heard myself say were, "Is your horse outside?" He disregarded my query and firmly shook my hand—his gray ponytail dangling beneath his cowboy hat.

Like I said, Bill Haljun was unique.

Bill drove a faded green 1972 Mustang convertible that his wife had given him new. His vanity license plates said "BLESS U," and his belt buckle sported a large Christian fish symbol. He was Episcopalian but rabidly evangelical. He also smoked cigars, drank wine with his dinners or when entertaining, and, when he deemed it necessary, used words that would have shocked my grandparents. He often wore patchwork pants that were custom made for him by a tailor in Andover, Massachusetts. Bill would pick a few wildly contrasting fabrics, send them to Andover, and a few weeks later a bizarre pair of pants would return. He had more than twenty pairs of custom patchwork pants. Twelve of them were Christmas-themed. To go along with all the Christmas pants, Bill had picked up on a trip to England a pair of green Doc Martens and a pair of red Doc Martens. Throughout the entire month of December, he would wear one red and one green Doc Marten, with a pair of Christmas pants and a bright green or red sweater. Whatever room he was in needed no further Christmas decoration.

"What do you want to do?" I asked after spending a few minutes getting to know him.

"I just want to do all the [expletive deleted] you don't want to do," he replied with a smile.

Other than the choice of words, I liked the sound of that. The more interest VeggieTales attracted, the more, um, [expletive deleted] there was that I didn't particularly enjoy doing.

I liked Bill. Everyone liked Bill. It was impossible not to like Bill, even while discovering that he wasn't as good at executing pesky operational details as you might have hoped. (Which, given the ponytail, car, and patchwork pants, probably shouldn't have come as a big surprise.) His eldest son was a William Morris agent in Hollywood, which immediately gave us ten times more connections in the industry than I had on my own.

Bill joined Big Idea as our vice president of licensing, and he and I hit the ground running with meetings in New York and Los Angeles. Traveling with Bill was interesting, as strangers would invariably ask him about his pants. After the fifth or sixth intrusion on one trip, and noticing that he didn't seem to particularly enjoy having to explain his pants over and over, I gamely suggested he print up business cards that said, "I am deaf. I'm glad you like my pants."

He didn't take me up on it.

Bill really shone when it was time to interact with people. At trade shows and industry events, Bill Haljun's patchwork pants and unflagging smile came to symbolize Big Idea almost as much as Bob and Larry. During the peak of VeggieTales mania, as we were signing licenses for everything from VeggieTales garden gloves to VeggieTales "sew-at-home" fabrics, Bill sent a bolt of bright turquoise fabric covered with little Bobs and Larrys to his tailor in Andover, who produced an entire, bright turquoise, VeggieTales suit. When Bill wore his "veggie suit" at tradeshows, combined with a huge cowboy hat made from balloons, fans ignored Bob and Larry and instead lined up for pictures with Bill.

I really liked Bill. To be honest, I envied Bill. All my life I'd been nervously checking how I looked in the mirror and wondering what others were thinking of me. Are they staring? What are they thinking? Does this shirt match these pants? Do I look *stupid*? And then here was Bill. He was wearing the goofiest pair of pants I'd ever seen, and he just didn't care. We had a lunch meeting with five or six Columbia Tri-Star Home Video executives on the fabled Sony Pictures lot in Culver City, and Bill led the group in prayer before eating. In the Rita Hayworth dining room. The stunned executives just bowed their heads and went along with it.

Behind Bill's complete lack of self-consciousness, not surprisingly, was his Christian faith. Yeah, he smoked cigars and drank wine and used questionable words every now and then, but he also went out of his way to help anyone who needed help. He would leave prayers on your voice mail or in your e-mail inbox if he was thinking of you. He provided meals for the animators during crunch time—usually at his own expense (earning him a "catering" credit on several videos). Over time he sort of became Big Idea's chaplain, with his door always open for heart-to-heart chats with hurting or disgruntled staff members. Before coming to Big Idea, he had used his own money to start a company to provide sewing jobs for underprivileged, inner-city moms. As much as I hated to admit it, this cigar-smoking, wine-drinking, swearing Episcopalian was behaving more like Jesus than most—if not all—of the strait-laced, teetotaling evangelicals with whom I had grown up. Including myself.

As you might expect, Bill's integrity was off the chart. Big Idea continued to grow, and it soon became clear that the front offices of the screw factory wouldn't hold us much longer. We were running out of electric and air-conditioning capacity, not to mention the fact that too many animators in one room—well—didn't always smell very good. Only problem—we still had six months left on our lease.

"What are you going to do about the lease?" Bill asked me. I already had a plan.

"Well, I've heard in situations like this you can negotiate. I'll go in and tell them we're leaving and offer two months' rent. They'll ask for four. We'll settle on three. It will save us three months' rent."

"You're not going to do that," Bill said with a smile.

"I'm not?"

"No. We're going to walk in there and tell them we're leaving but that we'll keep paying the rent until the end of the lease."

"We will?"

"Yes. Because that's the right thing to do."

Walking out of our landlords' office later that day (two likable screw makers who happened to be named Jim and Jerry—wink, wink), Bill turned to me and said, "Didn't that feel good?" I had to admit, it did. Especially seeing Jim's and Jerry's faces light up when they realized we weren't trying to pull a fast one—that we were going to pay everything we owed. They remained big VeggieTales fans ever after, happily calling us in our new digs a few months later to say they had noticed their "appearance" as two likable gourd brothers in our shows. Bill would play the role of "moral compass" in countless business meetings throughout Big Idea's amazing ten-year run.

By mid-1996, Big Idea was cranking. Our income from video sales was finally exceeding our expenses, even though the timing of payments often had us dipping heavily into Mr. Silent's line of credit. Christian magazines and TV shows were calling for interviews. The Southern Baptists initiated their Disney boycott, then promptly put me on the cover of their denominational magazine smiling wryly in my Bob the Tomato necktie. In the wide-ranging interview, I talked about Disney and my hopes for Big Idea. I was finding my voice, and people were responding. I spoke at churches, colleges, and industry events, and everywhere I went people lined up to tell me how much they appreciated what I had to say. I discovered that I loved inspiring people—pointing them to the "big picture" and painting a vision for changing the world. Suddenly people were asking for autographs and stuffing resumes into my hands. For a shy kid from Iowa, the response was a little overwhelming. They liked me. They really liked me.

As the business and marketing aspects of VeggieTales became more demanding, though, I had to find ways to pass off production duties to others. Luis Contreras took over storyboarding duties beginning with our fall release for 1996, *The Toy That Saved Christmas*. Late in the year, as we prepared to move to our new location, Joe Sapulich took over concept design, joined soon after by Daniel Lopez. As was typical in this period, as soon as I saw Joe and Dan's extraordinary art, I felt I never needed to lift a pencil again. I animated a few shots for *The Toy That Saved Christmas* to help make the deadline, then turned in my keys to the animation software. My ten-year run as a computer animator was over.

But if I was no longer an animator, what exactly was I? A writer? A producer? A "media executive"? The more I thought about it, the more I wanted to be like Walt Disney. He wasn't really a writer or a producer—or any of those things. And at the same time, he was all of them. And more. If he wanted to make a movie, his organization helped him make a movie. If he wanted to build a theme park, his organization helped him build a theme park. It sounded like my dream job. But how exactly did it work?

Lisa and I scraped together enough money to take our kids to Disney World for a break, and I spent a spare afternoon reading Walt's biography by the pool. Almost everything I read resonated with me. The letters Walt had written as a twenty-one-year-old entrepreneur—attempting to make his one-man shop sound big and legitimate when in fact he was on the verge of bankruptcy—sounded just like letters I had written in the early years of GRAFx Studios. Walt's interest in technology, his desire to tell stories that focused on the positive, even his late-in-life passion to build an entire city—they all resonated. (I had, in fact, become deeply interested in urban planning while sharing space with my friend, the space planner.) As I read of Walt's premature death and his longtime artists' memories of their last interactions with their friend, employer, and inspirer, I found myself wiping tears from my eyes. It shouldn't have come as a surprise to me that his biography ended with his death, but something about Walt's story moved me deeply.

I walked through Disney World with my kids, watching families laughing together in the environment Walt had conceived. The park was clean—the way it should be. Families were laughing together—the way they should be. Walt, it seemed, was in the business of making things right—of making them the way they should be. But as I thought more and more about what I was seeing, I couldn't help but wonder what Disney World would have been like with God in it—if the attractions celebrated God, rather than fairy tales, early American history, and Walt's optimistic view of the future. What would that look like? How would such a park affect families? And the big question—who on earth could conceive and build such a thing?

Me, of course. The answer seemed obvious. I could do that.

I came back from vacation inspired by Walt but frustrated that he hadn't led kids all the way to God. He stopped short—too captivated by human ingenuity and the American dream. He was a humanist. A modernist. And a ridiculously optimistic one, at that. And yet here in the mid-1990s it was clear that modernism was dying. People my age no longer bought into the notion that man could "perfect" himself through technology and progress. We'd grown up with computers, advanced medicine, and space travel, yet our newspapers were filled not with stories of utopia and flying cars, but of wars, genocide, and kids killing each other for bikes and overpriced sneakers. Whatever new media technology we developed (be it cable television, VCRs, or, later on, the Internet) was utilized to transmit depravity long before nobility. Christian videos didn't popularize VCRs. Porn did. And yet here was Walt's company, thirty years after his death, still parading around in Walt's hopelessly romanticized modernist clothes—telling kids their dreams will come true if only they'll "wish upon a star."

But all the wishful thinking in the world wasn't keeping kids alive in our inner cities. It wasn't feeding the poor or stopping the spread of AIDS. And it wasn't preventing half of America's marriages from failing. By the 1990s, the *majority* of American kids would see one of their parents walk out the door. Leave. What I had experienced as a kid was happening over, and over, and over. Yet Walt's scratchy old record just played on. "If you wish upon a star . . ."

Someone had to do something about it. Someone had to show the world how family entertainment could be freed from its hopelessly antiquated modernist trappings and reenergized with biblical truth—with a Christian worldview. As you can probably imagine, I quickly decided that someone was me.

How to go about it? Well, that part was a little fuzzy.

14

Life in the Nuthouse

Failure is no fun. I don't think anyone will argue with me on that point. But success brings its own set of challenges and pitfalls. Sure, it *sounds* fun, but the reality can be something else entirely.

The end of 1996 saw *The Toy That Saved Christmas* breaking sales records in Christian bookstores and Big Idea ensconced in our new home on Clinton Street just a few blocks west of Chicago's Loop. Our staff now numbered fifteen. Average age—mid twenties. Average salary—still around $30,000.

Leading people did not come naturally to me. There. Now I've said it. I know that's probably a huge disappointment to those of you hoping to glean valuable managerial insights from this book. You may, in fact, want to return the book now and exchange it for something by Ken Blanchard or Peter Drucker. I would not fault you for doing so. Before I continue, though, I must say that I loved the part of leadership where I got up in front of the troops and inspired them with a rousing speech about how we were going to "fight, fight, fight" and "win, win, win" and how the world would be a better place because of our efforts. I loved that part. I was good at that part. I'd speak, and folks would get all

excited and say, "We'll follow you anywhere!" and I'd think, *Great!
Just what I need!*

And then someone would ask, "So . . . what's the plan?" And
more specifically, "What should I be working on this morning,
'cuz I finished that other thing yesterday." And then I'd sort of
freeze up like a garden hose left outside in a Minnesota winter.

I played some backyard football when I was a kid, but I never
wanted to be quarterback. It wasn't because I couldn't throw or
run or anything like that. It was because I hated that moment
when you were in the huddle and everyone turned and looked at
you and said, "So, what are we going to do?" And then they'd just
stare at you, waiting for your brilliant plan. I hated that moment
when I was a kid, and now I discovered as the leader of a small
business, I still hated it.

I knew where I wanted to go, but I had only the vaguest of
ideas how to get there, and I despised the myriad tiny decisions
required to marshal the troops in any particular direction. For the
first few years, I tried several different management techniques
in fits and starts, but ultimately I began turning the day-to-day
leadership over to others, with wildly varying results.

By late 1996, Chris Olsen was more or less running the studio,
a task he performed fairly well. As we grew, Chris did a lot of the
early hiring. Chris was a great guy but not really a Christian in the
classic definition and, as such, wasn't specifically looking for
Christian artists to join our ranks. At this point, while I was calling VeggieTales a "Christian video series," I wasn't calling Big Idea
a "Christian company," and I didn't think an all-Christian staff was
necessary, or even legal. (Screening job applicants for religious
belief is, in fact, legal in only very specific ministry-related circum-
stances.) I knew I was and would always be in charge of the content of our videos, so demanding that every technical or support

position be filled by a Christian seemed unnecessarily narrow-minded and, especially in the early days, impractical. Very few people in the creative community had heard of Big Idea Productions as of late 1996, and even if they had, our low salaries precluded us from attracting anyone but the youngest and least experienced. While there were some Christian animators at places like Disney and Warner Brothers, the notion of them relocating their families to Chicago to work for peanuts on religious veg-etable videos they'd never heard of was laughable. So we made due with the folks we could find locally, who tended to be recent grad-uates of Chicago's art and film programs. Since only a tiny fraction of Chicago's art school grads are professing Christians (a reality we found true everywhere in the United States except the Deep South), the more we hired, the less Christian Big Idea became. Again, since I was firmly in control of the company and its con-tent, I didn't see this as a problem. History would prove me wrong, though not for the reasons you might expect.

While I wasn't involved in all the hiring of 1996 and 1997, it was fairly easy, when meeting new staff, to determine why they had come. Some were clearly excited about the Christian content of the videos and couldn't stop saying so. Others were just excited to have a job in animation that didn't require relocating to the West Coast. By early 1997 those excited by the Christian content appeared to be a distinct—and shrinking—minority, which had an unexpected side effect on my leadership. I was now speaking more and more outside Big Idea, and everywhere I went I talked passionately about my plans and goals for a Christian family media company committed to excellence. I talked at churches. I talked at Christian colleges. I talked at industry events. I talked everywhere except at Big Idea. I shared my passion for Christian ministry through creative media with everyone but my own staff, because, frankly, I wasn't sure many of the folks at Big Idea would buy into it. Would even care. That same insecure part of me that constantly asked, "Do I look stupid?" now kept me from sharing my real passion with my own employees. I could imagine it in my head: I'd give my pep talk about changing the world for Christ, and they'd snicker. Once I'd turn to leave the room, they'd laugh out loud. "What an idiot," they'd say, "Boy, did he look stupid!"

So even as I became more and more visible throughout the Christian world, I became less and less visible in my own company. When I stepped up to the podium at a Christian media event, I knew my audience was with me. I knew we were on the same page. When I walked out of my office into my animation studio, I was pretty sure we weren't. What's more, I knew my religious goals and motivations would make some of our artists uncomfortable—maybe so uncomfortable that they would consider leaving. Since Christian artists were so hard to find, I wasn't sure we could survive if our non-Christian artists left. So I worked hard not to make them uncomfortable. I measured my words carefully, saving the "hardcore" stuff for other audiences. Besides, I hated it when people I needed walked away. I hated the fact that others could mess up my life by leaving. I didn't want our interactions to drive them away, even if it meant not interacting with them at all. Here I was, the CEO of a thriving company. I was on the covers of magazines and on TV shows across the country. When I spoke, people lined up for autographs and pictures. Yet if I heard even the faintest rumor of a valued staff member considering other employment opportunities or showing the slightest sign of dissatisfaction, a pain stabbed through my chest that I would later link all the way back to the nights I lay in bed listening to my parents fight in the family room below, realizing my life could fall apart in an instant and there was nothing I could do to prevent it. In hindsight, my wounds were affecting Big Idea much more than I could have imagined.

The year 1997 was an explosive year for Big Idea. Externally, it appeared we could do no wrong. Our six existing videos now occupied the top six spots on the Christian video sales charts, completely supplanting Focus on the Family's titles. Our seventh video, *Madame Blueberry*, a delightfully subversive poke at American consumerist culture that marked Mike's first attempt at scriptwriting (with help from Lisa and me on the teaching and emotional parts), would be our best-selling title yet. I was writing a series of "Veggiecational" books for a major Christian publisher that would go on to sell millions of copies. A hastily compiled CD collection of songs from our first few shows had quickly gone platinum and would win the Dove Award for best Christian children's album. On the licensing side, Christian bookstores were ordering VeggieTales apparel and art and craft kits faster than our licensing partners could crank them out. Everything we touched was turning to gold. Externally, everything looked groovy.

Internally, chaos abounded. Personality clashes among the young artists were frequent, and Chris Olsen, barely out of college himself, was having a hard time keeping the crew rowing together. Bill Haljun was swamped in licensing contracts and executional details far outside his relationship management strengths. On top of that, he and I were now knee deep in interested distribution partners for the general market. The latest round of suitors had decided God could stay in the videos, but felt the Bible verse at the end was still too hardcore for a Wal-Mart shopper. We flew to meetings on both coasts and sifted through proposals. The massive success of Barney the Dinosaur had placed owner Dick Leach near the top of *Forbes'* list of America's highest paid entertainers and created a great deal of interest in preschool properties like VeggieTales. If Big Idea could achieve the kind of licensing and home video success that Dick's company, Lyrick Studios, had achieved with Barney, I was sure we could change the face of family entertainment. The sort of income generated by a big licensing hit like Barney could fund movies, TV shows—maybe even a Christian theme park. VeggieTales had the potential to be huge. Everyone saw it now. But how huge? And how on earth could we manage such growth? Bill, Chris, and I were hanging on by the skin of our teeth as it was.

Right about that time, I got a phone call that would have huge ramifications on the future of Big Idea. It was from Terry Pefanis, a finance executive at Gaylord Entertainment, the company that owned The Grand Ole Opry and neighboring Nashville theme park, Opryland, among various other newspaper, broadcast, and cable TV assets. Gaylord had recently purchased Word Entertainment, our Christian market distribution partner and one of the big three Christian music companies. Terry was calling to say they wanted to discuss buying Big Idea as well. Oh my. I spent the next few weeks getting to know Terry and the rest of the Gaylord company. Their new CEO, a committed Christian, was interested in using the company's formidable assets and competencies to pursue Christian entertainment in a big way. They owned assets in Christian music and music publishing, cable TV, and Internet. They were in negotiations to buy Christian pop star Amy Grant's management company and would soon bring in her two star managers to run all their Christian entertainment assets. They put me up in a suite at the massive Opryland Hotel and introduced me to Eric Westin, the newly recruited executive in charge of their theme park business. Eric had been a long-time Disney theme park designer (dubbed "imagineer" by Walt's goofy word department), taking a break from Disney only when invited by George

Lucas to oversee the construction of Skywalker Ranch, George's creative wonderland in Marin County, California. Eric showed me pictures of the work he oversaw for George and told me stories about being a young monorail driver at Disneyland in the early 1960s and meeting Walt. We talked about how Bob and Larry could find a home in their theme park. Eric sent me back to Chicago with an armful of theme park trade magazines to dream about the possibilities.

Hoo. I was jazzed.

A few weeks later, an offer letter came. Gaylord would buy Big Idea for $12 million. I would run it for them. We would immediately begin collaborating on multiple projects—TV, theme parks, you name it. If I could dream it and it made sense in a spreadsheet, they could fund it. Oh yeah—they could help with management too.

Obviously, the opportunity was too good to ignore. But I clearly lacked the experience to walk through the process of crafting this transaction unassisted. The right deal at this juncture would pave the way for everything I wanted to do. The wrong deal, conversely, would spell disaster. I needed help. Bill Haljun offered to bring in a couple of friends to give advice. One was the former chief financial officer of the Leo Burnett Company. The other was a friend from Bill's church who was, at the time, the chief executive officer of a $3 billion insurance company. Bill didn't tell me which was which. The first guy walked in—an older gentleman in a sharp suit, looking snazzy and polished. He talked and talked and talked. I listened. He left. "Must be the CEO," I thought. Then the second guy came in. Roughly the same age, he was short and unassuming, dressed casually in jeans and a polo shirt and wearing a big, down parka. Not nearly as impressive as the first guy. He sat down in front of me, took out a yellow legal pad, and started asking me questions. Questions about my goals, questions about

Big Idea, questions about Gaylord Entertainment. Everything I said, he wrote down. Several times I'd make a statement and he'd say, "Oh, I think that's important. *You* should write that down." After an hour he had to go, but he offered to come back again if I was interested. I was.

"I got a lot more out of that second guy than the big-shot CEO fella," I commented to Bill after the conversation was over. "Oh," Bill replied, "that second guy was the CEO." I was floored. Over the second half of 1997 I had lunch with Bill's friend, the "second guy," three or four times. I'd be in a jam, completely confounded about how to proceed, and I'd call him up. We'd meet down the street at Bennigan's, and he'd patiently listen and then sketch out on a piece of paper what he thought I needed to do. He didn't have any real experience with or knowledge of the entertainment business, but he had a truckload of general business experience and a whole lot of common sense. I would return to work from those lunches feeling calmer, like maybe I could do this after all. Needless to say, I grew rather fond of my new business mentor. The fact that he was old enough to be my father also may have played a role.

One of the changes we agreed needed to be made regarded the marketing of our videos. Everland Entertainment was increasingly frustrating me by failing to inform us of their VeggieTales marketing plans ahead of their execution, as was required by our distribution deal. When I walked into a Christian bookstore one day to find pictures on the walls of Bob and Larry in police mug shots, under the tagline "Veggies Most Wanted," I had reached my limit. Building trust with families was hard enough without your distribution partner portraying your key characters as felons. I informed Word that Big Idea would be assuming marketing responsibilities for VeggieTales, and hired a young marketing executive from the Christian music business named Ben Howard to lead the effort. Depending on how one characterized Bill Haljun, Ben may have been Big Idea's "first adult." Ben took over the responsibility for marketing VeggieTales through Christian bookstores as Bill and I zeroed in on the man we felt might be the perfect partner to guide Bob and Larry's launch in the mass market. He was Dick Leach, the father of Barney the Dinosaur.

The story of Dick Leach and Barney is a classic American success story. Dick started out in the Chicago area, where his father had founded a successful printing business in 1922. Wondering what to do with the time his presses were idle, Dick decided to start a business designing and printing posters for schools and churches. As a strong Catholic, he launched another company to publish Catholic textbooks and curriculum. If the publishing businesses failed, he figured, he could always fall back on the printing business. But the publishing businesses didn't fail, and as a result, he found himself in 1987 with ample resources to invest in a new idea his daughter Sheryl had just hatched—an idea for a preschool program starring a big purple dinosaur. By the time I was launching VeggieTales in 1993, Dick Leach was making tens of millions of dollars a year from the sale of all things Barney and using the proceeds to build a significant entertainment company a few miles from his new home in Plano, Texas.

In 1997, accompanied by Bill Haljun and our lawyer, Jim Vogler, I visited Dick in Plano. We talked at Dick's house, then followed him on a tour of Barney's nearby production facilities and the elaborate back lot they had recently built for the filming of *Wishbone*, their ambitious follow-up show. We met Lyrick's sales and marketing teams, populated heavily by Christians, due to the company's Texas location and Dick's own strong faith. I talked about my frustrations with Hollywood media and my goals for

VeggieTales and Big Idea, and the message resonated with Dick and many Lyrick staff members. Did they think VeggieTales could work in Wal-Mart, even with the Bible verses at the end? Dick wasn't sure, but he wanted to give it a try. At lunch Dick talked about the three days he had spent with several Walt Disney executives, who had expressed interest in buying Barney. Dick pointed to the table across the restaurant where he had declined their offer, explaining that he felt Lyrick should remain an independent voice in children's entertainment. According to Dick, one of the executives had then leaned forward and said, "We've just shown you how we could help Barney. We could also *hurt* Barney." It was shortly thereafter that the most vicious "Barney bashing" ensued. Was there a connection? Dick couldn't say for sure, but he clearly delighted in telling the story of standing up to "the Mouse." Dick was my kind of guy and, we quickly concluded, the best partner imaginable for our own battle against the secular media giants. By the fall of 1997, as sales of VeggieTales videos in Christian bookstores approached the 2 million mark, Bill Haljun was deep into negotiations with Lyrick Studios to bring Bob, Larry, and their Bible verses to the biggest retailers in America.

It was an exciting time at Big Idea for other reasons, too. Talks with Gaylord Entertainment about a partnership or a merger continued. Little plush Bob and Larry dolls, alongside numerous other VeggieTales licensed items, were the hits of the Christmas selling season at Christian retailers. For the first time in our four-year history, meeting payroll was no longer a concern. Money was coming in faster than we could spend it. Chaos still abounded inside our offices on Clinton Street overlooking the El tracks and the Lake Street station (where one rabid fan would stand waving a "Hire Me" poster outside our windows), but it was hard not to be optimistic. God had given me a dream—to tell the stories he put in my head. To share my brain's "weird thoughts" with the world. And that dream was working. It was coming to life. Big Idea could be big. Really big. Maybe even big enough to provide families with a legitimate alternative to Disney.

At the close of 1997, we had $4 million in our bank account and no debt. We had the financial resources to crank up the quality of our videos and consider launching other projects as well. A TV show? A feature film? A second home video series? I really wasn't sure what should come next. I wanted to do *everything*— to become the "new" Disney overnight. God had placed something extraordinary in my hands, and I didn't want to mess it up. But what was the best way to grow? Who did I need to hire next? What would be the wisest use of the money VeggieTales was generating? And how would I have the time to write all this stuff? Though Mike was taking on more writing responsibilities, I was still carrying the bulk of the creative duties, not just for the videos, books, and music, but also for the marketing materials and licensed products. (Our first series of neckties and T-shirts were, in fact, almost all my designs.)

I was working so hard to stay ahead of the veggie juggernaut that, in the middle of the night after *Madame Blueberry*'s wrap party, I found myself in the emergency room complaining of chest pain. After running an EKG, the attendants quickly paged the cardiologist and wheeled me into a bay marked "critical." "Why does that say 'critical'?" I asked. "Because you're critical," the attendant replied. I could tell from the look on his face he wasn't joking. For ten or twenty minutes I lay on a gurney, contemplating my own mortality and thinking about my kids. *Don't tell me this is how I will leave them.* The attendant finally returned with good news from the cardiologist. It wasn't a heart attack. An echocardiogram showed that instead, I was suffering from pericarditis, a viral infection in the lining of the heart, typically brought on by stress. Potentially fatal if undetected, the condition was, however, easily treated with medication. I returned to work after two weeks in bed, but my energy level would not recover for almost two years, and my ability to pull the all-night and multiday marathons that had made VeggieTales possible was gone for good.

I was still recovering from pericarditis when we drove up to my in-laws' house in Minneapolis for Christmas break at the end of 1997. Lisa and I had just bought our first house and brought home our third child, a girl named Sydney, joining big brother Jeremy and big sister Shelby. As the kids played with Lisa's mom and stepdad, I retired to the small desk in Lisa's childhood bedroom to rest and think. I pulled out a sketchpad to work up some ideas for VeggieTales rides at Opryland. I sketched an interactive VeggieTales fountain and a classic "Red Baron" plane ride converted to Larryboy's "Larry-Planes." I'd always wanted the opportunity to design a theme park, and here it was. But something was bugging me. Did I really think I could do all this work myself? Isn't that what landed me in the emergency room in the first place? How exactly was I supposed to do everything I felt God calling me to do? A Christmas present from a staff member caught my eye. It was a new, "hot" business book focusing on the characteristics of truly visionary, lasting companies. Companies like Sony, 3M, and Disney. Now that I was attempting to build a company, I thought, perhaps I should spend a little more time reading business books and a little less time sketching interactive fountains. I put down my sketchpad and picked up the book. Within a chapter, I was absolutely hooked. I couldn't put it down. This was exactly what I needed.

15

Built to Last

If you follow the world of "hot" business books, you have, no doubt already guessed the book I was reading was *Built to Last*. First published in 1994, *Built to Last* was, by 1997, not only sweeping through business circles, but also through the halls of Christian ministries and megachurches. Primary author Jim Collins was being invited to speak at Christian leadership conferences as if he was Jesus' long-lost thirteenth apostle bearing teachings vital to the advancement of the kingdom of heaven.

What *were* his teachings, exactly? Rather interesting, really. Jim Collins and his coauthor, Jerry Porras, were researchers at the Stanford School of Business who embarked on a comprehensive six-year study of "visionary" companies like General Electric, 3M, Sony, Ford, and, most appealingly to me, Disney. They wanted to know what made these companies tick—what made them consistently successful, and consistently visionary, even through multiple generations of leadership. For comparison, they chose a competitor for each target company who, while achieving at least moderate success, failed to sustain their market leadership over the long haul. For Sony they chose Kenwood. For

General Electric, Westinghouse. For Disney, Columbia Pictures. Each company had hit products at one point or another. Each company had "visionary" leadership at one point. But why, now in the mid-1990s, was Columbia Pictures just a logo alongside several other old film labels inside Sony Pictures while Disney was an independent, global powerhouse, far surpassing even Walt's grandiose dreams? The answers startled me.

Truly visionary companies succeeded, the research seemed to indicate, because their founders were more concerned with building great companies than great products. Truly visionary companies succeeded because their founders built their own personal goals and beliefs into the very culture of their organizations, from the highest vice president to the receptionist at the front desk. Columbia Pictures founder Harry Cohn was a visionary leader, but he did not build a visionary company. Once Harry was gone, Columbia Pictures quickly slid into irrelevance. Walt, on the other hand, didn't just stop at being a guy who loved great storytelling, innovation, and "feel-good, middle-American values." Within the studio that bore his name, he built an entire *culture* around great storytelling, innovation, and "feel-good, middle-American values." Make a cynical remark about a sweet, sentimental scene in one of Disney's films, and Walt would show you the door. Swear in front of a guest at Disneyland, and Walt would show you the door. As a result, the employees who lasted at the Disney Studios were those who shared Walt's values. Those with differing values and goals were either weeded out in the interviewing process or left the company of their own accord after noticing they didn't seem to fit.

Visionary companies, the research showed, were companies whose founders built their values into the culture of the organization. Into the ways they hired and managed their employees. Into the ways they celebrated successes and rewarded behavior.

In fact, IBM even had their own songbook at one point, filled with songs praising the big computer maker. Not into singing songs about IBM? You should probably look for work elsewhere.

All in all, the researchers observed, the cultures of truly visionary, lasting companies could be described as "cultlike." But rather than being cults of *personality*, rallying around a specific leader, they were cults of *ideology*, rallying around a core set of beliefs and values. If you were fanatical about customer service, you'd feel right at home at Nordstrom. Fanatical about coffee? Try Starbucks. Fanatical about middle-American values, great storytelling, and innovation? Disney was the place for you. (Disney's recent abandonment of its universal commitment to "middle-American values," demonstrated by Michael Eisner's expansion into non-Disney branded films and TV shows that many Americans find offensive, is the core motivator behind conservative Christian frustration with the company. The Southern Baptists aren't upset because Disney's values are now *worse* than the other Hollywood studios; they're upset because Disney's values used to be so much *better*.)

This was big stuff. It all made sense. But I was clearly at a crossroads. Was I building a visionary *culture* at Big Idea, based on my goals and values? Or was I just single-handedly creating visionary *products*? I glanced down at the interactive fountain I had been single-handedly creating earlier that day. Oh dear. It wasn't that I lacked strong goals and values for my work—my goals and values were the reason I got out of bed every morning. I talked about them every time I spoke on behalf of Big Idea. But where I didn't bring them up so much was within the company itself. Why not? Well, as I mentioned earlier, I didn't want to offend anyone. I knew a big chunk of our staff hadn't come to Big Idea to promote Christian values. I hadn't even mentioned my faith or values during their job interviews. As long as I was creating the product, everything would be fine. But did I want Big Idea to be only about my ideas and my projects?

I thought about two men I admired very much—Walt Disney and Christian author and apologist C. S. Lewis. Both were wildly creative and highly influential. Both were "visionaries" when it came to storytelling and communicating with an audience. But Walt had built a culture based on his strengths as a storyteller and innovator, whereas Lewis had been a "solo act." Lewis had left behind a collection of books—a great but finite collection. There would never be another C. S. Lewis book. Walt, on the other hand, had left behind a company capable of continuing his work—a group of people, aligned by gifting and ideology, who would continue to expand his influence around the world long after his death. What would God want me to leave behind? A bunch of great stories? Or a great creative organization capable of producing more and more great stories for the next hundred years? An organization that might one day exceed my wildest dreams in terms of societal impact and benefit? Staring out my wife's childhood bedroom window at the snowy Minnesota landscape, the answer seemed obvious to me. God would want me to build a great company. It was time to change my focus from the stories themselves to the company behind them. It was time to build Big Idea.

But how? The book said great organizations were marked by clearly articulated beliefs, values, and goals. I grabbed a pad of paper and started compiling the beliefs and values that were nonnegotiable for me. Within an hour or two I had my list.

Core Beliefs

- The irresponsible use of popular media has had a profoundly negative impact on America's moral and spiritual health.

- The same media, used responsibly, can have an equally positive impact.
- The best way to improve people's lives is to promote biblical values and encourage spiritual growth.

Core Values
- Personal and corporate integrity
- Creative excellence and design innovation in all we do
- The prioritization of people over products and profits

That much was relatively easy, since I'd been hammering those topics home in speech after speech. But now it was time for the biggie—our "purpose." What was Big Idea's purpose? Why did it exist? I knew my purpose in life was to draw others closer to God—to lead them to the abundant life found in the gospel of Jesus Christ. I'd known that since my first childhood Bible conference. But I also wanted to help parents raise healthier kids. Help families stay together. Help dads think harder about the choices they were making. How could I sum all that up in one sentence? I wanted to offset the negative moral influence of Hollywood media. At the same time, I wanted to help our culture reconsider the claims of historical Christianity, just as C. S. Lewis had done fifty years earlier with his wartime radio addresses on the BBC. Our purpose statement needed to clearly indicate that our objectives weren't simply moral but were also spiritual. But if we sounded too aggressively religious, I knew secular journalists would label our efforts "proselytizing" and write us off as dangerous, right-wing wackos. Too religious, and we'd never get a favorable write-up outside the Christian world. Not religious enough, and I'd fail to communicate what I was really about. Geez, did Walt have this much trouble?

After a few hours of laborious wordsmithing, I thought I had it:

Big Idea's Purpose
  • To markedly enhance the moral and spiritual fabric of
    our culture through creative media.

I sat back in my chair and smiled. That would work. Taken together with our core belief that "the best way to improve people's lives is to promote biblical values," it would be clear to our Christian fans that "enhancing the spiritual fabric" meant exclusively promoting Christianity. There would be no "VeggieTales for Buddhists." At the same time, the purpose statement itself was subtle enough to leave the feathers of all but the most cynical mainstream journalist unruffled. Perfect.

I went back to the exercise. I had my core beliefs, values, and purpose. Only one thing was left—a "big, hairy, audacious goal," or "BHAG," in *Built to Last* parlance. A "BHAG" is a seemingly impossible long-term goal that serves as a rallying point for a developing organization. Like Walt attempting to produce the world's first animated feature film. Like NASA aiming for the moon. "Big, hairy, audacious goals," according to Collins and Porras, were vital tools for visionary companies to inspire their troops to do the impossible. There was only one problem. I didn't have one. I mean, I was pretty sure God hadn't given me one yet. I knew I was supposed to use my gifts to try to make a difference. I knew I was supposed to tell the stories he laid on my heart. But I didn't have a strong impression of any giant, singular goal I was supposed to accomplish. I looked back at the book. A visionary company needed a BHAG to inspire its troops. What to do?

I'll make one up.

Just temporarily, of course, as an exercise. I'll make one up and put it down as a placeholder, and then, when God gives me my *real* BHAG (you know, like "build an ark and start loading animals"), I'll just swap it out.

In hindsight, I wonder why I thought this was a good idea. Hindsight, as they say, is 20/20.

My BHAG:
   To build the most trusted of the top four family media brands within twenty years.

That was it. My big, hairy, audacious goal was that in twenty years, if you were to ask Americans to name their four favorite family media companies, they would say something like, "Disney, Nickelodeon, Pixar, and Big Idea." Then if you went back and asked, "Which of those companies do you trust the most?" they would immediately say, "Big Idea." Being big enough to register alongside Disney and Nickelodeon in the minds of the public would mean we were having a huge impact. Being the most trusted of the "biggies" would mean we were consistently beneficial regardless of our size. It is relatively easy to be trusted if you attempt very little. Make only one product, sell it to only one person, meet that person's expectations, and then shut down the company, and you will be 100 percent trusted. But the more products you make and the more people you serve, the harder it is to consistently live up to all their expectations. The bigger you get, the harder it is to remain pure. That's what I wanted Big Idea to be—big and pure. It was only a "placeholder" BHAG, of course, but I liked it.

Big Idea now had its ideology. It was time to start building. Now I needed help. What I needed, I figured, was someone as comfortable in business leadership and decision making as I was in creative storytelling. I needed a partner. Immediately my Bennigan's lunch buddy, the insurance company CEO, came to mind. He seemed to have an answer for any business situation, no matter how baffling. He was also, Bill Haljun had informed me, in the process of merging his public company with another public company, after which he would depart and look for his next opportunity. I called him from Minneapolis and told him what I was thinking. I told him about my new values and purpose statement and about my goals for growing the company. I asked him if he'd like to help. We sat down face to face in Chicago the next week and talked it over. He said yes.

I was floored. Here I was, a Bible college dropout hanging on to a runaway business by my fingernails, and this seasoned, mid-fifties CEO of a $3 billion company who had worked at GE Capital under legendary "CEO of CEOs" Jack Welch was coming on board to help. I couldn't believe my good fortune. I asked him if his lack of entertainment experience concerned him at all, and he assured me it wouldn't be an issue, assuming we got good marketing, licensing, and finance people in place to help. It didn't seem right that someone with his experience should have to tell his friends he reported to me, a nobody, so we resolved that he would hold the titles president and partner in the Office of the CEO. I wasn't exactly sure what that last part meant, but I was so glad he was coming that I didn't really care. Help had arrived!

My new president joined Big Idea in early 1998, just before Lyrick Studios was to launch the first two VeggieTales videos into the mass market. Lyrick had forecast selling 300,000 units in the first twelve months, but early results suggested their predictions were low. Very low. Bill Haljun had hired a major PR firm to help get the word out about Bob and Larry, and the story was going over big. Christian magazines and radio stations were all over it, as you might expect, but mainstream journalists were also eating it up. "A kid in his spare bedroom? In the Midwest? Vegetables telling Bible stories? And he's sold *how many videos*? You're kidding me, right?" By the time Bob and Larry hit Wal-Mart, the story of VeggieTales was being told in newspapers across the country. I was flown to New York to tape an interview for *CBS This Morning*. The *Wall Street Journal* ran a story about VeggieTales that started with the line "Move over Barney!" Our PR firm sent us a three-ring binder filled with two or three inches of VeggieTales news clippings each month for five straight months. I had a speaking engagement in Los Angeles, and, knowing how long it had been since Lisa and I had gotten away together, Bill Haljun insisted Big Idea fly her out as well and put us up in a $500-per-night room at his favorite four-star beachside hotel. I sputtered at the price. "Nonsense," he said. "We can afford it, and you need to do something nice for Lisa." Needless to say, the hotel was unlike anything we had ever experienced before. Bill even had roses waiting in the room. What a guy. As we sat on the balcony overlooking the ocean the next morning, eating strawberries and wearing insanely squishy bathrobes, the phone rang. It was a reporter from *Newsweek*. They wanted to know if I had time to talk about VeggieTales.

It was like we had woken up in a dream. Sitting by the Pacific with my wife, eating strawberries and hobnobbing with *Newsweek* magazine. Could it get any better? As fun as it sounds, though, the press exposure played a critical role in the success of VeggieTales. Studies done in the late '90s showed that the average Wal-Mart shopper would look at the average product situated along a Wal-Mart store's prime circulation path—the fabled "power aisle"—for just over two seconds. In the case of a video, if they hadn't already heard something good about it, forget it.

They wouldn't even pick up the package. And that's only if you were lucky enough to get your product positioned along the power aisle in the first place. Get stuck "spine-out" in the in-line section, and the average shopper wouldn't see your video at all. You might as well be in the dumpster out back. The buzz about VeggieTales' unprecedented success in Christian bookstores earned us a spot in the coveted "new release" section on the power aisle, but it was the free publicity from all the newspaper and TV stories that made shoppers stop when they saw our package. "Oh—VeggieTales. I just read about that."

Instead of selling 300,000 videos in the mass market that first year, Lyrick sold 2.3 million. On top of that, sales in Christian bookstores didn't decline with the broader availability of VeggieTales as many had feared, but in fact almost doubled. My new president and I were ecstatic. If we could just get the right executive team in place, who knew how far VeggieTales could go? It seemed just like something God would do: Take a kid out of nowhere—a Bible college dropout, of all persons—and build something amazing around him. Something that could change the world.

It wasn't just my "BHAG" that was driving me, though. The more I learned about the media business, the more I became concerned about America's kids. By the late 1990s, the average American child was watching more than three hours of television each day. What concerned me even more than the quantity of media kids were consuming were the motives of the companies behind all that media—motives that directly affected the content of everything kids were watching.

By the mid-1990s, the media industry had consolidated so aggressively that the vast majority of children's entertainment was controlled by just three companies—Viacom, Time Warner, and Disney. Each employing more than 50,000 people, these companies were now so large that one industry analyst described working with them as more like working with nation-states than companies. The problem with these giant, publicly traded media goliaths isn't that they are *immoral*, but rather that they are profoundly *amoral*. They are valueless. They are simply too big to focus on any specific value system or moral code, and instead must be all things to all people. So Warner Brothers sells Bugs Bunny with one hand and Snoop Doggy Dog with the other. Viacom sells *Blue's Clues* with one hand and MTV with the other. Disney sells Mickey Mouse with one hand and *Desperate Housewives* with the other. We aren't talking about companies making blenders or farm implements here; we're talking about companies in the business of selling images and ideas—the business of influencing beliefs. And each is valueless! Why do they sell good values to preschoolers? Because there is money in it. Why do they sell lousy values to the same kids ten years later? Because there is money in it. When faced with the choice between doing what is beneficial and doing what is profitable, these companies choose profitable every time. Their shareholders require it.

I sat at a media conference in New York and listened to Viacom chairman Sumner Redstone explain to a roomful of Wall Street analysts how he intended to hook kids with *Blue's Clues*, then lead them through Nickelodeon straight to MTV. When I passed the eighty-year-old billionaire in the men's room a few minutes after his speech, I noticed how small he was. *I could take him*, I thought to myself. Not for the fun of it, of course, but for the sake of America's kids. The world's kids.

I decided that probably wasn't the solution God had in mind. (Moments earlier I had walked right past Michael Eisner and

Miramax chief Harvey Weinstein. Given their imposing bulk, I didn't even consider taking on that duo.)

Instead of grappling with octogenarians in the men's room, I continued talking about moral issues in kids' media everywhere I went. I was invited to speak in Washington, D.C., at the Annenberg Conference on Children's Media, where, during a lively panel discussion, I debated one of Nickelodeon's top executives on the impact of media consolidation on kids. The shy kid from Muscatine was mixing it up with the media "elite." Crazy, man.

But mostly, the more I learned about the state of the media, the more I was convinced the world needed Big Idea to be a legitimate alternative. A big family media company that actually cared about families. That valued benefit more than money. That would put the needs of kids before the needs of its shareholders. (As long as I remained Big Idea's controlling shareholder, I could ensure that statement was, in fact, true.) Big Idea would grow as big as possible while still being 100 percent beneficial, and then it would stop growing. Beyond a certain size, in the world of entertainment, you simply cannot afford to let morality govern your work. Your shareholders will not allow it. Regrettably, the Walt Disney Company had clearly now passed that size. After speaking about media issues at an event in the home of a wealthy West Coast family, the host's twelve-year-old son raised his hand and asked, "Could Michael Eisner be redeemed?" "Yes, he could," I replied, "but then he'd be fired."

Throughout 1998, my new president and I worked to put together a team of executives to build the "new" Big Idea, and the combination of my altruistic mission, VeggieTales' runaway success, and my new president's business pedigree proved extremely appealing. By the end of the year, we had an executive vice president in place, as well as an executive from Tomy Toys to develop our licensing business and a design director from the Disney Stores to oversee our in-house design studio. (Suffice it to say, I was no longer designing the neckties and T-shirts myself.) In early 1999, we would add a CFO from Price Waterhouse and a sales and marketing executive with extensive brand management experience at Kraft and Motorola. Another marketer jumped on board from Coca-Cola. It really was a pretty impressive group with tons of business experience. While they lacked traditional entertainment experience, the fact that VeggieTales was a product sold from store shelves made us all believe packaged goods experience would be just as valuable. (In fact, the growth in importance of Wal-Mart at that time had inspired even giant studios like Disney and Warner Brothers to hire packaged goods experts from places like Proctor & Gamble and Kraft to help shape their strategies.)

As we reviewed the business in early 1999, the new team excitedly realized we had now sold more than 8 million VeggieTales videos—6.2 million in 1998 alone. VeggieTales was now the best-selling Christian video series in history, and the number two kids' videos series in the world at that time, trailing only Pokemon. Eager to build on the momentum, our new executives began building their own teams. Suddenly, instead of having an "accountant," we had an entire finance department. Instead of two designers, we had a design studio. Instead of a lone "marketer," we had a marketing team with offices in Chicago and Nashville. At the end of 1997 our staff numbered thirty-six. Twelve months later, the number would reach eighty. Every other day, it seemed, I'd bump into someone new in the halls. "Hi, I'm Phil. What do *you* do?" The only thing I knew for sure was that they all worked for me. And somewhere down deep, that made me feel good. Big Idea was getting, well, *big*. The bigger we were, the more good we could do, I figured. The bigger we were, the more people would have to take us seriously. Take *me* seriously. The bigger we were, the more I felt, somewhere down deep, that I mattered. Invisible? Heck, no. Look what I'm doing now!

Even though life in the animation studio was still somewhat chaotic, the overall mood inside Big Idea was now wildly optimistic. Everyone believed Big Idea was on the right track. Everyone, that is, except "Mr. Silent" and our first full-time accountant, a soft-spoken fellow in his fifties named Don. Don had been recruited by Mr. Silent to take over Big Idea's books when the demands of our rapidly growing business began to overwhelm his own accounting team. Even though our revenue was exploding, the pace at which we were adding staff concerned Mr. Silent so much that he was becoming less and less silent every day. Shortly after my new president joined the company, we decided to write "Mr. Not-So-Silent" a check for $750,000 to buy back his 12.5 percent of the company. (The price was established by Gaylord's $12 million offer for 100 percent of Big Idea, with the customary discount for a minority interest in a privately held company.) In just under two years, Mr. Silent had seen his $25,000 investment multiply thirtyfold. Not a bad return by anyone's standards, and good enough to send Mr. Silent away smiling, silent at last. Don the accountant, however, was not so silent. He knew VeggieTales was selling well, but he saw more clearly than most the rate at which our expenses were ballooning. So with each new hire, his quiet voice would pipe up: "I think we're spending too much money."

"Silly fellow," I'd think to myself, "Doesn't he see how well we're doing?" Sure, we were hiring a lot of people, but we needed them to keep building the business—to become the "Christian

Disney" that more and more seemed to be our divinely preor-dained destiny. God was behind our success. He wouldn't let Big Idea fall apart. Besides, my CFO from Price Waterhouse and my $3 billion ex-CEO partner who worked for Jack Welch both said we were doing fine. For the next several years, Don's still, small voice kept echoing, "I think we're spending too much money." But the more he repeated his concern, the easier it became to tune it out like background noise.

At any rate, I had bigger issues on my plate than the unfounded worries of an anxious accountant. As our headcount soared toward 100, we were once again running out of space.

16

The Beginning of the End

I'd like to build a building," I said to my president, smiling nervously like a kid asking his parents for a pony.

I've always been an architecture and design nut, and the thought of actually building something from scratch was a longtime dream. After five years of moving from one hastily thrown together space to another, I desperately wanted to provide our growing staff with a real home. A really *cool* home. What's more, our customer service department (yes, we now had one of those) was receiving almost daily requests from families and church groups wanting to tour Big Idea—to see where the "magic" happened. We accommodated as many as we could, but our space clearly wasn't set up for public tours, and, even when we *could* fit them in, there wasn't much for kids to see. In my head, I saw a place that would engage our fans and our employees. It would have a Big Idea Studio store filled with our products. A veggie-themed restaurant for lunches. And a tour route designed right into the building, like Disney had done in their new Orlando animation studio. We could rehab an old warehouse or some other historic building, preferably in or near a pedestrian downtown with a train station, so employees could walk to shops and restaurants and easily commute by train into the city or out into the suburbs. It would be the coolest thing ever.

"Can we afford it?" I asked. My president and CFO ran numbers, and much to my delight—and surprise—gave me the thumbs up. At the rate our revenue was growing, they figured, a bank would easily finance a $10 million building project. Oh yeah. This was going to be great! We contacted Realtors and began a search. Within a few months we had located our site—a classic 1920s movie house in downtown Lombard, Illinois, a sleepy suburb along the western commuter train line that linked my home in Wheaton with downtown Chicago. The theater building included several storefronts with apartments above and a parking lot large enough for a major addition. With the help of eager city officials, we acquired the theater and two adjoining properties for about $2 million. We found a national architectural firm with a Chicago office and extensive experience both in historic restoration and new office/entertainment projects. Don the accountant was understandably concerned—was it too much? Too ambitious? As I saw it, though, it was God's will. The right home would become a huge part of Big Idea's culture and identity. Fans would come from across the country to visit Bob and Larry. They could see a movie in our classic old movie house, take a tour of the studio, buy something in the store, and have a meal in our café. School groups could come through for educational tours and screenings. New hires could buy homes within walking distance from the studio or anywhere along the train line from rural Geneva on the Fox River to downtown Chicago and get to work without a car. Besides, my CFO and president were sure we could afford it.

The architects were jazzed by my expansive vision for the project and quickly went to work drawing up plans for the theater's restoration and the adjoining studio facilities, attempting to meet our ambitious twelve-month schedule. Throughout late 1998 and early 1999, I spent every Friday afternoon with the architects, poring over plans and models, adding my own sketches to the mix as we crafted a headquarters befitting a new, major entertainment company. For several weeks I bounced back and forth between design work on the new building and a second major design project that would make it very clear we were a company with big dreams.

It had bright yellow and orange walls fifteen feet high, swooping in playful curves. It had a huge video wall facing a row of curved, bright yellow benches supported by fiberglass peas. But its crowning glory was a twenty-foot tower topped by spinning "Big Idea" logos and a six-foot-high fiberglass Larry the Cucumber and four-foot-high fiberglass Bob the Tomato. It was our new tradeshow booth that we premiered in July of 1999 at the Christian Booksellers Association convention, and amid a sea of Bible salesmen on the convention floor, it looked like Disney World rising out of the orange groves. Ironically, the convention that year was in Orlando, just a few miles from the Magic Kingdom itself. The location couldn't have been better for the introduction of the "new" Big Idea. Looking to make a splash at the convention, we flew down twenty staffers to work the new booth and attend meetings. We also flew down ten animators and their families, as rewards for their hard work finishing our newest video, *Larryboy and the Rumor Weed*, which would premier at the show. Conventioneers, often with kids in tow, flocked to our snazzy booth and filled the pea benches in front of the video wall to watch clips from the new film and clips of me standing in front of the theater in Lombard talking excitedly about our plans for the new headquarters. The buzz on the floor was palpable. Big Idea was big.

In an ironic twist, Disney invited me to speak at their

Orlando animation studio while I was in town, as part of their "visiting artist" lecture series. I drove from our "mini-Disney World" tradeshow booth over to Walt's Magic Kingdom, where I spent an hour showing VeggieTales clips and talking about the creation of the first video. After my talk, I found myself surrounded by five or six Disney animators, all Christians and already big VeggieTales fans. Resumes from Orlando began arriving at Big Idea the following week. (When two artists announced within days of each other that they were leaving the Orlando studio for Big Idea, word came down from Disney animation headquarters in Burbank that no additional artists would be freed from their contracts if their destination was Big Idea Productions. We had been officially "noticed" by the Mouse.)

The real highlight of the convention, though, was the premier of *Larryboy and the Rumor Weed*. The new film was by far our most ambitious and cinematic effort yet, and to premier it in style we rented the Hard Rock Live—the huge Hard Rock Café restaurant and concert venue at Universal Studios' City Walk complex—and bused in seven or eight hundred bookstore owners and industry folk from the convention center. The crowd noshed on free food and drinks while several live bands performed music recorded for the new video. Then the lights went down, and I took the stage, backed by a giant Big Idea logo.

I read excerpts from Time Warner's latest annual report, where the media behemoth talked about the "importance of values" in business. What exactly were Time Warner's values, I asked? I skipped further down the page and read about the new committee Time Warner was setting up to "identify" the company's values. I stopped reading. "The world's largest media company," I said, "is admitting that it has *no values* and is setting up a committee to find some." The audience hooted.

I then talked about the Millennium Celebration under way at Walt Disney World, just a few miles down the interstate. I read from a Disney press release that described, in typical Disney-speak, the sense of "wonder" and "hope" Disney's millennial bash would generate for its guests. I contrasted Disney's irrational optimism with current statistics about crime and failing marriages. "If I were Disney," I said, "I'm not sure I could come up with any reason to be hopeful. But we're not Disney. We're Big Idea."

The audience burst into enthusiastic applause, and in that moment, I knew I had done it. Almost since the beginning, bookstore owners and Christian market industry folks had been excited about VeggieTales. But my real goal for the prior few years and, in particular, for that convention was to move their excitement from a video series that was making them a lot of money to a new Christian family media company that was ready to go head to head with Disney and Time Warner and make a real difference in the world. I knew my ability to build a trusted media company depended on moving our audience's growing trust for Bob and Larry to Big Idea itself so they would trust new non-VeggieTales projects as well. (This was, in fact, the reason I had placed Bob and Larry in the Big Idea logo in the first place.)

"We know where our hope comes from," I continued. "There is a God who made us special and loves us very much." I thanked them for coming and left the stage to a rousing ovation, bringing to mind ovations my father had received at Bandag sales conferences years earlier. His were about tires. Mine was about a media company that was doing God's work. Either way, it felt really good.

The new film was a big hit. As the credits rolled, one of my executives sidled up to the Hard Rock employee manning the sound board, a grizzled, tattooed biker dude. "What did you think of the movie?" he asked. The biker dude turned and grinned. "It's got a great message, but it's funny as hell!" To this day, that is still my all-time favorite quote about VeggieTales.

Spirits were high at the VIP party after the event. Lisa and I posed for pictures with the night's musical artists and with various Christian market bigwigs. One of my original animators came up to me in between photos, his face positively glowing. He clearly wanted to say something but was struggling for words. "It feels like—," he said at last, "it feels like we could do *anything*." I couldn't help but agree.

Today I look back on that moment as the high point in the history of Big Idea. We were the "toast of the town" so to speak—a ministry with the creative moxie and business savvy to mix it up with the big boys in the nasty, amoral world of media. Our thirteen customer service reps were responding to more than four hundred pieces of fan mail each day, many with messages like "Who needs Disney when we've got Big Idea?" Everything, it seemed, was working. God was blessing my efforts beyond my wildest expectations. Shortly after the event, *Animation Magazine* would name Big Idea one of ten studios to watch in worldwide animation. A PBS special had just named me one of ten people to watch in worldwide religion. My dream was coming true.

But as Lisa and I stood basking in the afterglow of the Hard Rock event, leaning on a railing overlooking Universal's theme parks, my eyes were burning like mad, a post-pericarditis indicator that my energy was seriously depleted. The year after I had pericarditis, I contracted strep throat. The year after that, shingles. All stress related, the results of an increasingly maniacal schedule that had me bouncing between press interviews, speaking engagements, and endless meetings with animators, marketers, licensors, architects, and designers. My days were now scheduled down to fifteen-minute increments. Even the tasks I should have enjoyed—the creative writing projects or strategy sessions—were no longer fun. Big Idea was now creating toys, books, greeting cards—you name it. Exactly what I had wanted. But my time was so stretched now that the only projects I could handle personally were the videos themselves, and even those I did only by locking myself away in a nearby hotel for intense two-day writing marathons characterized more by stress than joy. And the strategy sessions with my executive team, sessions that sounded so fun going in, were routinely devolving into extended and unresolved arguments.

"Who do we believe is our core audience?"

"That's easy," I'd respond, "Christian families."

My marketers pushed back. "How do you know that? Have you done a segmentation study?"

I didn't even know what a segmentation study was.

"Until we've done a full segmentation study, you can't say for sure who our audience really is. We believe our real core customer isn't Christian families at all, but rather 'moral active' families."

Huh? Moral *what*?

I went to our Web site one day and noticed that almost everything I had ever written had been rewritten by our marketing department. "It sounded too Christian," our marketing VP explained to me, "It would limit our growth."

Oh. Sorry. Didn't mean to limit our growth. "You want Big Idea to grow, right?" Well, sure I did. "Then we need to be careful we don't sound too Christian. We believe the 'moral active' audience is much larger than the 'Christian' audience."

I went to my president and complained. "It's their business," he said. "You need to let them run it." Right. It's their business. We hired our head of sales and marketing for his expertise in marketing, and I needed to get out of his way so he could grow

VeggieTales video sales. We hired our head of licensing to build our licensing business, and I needed to get out of her way so she could do just that. I was getting in the way.

I tried to "lay off"—to stay out of their way. Otherwise, I'd send the message that I didn't trust them, and they might get frustrated. They might leave. And I hated it when people left—especially people I was convinced I needed very much. "I'm 95 percent with you," our licensing VP told me several times after hearing my point of view in a strategy meeting. "Hmm," I remember thinking at the time, "95 percent is pretty good." What she really meant with that statement, I now realize, was, "I'm not quite with you." And having your key leaders "not quite with you" in the heat of battle is pretty much the same as having them not with you at all.

My president, CFO, marketing VP, and licensing VP began meeting weekly without me. When our new VP of human resources joined the company in the fall of 1999, he was invited to join the weekly "no Phil" meetings. He declined. Our executive vice president, a good friend of mine with a background in Christian ministry, was never invited. I had no idea the meetings were even taking place. Lines were being drawn. Sides were being chosen. People, I was learning, were nothing like computers.

17

The Middle of the End

We Americans love to be ranked. *People* magazine keeps track of our "50 Most Beautiful People." *Forbes* tracks the "400 Wealthiest Americans" and the "200 Highest-Paid Entertainers." Not to be outdone, every year *Inc.* magazine puts out a list of the five hundred fastest-growing private companies in America. These companies tend to be on the small side, but for whatever reason, they're growing like gangbusters. *Inc.* tracks and ranks them all, and then the entrepreneurs behind each company can hang the magazine cover in their conference room and beam like proud parents when their friends notice their amazing fast-growing-ness.

If I had put a lot of value on such lists or if *Inc.* had noticed us, it's fairly likely Big Idea would have made the list a year or two. Between 1996 and 1999, our revenue grew by 3,300 percent, from $1.3 million to $44 million. Pretty impressive by anyone's standards. But by early 2000, just as our first feature film, *Jonah—A VeggieTales Movie*, was headed into production, the company was in serious financial trouble. How could that be, you ask? Good question.

It's interesting to note that only one out of three companies that makes the *Inc.* list repeats its appearance the following year. What happens to the rest? Many see their growth stall, never to fully recover. Others simply cease to exist. Vanish. You see, when a small company experiences extremely rapid growth, it soon ceases to be a "small company." Yet just because it no longer qualifies as "small" doesn't necessarily mean it is now "big." In other words, just because you're no longer "Tim's Software Hut" doesn't necessarily mean you're "Microsoft." And somewhere in the middle, many, many companies fail.

Inc. magazine noticed this dynamic and had several business researchers look into it. What emerged was a picture of a treacherous period in any business's growth when a company finds itself "too big to be small yet too small to be big." The researchers dubbed it "No Man's Land."

"No Man's Land" threat number one, according to Inc.'s experts: Small companies, experiencing rapid initial growth, attempt to make the leap to being "big" without having a clear plan for sustaining that growth. What got you to $10 million in sales won't necessarily take you to $100 million.

We sold more than six million VeggieTales videos in 1998. Unable to imagine selling more than that, I entered 1999 assuming Big Idea's continued growth would depend on expanding into other areas like television and feature films. Unfortunately, the executive team I put together had no experience in television or feature films; they knew how to sell things through stores. Rather than wade into unknown waters, they stuck to their belief that future growth would come from selling even more VeggieTales videos using marketing techniques borrowed from the world of packaged goods. The team quickly discovered through research that even though we had sold more than eight million videos by the end of 1998, only one-quarter of American mothers of young children had even heard of VeggieTales. Given that fact, they reasoned, increased awareness would result in increased sales.

As a result of the difference of opinion, 1999 saw us moving down two separate tracks. When I wasn't penning the next video, designing the new headquarters, or dealing with the press, I began aggressively investigating the TV and feature film businesses, looking for points of entry for Big Idea. I was working on these efforts more or less alone, though, as my executive team was busy building a large marketing group to launch an even larger VeggieTales awareness campaign to expand home video sales. Between 1998 and 2000, our marketing department grew from one person to thirty people. We gave away 400,000 VeggieTales videos at the grand openings of malls and Target stores and took out two-page ads in *People* magazine to introduce America to the concept of VeggieTales. As a result, our marketing expense grew from $3 million in 1998 to $13 million in 2000. No problem, though, since the team estimated the increased awareness would double our sales within twenty-four months, from six million videos a year to twelve million videos a year.

With this massive sales growth in mind, my president charged our brand new vice president of human resources to build a human resources team, "assuming we will have five hundred people on staff." (Yet another conversation I wouldn't learn about until several years later.) My marketing chief developed a plan for an inbound telemarketing center with a full-time staff of twenty to field customer service calls from an 800 number he intended to put on the back of every package. You know, like Proctor & Gamble. Based on this plan, my president approved the purchase of a new phone system big enough to handle 250 employees, plus the telemarketing center—all of which, of course, was to be paid for by the cash generated from the huge increase in video sales.

As of mid-1999, though, the sales growth wasn't happening. After achieving revenue growth of more than 200 percent per year for five straight years, 1999's increase looked to be less than 10 percent. "No problem!" my marketing chief exclaimed. "Just wait until we execute our plan!" He was smiling, but I was worried. Our expense growth was now far outstripping our sales growth. In the prior eighteen months, in fact, we had doubled the number of artists working on our films and doubled their average salary in order to better compete with high-paying West Coast studios. Since we were still only producing two videos per year, the net result of our hiring and pay increases was a fourfold increase in the expense of each video. The video that cost $250,000 to produce in 1997 now cost a cool million. Lying in bed at night, I wondered if my executive team really had Big Idea on the right track. When I asked my marketing VP in the hall one day why he thought we could still achieve significant growth in home video sales, he simply smiled and responded, "Because I'm here!"

Meanwhile, though, I wasn't doing much better getting us into new businesses. Intrigued by the strategic possibilities of having a home in television, I began talking with the newly launched family network Pax TV about taking over their entire Saturday morning block. They seemed genuinely interested, given VeggieTales' huge success. I spent time crunching numbers and identifying other shows that could fill out a block alongside VeggieTales and be introduced by Bob and Larry. The pieces were falling into place, when suddenly Pax announced they weren't interested in a Big Idea Saturday morning block but would much rather we supply them with an hour of programming for prime time. Since none of the shows I had been considering for Saturday morning would work well in prime time, I was back to square one.

As a hedge against the possibility that a TV strategy might

not pan out, I also was trying to chart a course to take our animation studio toward feature film production. In late 1998 I had put
Larryboy and the Rumor Weed into production, our most cinematic
half-hour video yet. It was my plan, in fact, that it would be our
last half-hour video. It was time to move on. With that in mind,
Mike and I had already begun work on an elaborate forty-five-
minute script based on a classic Bible story that would take us
one step closer to the world of feature films. The story was Jonah
and the whale.

"Wait a minute," you say. "Wasn't *Jonah—A VeggieTales Movie*
conceived as a movie?" No, not originally. I thought jumping from
Larryboy and the Rumor Weed straight to a feature-length, film-
resolution project would be too ambitious. The next logical step,
I decided, was a forty-five-minute video project that would be
longer and more elaborate than anything we had done before
(thereby justifying a bigger marketing budget to create more buzz
and a higher sale price to cover the added expense) but not as
complex as a feature film. Our first real, honest-to-goodness
movie, I figured, would come further down the road.

So what happened? How did *Jonah* wind up on the big
screen? That would be my doing. As *Rumor Weed* headed into production, Mike and I worked out an outline for a forty-five-minute
Jonah. It was at this point that we decided to "bookend" the biblical story within a modern-day setup/wrap-up involving Bob,
Dad Asparagus, and a van full of veggie kids on their way to a
Twippo concert. (Although technically, Mike first had them heading to a "Tweezerman" concert. Why Tweezerman? Like many of
his ideas, Mike could never really articulate where the name came
from. We changed the name during the film's production when
someone noticed that Tweezerman was the registered trademark
of a company that manufactured—you guessed it—tweezers.

Mike then proposed "Twippo." Where'd that one come from? Again, he had no idea.)

Mike started writing the setup as I was directing *Rumor Weed*. As brilliantly funny as he is, Mike at that time wasn't the most disciplined of writers, and seventeen pages into his script he was still in the modern-day setup. He was just having too much fun with a van full of veggies and a weird old seafood restaurant. My first thought was, "Well, he'll just have to throw it away and start over again." But when I read it, I really liked it. It was fun stuff. So here's where I made a large mistake: I let my fondness of Mike's pages overrule my business conviction that we were *not* ready to make a movie. Instead, a little voice in my head was whispering, "Well, maybe just a *little* movie . . ."

I ran some numbers. The recently released Christian film *The Omega Code* had surprised everyone by grossing $13 million at the U.S. box office with a tiny marketing budget of less than $2 million. Using *The Omega Code* as a model, I estimated a small VeggieTales film with a $7 million production budget and a $7 million marketing budget needed to do $18.5 million at the box office and sell 3 million videos and DVDs. I figured the 3 million video mark was achievable since our relatively low-budget half-hour VeggieTales Christmas video had already passed the 2 million-unit mark. As for the $18.5 million figure, it was only 40 percent more than *The Omega Code*, and our film had a large built-in audience and would launch with a much larger marketing budget. The great thing was that if we hit these numbers, not only would our investment be returned, but we'd also make about half the money needed to fund our second movie. Looking at the numbers, it seemed like a no-brainer. Write on, Mike! Write on! We're gonna make a movie!

In my excitement, the question of whether we were *ready* to make a movie somehow escaped me.

As small companies grow, the experts at *Inc.* magazine observed, their *need* for top-notch management often arrives years before their ability to attract or even *afford* top-notch management. Many small companies fail to survive "No Man's Land" because they either never find the management talent they need to make the leap from "small" to "big," or even worse, they bring in the wrong management.

In 1999, as I pointed the company toward our first feature film, no one was running the animation studio. The last head of the studio had departed in 1998, moving directly from Big Idea into several months of therapy. He was, in fact, one of three executives to follow his tenure at Big Idea with extended therapy engagements. One senior designer, worn down by countless conflicts with our licensing executives, abandoned art altogether and moved back to his parents' farm to pick olives. What was it about the home of sweet little Bob and Larry that was chewing up and spitting out managers at an alarming rate? Big Idea had long been a tricky management environment because of the broad range of motivations that brought people to our doors. With the heightened visibility brought by our success, though, most new hires from 1998 on were huge VeggieTales fans and, like myself, deeply committed evangelical Christians. "Great!" I thought. "This will make everything easier because we'll all be on the same page!"

If only it were so simple.

Once again, chaos reigned. The evangelical Christians joining the company assumed *everyone* at Big Idea would be an evangelical Christian and were sometimes deeply confused when they learned this was not the case. "When are the prayer meetings? Don't we have all-company prayer meetings?" Well, no, we don't. Why? Because in the old days, only half the company was *any* kind of Christian, much less the "prayer meeting" variety. But given our Christian mission, a prayer meeting every now and then probably made sense. So we proposed a quarterly prayer meeting, going out of our way to say, "All invited, none compelled." But no matter how often we repeated our "All invited, none compelled" mantra, a significant group of non-Christian and marginally-Christian employees was absolutely convinced that failure to attend would inevitably result in being passed over for raises and promotions. "We know you keep track of who's at those meetings," they complained.

The party planners in our human resources department managed to deeply offend our Catholic contingent by holding a wrap party in a goofy Italian restaurant, where employees could have their pictures taken with a bust of the pope in the restaurant's tongue-in-cheek "Pope Room." The resulting pictures were quickly and sheepishly removed from a company bulletin board and a formal apology issued. Things got even messier when several evangelical Christian employees began witnessing to their non-Christian coworkers during work hours. When they were supposed to be animating. Evangelistic tracts were left on desks. Feelings were hurt. Our vice president of human resources had never experienced issues like these in his Fortune 500 days. Few companies, I imagine, have ever found it necessary to write a policy on "the appropriate time and place for witnessing to your coworkers." In the end, some non-Christian artists left Big Idea because it was "too much like a church." Some Christian artists left because it was "not enough like a church." My mission statement, intentionally vague to keep cynical journalists from writing us off as radical right wackos, proved equally adept at allowing employees to draw various, often contradictory conclusions about what it actually meant. "Is Big Idea a Christian ministry?" Ask twelve different employees and get twelve different answers. Yes. No. Sort of. What do you mean by "ministry"? Even I wasn't entirely sure.

I knew my life was a ministry, but my company? A ministry? No, my company was a *mess*.

Attempting to manage a team at Big Idea was extraordinarily difficult, and as a result, as *Jonah* rolled into development, no one was running the studio, and our search for a new chief was proceeding excruciatingly slowly. The world in 1998 was not awash with seasoned CGI animation studio chiefs. The pool of those willing to relocate to Chicago to make biblical films was even smaller. Pathetically small. In lieu of a production head, the studio was being managed by a committee composed of the studio's team leaders, most of whom were quite young and only one of whom had any previous management experience. The process quite often resembled *The Lord of the Flies* more than *The Art of Management*. In the end, the studio would go "headless" for more than a year as our recruiter scoured Hollywood for the right person and *Jonah* barreled toward production like a runaway locomotive.

Our search finally ended in 2000 with the arrival of two seasoned industry veterans from Dreamworks Feature Animation. One would act as *Jonah*'s producer while the other ran the studio. Given that the new studio chief had never actually run an *entire* studio before, and the producer had only worked on traditionally animated films (and never in the role of overall producer), both faced a steep learning curve. *Jonah* would be well into production before the two had enough of a grasp of our unique production system to assemble a budget for the project. They were inheriting a process and a crew that had been built and rebuilt over the years by a series of managers. On top of that, a fair amount of hiring had already taken place with *Jonah* in mind. Some department leaders had carefully thought through their own plans for *Jonah* and had begun hiring accordingly. Others later admitted they started hiring simply "because everyone else was." The first budget forecast came in at $10 million. I gulped. Not the $7 million I was hoping for, but—heh, heh—it could be worse.

Within a few months, it would be.

Throughout 1999, as *Jonah* moved through pre-production, the new Big Idea leadership team was being assembled. Strategy meetings were taking place. Numbers were being crunched and trends analyzed. Even though there was still no official plan and no real budget, hiring was already well under way as the new leaders each built support staffs. By late summer—shortly after the *Rumor Weed* premier in Orlando—the team was finally in place.

We were all grins as we attended the groundbreaking ceremony for the new building in Lombard. We handed out balloons to the kids. The mayor spoke, my president spoke, I spoke. The *Chicago Tribune* and several local papers carried the story. The excavating crew was scheduled to begin digging the foundation the following week. Everything looked great, except for the fact that we still didn't have a budget for the project, or a financing commitment from our bank. Finally, the budget came in, based on our completed drawings and renovation plans: $17 million. Gulp. That was quite a bit more than the $10 million we'd been hoping for. Well, we told ourselves, if the bank was willing to write the mortgage, maybe we could still move ahead. All we needed was the bank's appraisal, which would determine the amount they would underwrite. Then the appraisal came in, and our hearts sank. The project was too unconventional, they said. It was too far from the nearest freeway. It didn't have enough parking. And who would want to buy an office building connected to an old movie theater? What the appraisers were trying to determine, of course, was not the value of the project to Big Idea, but the value of the project on the open market if Big Idea were to default on its loan. The final figure was a knife in the heart: $10 million. That's what the appraisers felt the finished project would be worth. The bank would loan 80 percent of the appraised value of the project. So we could borrow only $8 million to complete our $17 million building. We were dead.

The next day we called the mayor in to our offices and broke the bad news. We couldn't afford to proceed. He later admitted that he went home that night and cried. Great. I made the mayor of Lombard, Illinois, cry. The news flashed across the papers, inciting a flurry of response. "Big Idea pulls out of theater project!" Angry citizens wrote letters to the editor. "Make Big Idea keep its promises!" Angry letters poured in to Big Idea. One Christian family wrote me directly, angrily explaining how my "lack of integrity" would forever affect their Christian witness before their Lombard neighbors. For my wife and I, the experience was brutal. Rather than ensure the historic theater's demise by selling the property to a developer, we chose instead to donate it to the Village of Lombard, hoping they could raise the money for restoration. Our $4 million investment ($2 million for the property, plus $2 million for plans, tenant relocation, and initial renovation) was a total loss. It was the first unqualified disaster of my VeggieTales experience.

Traveling in Los Angeles on business shortly thereafter and still smarting from the Lombard debacle, it suddenly dawned on me that it had been ten years since I had started GRAFx Studios, the company that would become Big Idea Productions. A full decade of my life had gone into this often exasperating pursuit of the stories I felt God wanted me tell. For the first time, I really felt the weight and fatigue of building and attempting to run the company alone for so long—a task I had seldom enjoyed. Sitting alone in a hotel room somewhere in Los Angeles, I found myself breaking down in tears. I was exhausted.

Back in Chicago, I told my president I needed some time off. We

agreed that I would take the month of October off to rest and recu-
perate. The team was in place. They could manage the business
without me. October came, and Lisa and I headed to Hawaii for a
week of blissful rest. I had intended to spend the rest of the month
playing with my kids, taking pictures, and studying the Bible. The
distance from Big Idea, though, gave me ample time and space to
think things through, and I began to doubt that things were going
as well as I had thought. One clue that perhaps they weren't came as
I returned from Hawaii and was called in because my president and
executive vice president, locked in a dispute over their stock awards,
were no longer speaking to one another. Over the rest of month I
noticed more and more concerning issues—so many, in fact, that
upon my return, I called all the leaders together and laid out my concerns about our direction one by one, in front of the entire team.

The reactions were swift and strong. Several leaders were
embarrassed that I had mentioned concerns about their areas in
front of their peers. Another leader called it "the most important
meeting he had ever attended." Our brand-new head of human
resources said it was "exactly what he expected Big Idea to be
like." My president, however, did not speak to me for two days.
When he finally did, he declared it "the biggest leadership disaster he had ever seen." The next day he instructed our new head of
human resources to help me write a full retraction and apology. I
was confused. For the first time I felt like I was leading boldly, but
the man I had hired to help me lead—the man I looked up to for
his wisdom and experience—described my bold leadership as a
"disaster." I agreed to apologize for any embarrassment I had
caused by addressing concerns so publicly, but I stopped short of
issuing the full retraction my president had demanded. It was
clear the two of us didn't see eye to eye, and our relationship
would be strained from here on out.

Christmas 1999. Due to the rapid growth and hiring, we were a little short on cash, so our annual Christmas party was held at Big Idea's new temporary offices in an old Woolworth's store in a mall near the new building site in Lombard. Toward the end of the evening, my good friend, the executive vice president, pulled me into his office and said, "Wanna see a joke?" He dropped a thick, three-ring binder on the table in front of me. The cover read, "Big Idea Productions—2000 Budget." Up to this point, Big Idea's growth had been so unexpected and chaotic that we had never even attempted to put together an annual budget or sales forecast. Now that the leadership team was in place, though, it was time to start running things like a "real company." So while I was taking October off, the team had started the budget process that had produced the tome sitting in front of me.

Curious (I had been completely uninvolved in the process), I turned to the summary page and felt my jaw drop. Our sales in 1999 had totaled roughly $38 million, a staggering amount in my mind. The new forecast for 2000—$77 million. *Egads,* I thought, *who's going to buy all those videos?* Then I looked at the expense side—the costs needed for the team to meet its sales forecasts. Our expenses in 1999 had been somewhere around $25 million, leaving the company with a very healthy $13 million profit. (Half of which had gone to cover my president's tax bill for his stock awards, the rest reinvested in new people, projects, and the Lombard building.) For 2000, the team projected expenses of $73 million, including staff growth from 1999's 150 to an unbelievable 315. I was speechless.

As soon as we returned from the Christmas break, I called the executive team together and posed a simple question: "What *exactly* are we building here?" We were proposing to triple our expenses while only doubling our sales. More concerning, we were proposing to double our staff size without increasing our ability to produce films. Of the 165 hires being requested, only a handful were in the animation studio. Ninety percent were in finance, human resources, marketing, licensing, and design. So at 315 people we would be able to produce no more videos per year than we had produced five years earlier with a staff of 10. The meeting ended with no answers and very little real discussion. It was as if my executives just wanted me to go write the next video and leave the business up to them. Stop meddling, we're professionals. My president assured me the budget wasn't yet approved and we wouldn't be hiring anywhere near that many people. Don't worry. We know what we're doing.

A few weeks later, the sales results for the month of January came in. The team missed the number they had forecast in the 2000 budget by 80 percent. Not by 20 percent—by 80 percent. The team had sold one-fifth the number of VeggieTales videos they had planned on selling. Yet they had spent significant monies on marketing plans and awareness/sampling programs to generate the sales they were forecasting. Something was seriously wrong. I ran into the president's office to express my alarm. "Don't worry," he assured me, "I've told the sales team they need to make up those lost sales in the second half of the year." Make up the sales later in the year? How on earth would they do that? It didn't seem possible.

By now I realized I had made a huge mistake: I was running the company blind. Ever since I had created that first spreadsheet to figure out how much money I would need to launch VeggieTales, I had maintained my own financial model of the business. For five years, I called Word Entertainment every other week to get the latest sales report for each video we had produced. Every other week, I fed that data into my spreadsheet, recalculating our financial health. When we finally hired our own accountant, he looked over my spreadsheet and was amazed that, even though none of my individual categories were quite right, the total was always dead-on. I knew exactly how much money we had and exactly how many videos we had sold at any given time, and I carefully pored over the trends to project our probable health over the coming year. As the business grew more complex, though, it became harder and harder for me to keep my model accurate, so when our CFO walked in the door from Price Waterhouse in 1999, I gave a huge sigh of relief and said, "Now *you* can keep track of the money!" and I stopped updating my model. Theoretically this shouldn't have been a problem, as my CFO should have fed me whatever information I needed as often as I needed it. But it was a problem. Under my president's direction, my CFO built his own model for the business and began cranking out monthly reports. The problem? I couldn't read them. They didn't make any sense to me. I held the first one up and turned it upside down and sideways and backward and kept saying to myself, "Where's the part that tells me how many videos we've sold?" But his reports were full of "net"-this and "gross"-that and amortization and depreciation and capitalized expenses and. . . . And nowhere did they say, "We sold this many videos and now we have this much money." What's worse, I was too embarrassed to admit it. I was the CEO, after all. I should be able to read a basic financial statement, shouldn't I? So instead, I turned to my president and said, "How are we doing?" And he said, "Great!" And I went blind. When I wanted to build a building, I went to my president and said, "Can we afford it?" and he said, "Yep!" When I wanted to make a $7 million movie, I went to my president and said, "Can we afford it?" and he said, "Yep!" I allowed myself to go blind, relying entirely on the fact that my executives were much older and wiser and therefore would keep us out of trouble. But now here I was, confronted with the fact that they had missed their numbers by 80 percent in the first month of the first year completely under their control. And I realized I had made a terrible mistake. I needed my sight back.

Over the months of February and March 2000, I dug through reams of sales and financial data and painstakingly rebuilt my own financial forecast for the company. I based my forecast not on the leadership team's optimistic projections, but on the real expenses we were incurring and the real sales that we appeared to be achieving. With *Jonah* just recently greenlit, and sales at a fraction of the forecast used to justify its production budget, my forecast looked bad. Really bad. We weren't going to be able to keep the company going long enough to finish *Jonah*, according to my forecast, without bringing in nearly $20 million in cash from some external source. In fact, we were just five or six months from running out of cash and shutting down.

In April of 2000, I ran to the president and CFO with my new, deeply disturbing forecast. They both looked it over and handed it back to me. They had their own forecast that looked much better than mine, and, more important, they had already given their forecast to several major Chicago banks. If they changed the numbers now, it would make us look bad with the bank, which would not be good since we desperately needed a very large loan in order not to run out of cash in five to six months if sales didn't turn around.

Desperate for cash, we pressed ahead with the bank loan process until finally in August I found myself sitting in our dead-Woolworth's conference room with my president, CFO, corporate attorney, and a large stack of legal documents. It was the bank loan, ready for signing. Our attorney looked at me.

"Before you sign this, are you comfortable with the covenants?"

"What covenants?" I replied. His face whitened. My president and CFO shifted uncomfortably in their seats. I knew we were trying to borrow a lot of money from our bank. What I wasn't so clear about was that when a company borrows money from a bank there are certain financial requirements placed on the company to keep the bank comfortable with its financial health. Fall out of compliance with those requirements, and the bank has the right to call the loan and, effectively, take over the business.

"Well, there are certain hurdles we have to meet to remain in compliance with the loan agreement," my CFO said. "Like . . . what?" I asked. The room was a bit tense. "I don't know them off the top of my head, but I could go get them if you'd like," he replied. "Yes. Go get them," I responded. In a few moments, the CFO was back in the room with the list of performance covenants. He read them in English, but they sounded like Greek to me. And I got kicked out of Bible college long before I mastered Greek. "Our blah-to-blah ratio needs to be no more than blah. . . . Our blah-blah-blah shall not exceed blah-point-blah. . . . Our twelve-month rolling EBITDAE (I remember that one) must be blah-blah-blah."

He finished the list. Everyone stared at me.

"So . . . can we make those numbers?" I asked, not entirely comfortable admitting I had no comprehension of what he had just read. "Sure," he responded, "we can make those." Keenly aware that we were just weeks away from running out of cash, I swallowed hard and signed the documents. Did I understand exactly what I was agreeing to? Not really. But my president and my CFO were convinced we could make the numbers, and they were much smarter than I was.

One month later, our financial analyst walked into a senior leadership meeting and said, "We aren't going to make those numbers."

I signed the loan agreement in August of 2000. By late September of that year, we were already out of compliance, effectively giving LaSalle Bank the right to shut down the company and sell off all of its assets, including, of course, Bob and Larry.

I was not happy.

18

The End of the End

So there we were in late 2000. Sales were declining. Expenses were skyrocketing. *Jonah* was heading into production, but we were $20 million short of being able to complete it. (A fairly remarkable thing, given the fact that it was only supposed to be a $7 million film. The rest of the money was needed to cover all the staff we had added to nonproduction areas of the company.) Our bank could pull the plug at any moment. We were in deep doo-doo.

It was clear to me that changes needed to be made to my leadership team. Though they were all good people whom I liked very much, their lack of experience in the entertainment business, coupled with my lack of experience in the entertainment business, was not going to get the company through this crisis. Nervously, I asked my president and my head of sales and marketing to step down. My CFO left in protest, saying I was "throwing world-class people out the window." I put my licensing vice president, who had developed the habit of making our designers cry with her sometimes brutish manner, on a performance plan. She resigned the following day. By the end of 2000, only my executive vice president and head of human resources remained. My executive vice president and I quickly brought in a freelance CFO to keep the bank from panicking and shutting down the company. We then went on a tear, trying to raise $30 million in less than 120 days. We sent out information packets and visited with wealthy VeggieTales fans across the country. The reaction was not good. Though they loved the company and the films, the financial situation Big Idea now faced did not inspire confidence. One potential investor, after reviewing the company's financials, simply shook his head and muttered, "What did you do to VeggieTales?"

At a Christian media conference in April of 2001, one of my employees met an experienced Christian executive from Hollywood who wanted to help. In dire need of someone who really knew the entertainment business, I hopped on a plane to Los Angeles and spent several hours with him in his home in Bel Air. Less than forty-eight hours after meeting him for the first time, I offered him Big Idea's presidency. He flew in the next week and hit the ground running. Sharing an office in the basement of our old Woolworth space with our freelance CFO, the new president soon discovered that the situation was worse than my executive vice president had led him to believe. According to their new forecast, the company would run out of cash and be forced to shut its doors by the middle of June, just sixty days away.

Drastic steps were needed. The new president recommended immediately cutting staff to preserve cash. My heart dropped. There had to be another way. I thought about all the people who had joined Big Idea, many uprooting their families and moving across the country to be a part of something inspiring, many coming specifically because I had inspired them, either through my work or through my writings and speeches. The thought of sending them packing was almost more than I could bear. I'd be letting them down. I'd be the one walking out on them. It was painfully clear, though, that our expenses had to drop drastically if we were to continue the ministry God had begun. But how could hurting people be God's will? I wracked my brain for another solution but came up empty. Big Idea was horribly over-staffed given our actual sales level. Many of our leaders had built their teams based on sales forecasts that simply never came to pass. The unthinkable was now the only way out.

In early May of 2001, I stood before the entire company and explained the choices we were forced to make. What began as a typically upbeat all-company meeting soon turned into a funeral. The whole room wilted before my eyes as I explained that it would be the last day at Big Idea for some of those gathered there. Some burst into tears. Others sat in stunned disbelief or hard-ened into anger. For everyone, a part of Big Idea died that day. A part of me died, too, as I found myself overwhelmed with the feel-ing I had let everyone down. After the meeting I drove to a nearby park, sat on a park bench, and cried.

Thirty really great people—about 15 percent of our staff—lost their jobs that day. My president and CFO had a sinking feel-ing it wasn't enough, but they had yielded to my insistence we go no deeper. History would prove them right.

At this point, we really had just two options. The first was to press ahead with the current plan—to raise enough money to complete *Jonah* and hope that this film about a waterlogged prophet would bring in enough money to keep Big Idea's own leaky boat afloat. The second was to radically cut back. Stop production on *Jonah*, shut down the animation studio, cut the company down to a core team of thirty to forty people, and go back to producing just one or two VeggieTales videos per year. Both my new president and our freelance CFO recommended this second, radical option. Frankly, it was the option most likely to save the company—at least what would be left of it. But I couldn't do it. To pull the plug on *Jonah* and shutter the animation studio—the animation studio I'd been building for nine years—seemed like a decision I would make out of a lack of faith. Surely God was pleased with the impact we were having. Surely he was pleased by our efforts to have even more impact. Surely he could use *Jonah* to cover up the "sins" of our past, erase our fiscal shortcomings, and set us on the road to renewed health and ministry. The way I saw it, to choose the second option was to lose faith in God. I wouldn't do it.

That decision made, we needed to come up with a lot of money very quickly. My new president knew it would be impossible to raise the money we needed from investors in ninety days. We all knew raising money directly for *Jonah*'s production wouldn't work, since the amount of money we needed far exceeded *Jonah*'s production budget. (Want to look like a fool in Hollywood? Tell people you need to raise $20 million to produce a $10 million film.) The only potential source for the money, my president reckoned, was our distributors. VeggieTales videos were still among the best-selling kids' videos in the world. Retailers wanted more. Distributors wanted more. The market's desire for more of our product appeared to be the only asset we had left.

Within a few weeks, my new president had a plan. We could raise millions if we could create a new series to offer to a new distribution partner. We had previously toyed with the idea of spinning off Larryboy as a separate series. Given his television experience, my president figured a new series of videos could be produced more like an animated television show, greatly reducing production expenses compared to our big-budget VeggieTales productions. The Cartoon Adventures of Larryboy was born and placed in the hands of a gifted ex-Disney animator who had recently joined Big Idea.

But that alone wouldn't be enough to save the company. The distribution rights to VeggieTales videos were worth much more than a new series but were locked up with Word Entertainment and Lyrick Studios. The Word deal was locked up tight, but the Lyrick deal, our lawyers pointed out, was still unsigned. Lyrick and Big Idea had been working together for almost two years without a signed contract. Numerous drafts had floated back and forth between the companies' lawyers, but none had been signed and negotiations were still, in fact, ongoing. "You might be able to move VeggieTales elsewhere—or at least call for a major renegotiation," our lawyers advised. But that option didn't seem right to me. I couldn't do that to our old friend Dick Leach.

As I explained earlier, we chose Lyrick because of Dick Leach's personal faith and commitment to keep God in our videos. Because of the value we placed on his convictions and dedication, we had requested that two special provisions be added to our contract. First, if Dick Leach ever left leadership at Lyrick, we wanted the right to walk away too. Second, if Dick Leach ever sold Lyrick Studios to someone else, we wanted the right to walk away. Our message was very clear. If a big company like Disney or Viacom bought Lyrick and/or Dick Leach left leadership, we wanted the right to leave too. Lyrick agreed.

That point was about to become very important because right about this time, the phone rang. It was our entertainment lawyer in Los Angeles. "HIT Entertainment is buying Lyrick," he said. We were stunned. Dick Leach was selling the company? This was the man who had refused Michael Eisner's offer to make Barney as big as Mickey Mouse if he would sell his company to Disney. This was the man who had sat in a restaurant with top Disney execs and said, "No thank you. I'm not selling." So why was he selling now?

The answer could apparently be summed up in two words: estate planning. Now in his seventies, Dick was ready to slow down and needed to find a way to resolve ownership of Lyrick. None of his children wanted to run the company, and passing it on to them would create huge tax implications. Selling his company to a large publicly traded company would exchange the value of Lyrick for stock that could be transferred to his kids in creative ways, avoiding significant inheritance tax. Dick also had lost millions of dollars on the *Barney* follow-up show *Wishbone*, an experience that had taken more than a little of the spring out of his step. He just wasn't enjoying the business like he used to. Regardless of the reason, we were about to be in business with a whole new set of people.

I was very familiar with HIT Entertainment, and the news wasn't encouraging. A large, publicly traded British media company, HIT was the owner of *Bob the Builder* and was actively and aggressively trying to corner the world market on preschool properties. Being London-based, I knew their knowledge of and interest in the American Christian market would be weak at best. One of their top executives had recently told *Variety* magazine that HIT was no longer interested in working with properties they didn't own. From now on, they would be buying, building and managing their own properties around the world. (Shortly after buying Lyrick to get *Barney and Friends*, HIT bought the company behind *Thomas the Tank Engine*.) In other words, unless they could own a property, they weren't very interested in helping a property. Since Bob and Larry were not for sale, this didn't bode well for the new relationship.

At this point, someone pointed out the clause in our agreement that allowed us to leave if Lyrick was sold. Hmm. At the very least, we thought, we were free to renegotiate our relationship with HIT. (We had discovered several matters in the relationship with Lyrick that we felt needed addressing, not the least of which was the fact that the huge volume of duplication business VeggieTales brought them was earning them large cash bonuses from their duplication company, bonuses they were failing to share with, or even report to, us.)

Then another call came. Dick Leach, while walking through the Dallas airport, had fallen, struck his head, and died. We were shocked and saddened to lose such a good guy. Bill Haljun, the Big Idea executive who had initiated the Lyrick relationship, flew down for the funeral in Dallas. This development made us even more concerned about giving our distribution rights to HIT. Without Dick on the board and with HIT's stated disinterest in "other people's properties," it seemed Bob and Larry were destined to become unloved stepchildren at HIT, picking up whatever table scraps were left after the "true children" had eaten their fill. (We had already noticed this dynamic at Lyrick when we started accompanying Lyrick staff on sales calls. If Lyrick had an hour with the Wal-Mart buyer, for example, they would often spend the first forty minutes talking about Barney and the last twenty talking about VeggieTales. Even when VeggieTales sales surpassed Barney's, the "owned property" still got the lion's share of the attention. This problem would only get worse, we reckoned, at HIT.)

After a few weeks talking with HIT and several other distributors, it was clear that HIT would not be the best home for VeggieTales. We announced in early summer of 2001 that VeggieTales' new general market distribution partner would be WEA, the music distribution company at Warner Brothers. WEA owned no children's properties of their own, so Bob and Larry wouldn't receive "stepchild" status. On top of the attention we would receive, WEA offered advances large enough to guarantee *Jonah* could be completed and the company could continue long enough to get back on its feet. Optimism returned to Big Idea for the first time in many months. We all started breathing easier.

Ten days after we made the announcement, HIT Entertainment filed suit against us in federal court in Dallas, claiming breach of contract. Barney the Dinosaur was hopping mad.

Late 2001 and early 2002 were a mind-boggling flurry of activity. In addition to the storm of legal briefs, motions, counter-motions, and depositions required to respond to HIT's lawsuit, my new president was opening a Big Idea office near his Bel Air home (one of his conditions for employment) and hiring support staff and two creative development executives from the television business to oversee 3-2-1 Penguins and The Cartoon Adventures of Larryboy. 3-2-1 Penguins was now in production at an animation studio in Canada in an attempt to bring production costs down to a manageable level. (Initially budgeted at $450,000 per film, the latest Penguins video had actually cost $1.2 million.) Larryboy 2D, as the new series was called internally, was in production at a studio in Los Angeles, using inexpensive Flash animation technology typical of TV shows like *Dexter's Laboratory* and *Powerpuff Girls*. A new publishing deal with HarperCollins' Christian unit, Zondervan, required the writing and production of more than twenty books in the first year alone.

And then there was *Jonah*. Less than six months from its required delivery date, the production was almost hopelessly behind schedule. No matter what we tried, we couldn't seem to get a grip on the situation internally. Desperate, we finally brought in a "finishing consultant" from Los Angeles—a specialist in the computer-animation world with extensive experience helping the major studios set up CGI production pipelines. The consultant quickly determined that *Jonah* would not be finished on time unless we brought in more artists and a lot more rendering computers. Our $10 million budget now walked out the front door, got in my car, and drove away. My original $7 million budget was turning into a ridiculously funny joke. The production was woefully behind schedule on lighting and final rendering, so we brought in lighting artists from Blue Sky and DNA, the two studios that had just wrapped *Ice Age* and *Jimmy Neutron*, respectively. Our render farm ballooned from 150 computers to more than 500.

Out of space and electrical service in our old Woolworth's, we rented another shuttered store at the other end of the mall and transformed it almost overnight into a second high-tech data center (although I'm fairly certain it was the world's only high-tech data center that could be accessed only by walking through a mall food court and the back room of a Dairy Queen). A fiber optic link was run almost the entire length of the mall, connecting the new "satellite" data center with the mother ship. Several rooms were stuffed with temporary lighting artists working in almost complete darkness (for color integrity issues) and living in temporary housing. They began to look like moles.

All of this was paid for by almost $20 million in advances my new president had brought in from new distribution and publishing deals, a remarkable achievement accomplished in very little time. It was very clear now that Big Idea was going to explode— either in a good way or a very, very bad way. We had never released more than three videos in any one year, and now in 2002 we would release one veggie video, three penguins videos, and three Larryboy videos, on top of more than fifteen books, an elaborate live touring stage show, a vacation Bible school curriculum, four sing-along albums, and a flurry of related merchandise, including apparel, games, housewares, sew-at-home fabrics, garden gloves, and a really cool pirate ship play set that, like the rest of the product, had been designed entirely in-house by Big Idea designers. Oh yeah—we were also about to release our first the-atrical feature film.

Did I want to release all of these products? Did every last bit of it have a compelling ministry objective? Did it all fit into my "master plan" to benefit America's kids? Frankly, no. None of it was *against* our mission, and most of it promoted a biblical value or virtue in some way, shape, or form, but the sheer volume was driven not by mission, but by a desperate need to keep Big Idea from collapsing. Many of us felt the tension between our ministry-driven mission and the vast amount of merchandise we were attempting to drive into the market. The pace of work, however, left precious little time for introspection.

What was clear to me was that if all this new product worked, Big Idea would be healthy again and we could refocus on doing only the things that mattered. If it didn't . . . well, I didn't like to think about that one.

Everything did not work. The Cartoon Adventures of Larryboy hit stores and was roundly drubbed by our fans. "It looks cheap!" "It looks like something my kids can watch on the Cartoon Network for free!" Our experiment in lower-cost production methods was not going over very well. Within an episode or two, it was clear that Larryboy in 2D was not going to save Big Idea.

3-2-1 Penguins had launched in 2000 with much fanfare. In a very fun marketing move, we had rented the Kennedy Space Center for a world premier event and produced a one-hour live radio show from beneath the giant Saturn V rocket. It was carried on more than a thousand Christian radio stations. The first episode launched with the biggest numbers ever achieved by a new video series in the Christian market. But the second episode sold 25 percent less than the first, and the third, 25 percent less than the second. When sales finally stabilized, the shows were still selling better than any nonveggie series but not enough to cover their $1 million production budgets. 3-2-1 Penguins was not going to save Big Idea.

Produced by Clear Channel, America's leading theatrical production company, *VeggieTales Live!* opened to near-sellout crowds in Minneapolis. "It's working!" we hollered. But as the show moved from city to city, it didn't appear to be making any money. In fact, it was losing money. The producers at Clear Channel had approved elaborate sets and overscaled props for the show that ultimately filled four semitrucks, rather than the more typical two. The show, it seemed, was doomed to barely break even because of the expense of the two extra trucks, extra union labor for eight-hour load-in/load-out marathons at each venue, and even an extra full-time staff member to travel ahead of the tour, planning load-in strategies for each upcoming site. Like Big Idea itself, the show was just too big. We worked with Clear Channel to try to simplify the show as it toured, but the damage was done. *VeggieTales Live!* would not save Bob and Larry.

Through it all, *Jonah* lurched ponderously toward its release date, like a . . . well, like a nauseated whale. But now it would need to do much more than just justify its own existence—it would need to save the company. We huddled together with Artisan Entertainment, *Jonah*'s new distribution partner, to plan our strategy. My original plan to spend $7 million to release the film, they assured us, wouldn't give the film a fighting chance. Although the production process had been chaotic, the finished shots that were beginning to roll out of the studio looked good. Really good. Like a real movie. Like a movie that could do much more than $18 million at the box office. "We need to spend $12 million if you want to give it a chance," Artisan said. Yikes. $12 million was a lot more than $7 million. If we spent $12 million to release the film, it would have to do much more than $18 million at the box office. But those pictures—they looked really good. Maybe this was how God was going to save Big Idea—by taking what was supposed to be a modest, forty-four-minute video and turning it into a surprise box office hit. A big hit. Wouldn't that be just like God?

My new president recommended I approve the budget. I agreed.

Meanwhile, back at Big Idea, we were having a bit of a problem. We were running out of cash again. The $20 million my new president had raised was paying for new 3-2-1 Penguins videos, Larryboy videos, VeggieTales videos, the *Jonah* production, and the rest of the company's overhead in marketing, design, human resources, and other areas—not to mention our new office and staff in Los Angeles. At the rate we were spending, we were going to run out of money before *Jonah* even hit theaters. But wait, weren't we still selling VeggieTales videos? Didn't we still have a hit children's property, selling millions of books, videos, and little stuffed cucumbers and tomatoes? Yes we did. But there was a catch. The $20 million we had raised was in the form of advances on future income. What we had done was the equivalent of getting an advance on your next paycheck. It's a great way to solve this week's problems, but you'd better have a good plan for next week, because when you get there, there isn't going to be a paycheck. We were still selling hundreds of thousands of VeggieTales videos, but our distributors were keeping all the money to recoup the advances. Our new books with Zondervan were selling like hotcakes, but Zondervan was keeping all the money to recoup their advance. Our cash flow had dropped to a trickle. And the $20 million was going very, very quickly.

Now wait a minute, you're thinking; *didn't you guys see that coming? You weren't that dumb, were you?* Yes, we knew we were borrowing against our future and our actual income would be greatly reduced until the advances were recouped, but frankly, we didn't see another option. It's sort of like when your house is on fire and the only escape route is to jump out the window into your neighbor's yard, but you know your neighbor has a rather ill-tempered pit bull. The hotter it gets, the more likely you are to say, "Let's solve the fire thing first and worry about the pit bull later." It isn't a perfect plan, but if it's the only plan you have . . .

It was clear now that we had escaped the fire, but the pit bull had us by the leg. This new crisis led us to the most painful decision I ever had to make. We had a second feature film in development— *The Bob and Larry Movie*. If *Jonah* was a Sunday school lesson on steroids, *The Bob and Larry Movie* would be our *Toy Story*. It was funnier, more exciting, and more emotionally involving than *Jonah*. It was really good. We already had a team of about ten people working on it, designing sets, props, and characters. Test animation on some of the lead human characters (yes, it involved humans!) was being done. Except we didn't have the money to continue the work. We had to shut it down, which meant that most of the artists in the animation studio would have nothing to do once their work on *Jonah* was completed. You see, when you own an animation studio, lacking the money for your movie really means you lack the money for your animation studio. The next choice became painfully clear, and painfully . . . well, painful.

In late summer of 2002, just a few weeks before *Jonah*'s release date, we staged a premier event just for the company and production crew. The film was done. It looked great. Even many of the freelancers flew in to see the finished product and attend the wrap party on a boat in Lake Michigan the next night. We rented the "big room" at the McClurg Court theaters for our premier—the room that had been set up for digital projection by George Lucas's company for one of their events. The film looked and sounded amazing. The crowd was thrilled, and thunderous applause followed the credits. But I barely made it through my speech thanking everyone for their work, because I knew, along with just a few other leaders in the room that night, that the next morning we would announce that the wrap party was canceled, *THE Bob and Larry Movie* was postponed indefinitely, and more than half the studio would be laid off. For those of us who knew what was about to happen, it was the most bittersweet night imaginable.

The next morning, Big Idea's nine-year effort to build a feature animation studio ended. Worst of all, the folks who got laid off were many of those who had worked the hardest on *Jonah*. People who had put their lives on hold to help launch Big Idea into the world of feature films, who had just fallen across the finish line in exhaustion, found themselves rewarded with pink slips. Many were understandably angry. One artist sent out an e-mail to the whole company as he was packing his things saying simply, "Has anyone seen my copy of *Where's God When I'm F-f-fired?!?*" Another said he would never again work so hard for an employer. But others were remarkably gracious, pointing out to their peers the friendships that were forged at Big Idea during *Jonah*'s production. I honestly wondered if keeping the company alive was worth the emotional toll on those let go as we tried to save it. But throughout, I clung to hope. "If *Jonah* works," I thought, "I'll bring them all back."

It was a nice thought. It would only take a couple of weeks to find out if it had a snowball's chance in you-know-where of actually happening.

Friday, October 4, 2002: *Jonah*'s release date. It's amazing to find yourself in a position where three years of hard work will be justified—or not—in one day. While opening-day box office doesn't necessarily tell you exactly how a film will perform, it tells you a lot.

For *Jonah* to pay back its production and marketing costs and have any hope of returning additional monies to stabilize Big Idea, we figured we needed to gross at least an $8 million on opening weekend. Given that Artisan planned to release our small film on only 800 screens initially (as opposed to the more than 3,000 of major studio family films), an $8 million gross was aggressive, though theoretically achievable. More important, that kind of gross would get noticed by the newspapers, which would get people talking, which could lead to the kind of buzz that can boost a film to a whole different level. Suffice it to say, we all were a little tense.

The first call from Artisan came in at about 2:00 p.m. central time, just a few hours after the film had opened on the East Coast and in the Midwest. Three or four of us huddled in a marketing room to listen. The numbers were off the chart. Huge. Moms with preschoolers were evidently turning out in droves—selling out afternoon screenings. We were so happy we felt like crying. And dancing. If those numbers held up, we could be looking at a $10 million–plus opening weekend, which would place *Jonah* in the top two or three films that weekend and earn us lots of free press in newspapers across America. Perhaps God was going to use *Jonah* to save Big Idea after all.

The second call came at 4:00 p.m. Something had changed. The numbers now didn't look nearly as good as just two hours earlier. While some theaters were selling out, others appeared to be half empty. The first numbers from our 120 screens in Canada were horrid. Our visions of a $10 million opening weekend melted. Even $8 million didn't look very likely. Artisan believed we were headed somewhere in the vicinity of $6 million. We deflated. While respectable, $6 million probably wouldn't put the film on track to recoup its investment, much less bail out the rest of the company. In two hours we had gone from the top of the world to the bottom. *Jonah*'s theatrical release wasn't going to save Big Idea.

The final number for opening weekend was $6.5 million, below the $8 million we were hoping for but good enough to earn Artisan congratulatory calls from competing studios. Conventional wisdom in Hollywood had *Jonah* opening at about $3 million. Artisan was thrilled and immediately requested approval to spend another $3 million on TV ads to keep the momentum going. Perhaps *Jonah* would have the "legs" of a *My Big Fat Greek Wedding*, they reasoned. Additional ads could carry quotes from the generally positive reviews we were receiving. While I had serious misgivings about spending any more money on the film, I couldn't help but wonder if an extra boost at this critical moment might be the thing that would push *Jonah* over the proverbial hump. Maybe that $3 million would mean the difference between a $20 million gross and a $40 million gross. My new president recommended that I approve the additional spend. I agreed.

In the end, *Jonah* grossed about $25 million at the domestic box office, establishing a new record for Christian films that would stand until Mel Gibson decided to try his hand at a Christian film a few years later. Since half of that money stayed with the theaters, though, Artisan received a little more than $12 million, which wasn't enough to recoup the $15 million they had spent marketing the film. (Artisan wasn't worried, of course, since they knew they would continue recouping that money from the home video release.) On the one hand, $25 million was a lot more than the $18 million I had originally projected. *Jonah* was the sixth-highest grossing movie in America on opening weekend (bumped out of the top five by the surprise success of the urban comedy *Barbershop*) and the number two film in America in terms of gross per theater. Virtually everyone in Hollywood was surprised by our performance, which would help us immensely in trying to put together subsequent films. But the reality was clear that *Jonah* was unlikely to return its own investment, much less fund the rest of Big Idea.

"Well," I thought, "maybe if the home video does really, really well . . ." I was beginning to sound like a Cubs fan.

The winter of 2002 was an immensely difficult time at Big Idea. With *Jonah*'s theatrical release behind us, we nervously awaited the home video launch in March. Spirits were not high aboard the good ship *Veggie*, though. The Lyrick lawsuit had cost us $2 million in legal fees in 2002, and the bills kept coming. 3-2-1 Penguins and The Cartoon Adventures of Larryboy were shut down. *The Bob and Larry Movie* was indefinitely postponed. Two more rounds of layoffs rocked the company as we desperately tried to preserve cash. Noticing the water rising in the hold, artists started jumping ship. Blue Sky Studios in New York was just starting production on *Robots*, their follow-up to the surprise CGI hit *Ice Age*. One Big Idea artist left for Blue Sky, and several others immediately followed. Eventually so many Big Idea artists jumped at the project that we began referring to any studio sick days as "Blue Flu." Since any effort to raise or borrow additional money was blocked by the outstanding lawsuit with Lyrick, settling the suit became our top priority. Lyrick's new owners at HIT wouldn't budge, though. As a last resort, we explained our financial situation to HIT's CEO, Rob Lawes. We had $500,000 set aside to try the case in court. We offered HIT that money as a last-ditch settlement offer, confessing that if the suit went to court and we lost, we would be forced into bankruptcy and Lyrick would receive little or nothing. We were out of money. Rob refused to settle, and the case was scheduled for April in federal court in Dallas.

Tensions were rising higher internally as we searched for ways to cut costs. My president in Los Angeles thought our Chicago operations could be cut back significantly. Given the death of 3-2-1 Penguins and Larryboy 2D, I wondered why we still needed the staff in Los Angeles hired to oversee their development. He wanted to shut down the animation studio in Chicago. I wanted to curtail his development efforts in Los Angeles. Unable to resolve our differences, we parted company. The Los Angeles office closed shortly thereafter. The changes saved us some money, but now I was the only one left at the company with enough knowledge of our distribution experience to represent Big Idea at the Lyric trial. Our Dallas attorneys flew to Chicago to prepare me for my first experience in litigation. Bob the Tomato and Barney the Dinosaur were about to mix it up in front of a jury of their peers.

Meanwhile, back in the world of retail, the *Jonah* home video and DVD hit stores on March 4, 2003. Like the film in theaters, it performed solidly if not spectacularly, selling about 2.5 million copies. I had hoped for 3 million, but the four years since I had made my original projection had seen a steady weakening in VeggieTales' sales. Every property has a "life cycle," and *Jonah*, conceived at VeggieTales' peak, was hitting home video about two years late. Even worse, my original forecast was ignorant of the fact that *Jonah*'s two-disc format and shiny "holofoil" packaging, plus Artisan's use of Fox Home Video for certain fulfillment services, would add an extra $1.50 to the cost of each DVD. The result was significantly less money coming back to recoup Artisan's marketing expenditure and, ultimately, our investment. In the end we sold 2.5 million copies of *Jonah* on VHS and DVD and didn't see a single penny of revenue. Our $14 million investment ($12.5 million for production plus another $1.5 million for computer gear we assumed we'd use on future movies as well) was a complete loss.

By early April 2003 only 65 people remained at Big Idea, down from 210 just six months earlier. Thirteen of us gathered for an evening prayer meeting just a few days before I was to head down to Dallas for the trial and prayed earnestly for the survival of Big Idea. The next week I walked across the mall from our offices and picked out a suit to get me through the projected two to three weeks of sitting in court. I called it my "law suit." I arrived in Dallas and checked into the Hampton Inn across from the Federal Building. It had been fourteen years since I started GRAFx Studios, initiating my quest to tell stories and make a difference in the world. Now it appeared it would all be decided by eight Texas strangers sitting under cold fluorescent lights in a courtroom that brought to mind an old *Matlock* rerun.

The first day was jury selection. Two women quickly identified themselves as huge VeggieTales fans and confessed that they couldn't possibly imagine Big Idea doing any wrong. They were quickly excused from the room, never to be seen again (no doubt devoured by an angry purple dinosaur in the parking lot). At lunch, my lawyer told me to try to look more "interested" in the jury selection process. As if wearing a suit every day wasn't punishment enough. It's not that I wasn't interested, of course, it's just that, after four or five hours of listening to lawyers ask truck drivers if they have any strong preconceived notions about Barney the Dinosaur, Bob the Tomato, or the moral reliability of Christians, one's mind can wander. I tried harder.

Over the next week, I would be asked not to look around the room casually. Not to bounce my knee. Not to exhibit excessive interest in the light fixtures overhead. I was beginning to think I might not be cut out for this line of work. The court proceedings themselves vacillated between painfully boring and extremely aggravating. Lyrick's lawyer at times made me so angry I wanted to jump up and yell, "That's crazy!" But by then I had learned that my job was to sit still and look interested. Nothing more, nothing less. So on the outside I appeared interested. But on the inside I was asking God to cut the power to the Federal Building so we could all go home.

In the end Lyrick's argument boiled down to this: even though our contract had never been signed nor even fully agreed upon, and acknowledging that copyright law precludes the transfer of any rights without a signed document, there was, in fact, a binding agreement between Lyrick and Big Idea based on the original offer letter bearing the signature of Lyrick's president and a return correspondence from Bill Haljun that carried his signature on a fax cover sheet. Even though their president's letter clearly stated that there would be no "binding relationship" until a formal agreement was signed by both parties, Lyrick argued that their letter and our fax cover sheet, taken together, constituted the binding relationship. *What?* I thought to myself, *A binding contract made out of signatures on two different documents, one of which clearly says it isn't binding? Nice try.*

Furthermore, they argued, even though the unsigned draft agreement clearly stated that we could walk away if we did not approve of a new owner or replacement for Dick Leach, Lyrick's lawyer pointed out that they had added the wording "approval of which Big Idea will not unreasonably withhold." We pointed out that we had never agreed to such a vague phrase (which, in fact, was one of the reasons the contract was still unsigned and under negotiation). Now Lyrick went for broke. Big Idea didn't walk away because we didn't like HIT Entertainment, they argued. HIT Entertainment was a perfectly acceptable partner. We didn't walk away because HIT chairman Peter Orton wasn't an acceptable replacement for Dick Leach. Dick Leach was hardly active in the business anymore. No, Big Idea walked away because we wanted more money. Lots more money. Big Idea didn't walk away because of philosophical convictions, Lyrick explained to the jury. We walked away because we were greedy for money. And that was not a "reasonable" reason to walk away. Yes, Big Idea had the right to approve of HIT's purchase of Lyrick. But we "unreasonably withheld that approval." I eyed the jury. *They can't possibly be buying this. Not after hearing how important Dick Leach's faith was to us.*

Finally, recognizing that VHS sales were declining rapidly and damages from lost VHS sales would be minimal, Lyrick argued that we had given them DVD rights to all our videos, even though the draft contract clearly stated "videocassette only." Their evidence: the two videos we had allowed them to release on DVD to test audience interest in the new format. Lyrick's lawyer showed the two DVD cases to the jury, highlighting the Lyrick logos on the back corner. "See? They gave us DVD rights." *Hoo-boy,* I thought to myself, trying not to laugh out loud, *No way they'll go for that one! They know those two DVDs were just a test!*

The jury headed out for deliberation. I flew back to Chicago to spend time with my kids. The following week we all returned to the courtroom to hear the verdict. Before the jury entered the room, the judge called both attorneys into her chamber. "Okay, God," I said under my breath, "time for you to ride in and save the day."

When Big Idea's lawyer reentered the courtroom a few minutes later, he looked pale. Like he'd just been mugged.

"They're giving them everything they asked for," he muttered under his breath. Before I had time to even process what he had just said, the jury entered the room.

"Was there a binding agreement between Lyrick Studios and Big Idea Productions?" the judge asked.

"Yes."

"Did Big Idea Productions have the right to approve the sale of Lyrick Studios to HIT Entertainment?"

"Yes."

"Did Big Idea Productions 'unreasonably withhold' that approval?"

"Yes."

And finally, the kicker: "Did Big Idea Productions grant Lyrick Studios the right to distribute DVDs in addition to videocassettes?"

"Yes."

I couldn't believe my ears. They gave them everything. Everything they had asked for. Fourteen years' worth of work flashed before my eyes—the characters, the songs, the impact, the letters from kids all over the world. It all flashed before my eyes, then it all vanished.

The gavel came down awarding Lyrick $11 million in damages. All their legal fees plus every penny they estimated they would have made selling VeggieTales DVDs over the remainder of the term stated in our unsigned draft agreement. Lyrick's lawyers were ecstatic. As for me, I knew it was over. Three strikes. I was out.

Our lawyer, a great guy who was deeply impacted by the loss, offered to drive me to the airport for a long, painful flight back to Chicago. Big Idea Productions was dead. It was finished.

19

Dreams, Part I

I had a dream once. If *People* magazine is to be believed, my dream came true. But then I watched it die—crumble and fall apart right before my eyes, like time-lapse photography of a flower wilting, or that Internet footage of the Seattle Kingdome crashing to the ground. Boom. Crash. Ouch. You wonder if the crashing sound is your dream breaking or your heart. Some people get angry when they lose things. I got numb.

Once the verdict came in, there wasn't much left to do except get out of the way and let the lawyers argue over who got what. Big Idea Productions was headed toward liquidation. Rather than allow the company to be stripped in the alley like a cheap Yugo, though, we opted to attempt to sell it in one piece in a tricky maneuver called a "363 bankruptcy sale." I'm not sure what the "363" stood for, but it gave the proceedings a nice ring—like a trick football play. ("We're going to run the ol' '363.' Johnny, you button-hook around the swing set. Carlos, you fake left and then hide in the dumpster until you hear me yell, 'Barbara Walters.' Ready? Break!") The goal was to keep the assets together so that a friendly buyer might be able keep the company operating and allow me to continue to guide it, if they saw fit. So over the summer of 2003 we ran the ol' 363, which involved sending out information packets on the company to anyone and everyone who expressed an interest, then sitting back as they all came into town to sniff around, kick the tires, and check Bob and Larry's teeth. To Lisa and I, it felt a bit like our children were being put up for auction. Like we'd lost the family farm, and now the neighbors were all coming over to see if they wanted to bid on the kids. It hurt.

Perhaps the "highlight" of the process came early on in a meeting with our bank. Since the sale process would take three to four months and the price the bank would get for the company would decrease significantly if the company ceased operations, the bank needed us to keep the team together. We calculated that Big Idea needed about $4 million to keep operating and keep the staff on board through the sale. Our bank agreed to lend the money (which would be fully recouped out of the sale price—assuming the company was successfully sold) but then turned to me and asked that I personally guarantee the loan. I gulped. They gave me a few days to think it over. I was in the process of losing everything I owned except my house, and the bank was effectively asking me to, in exchange for their assistance in my losing everything except my house, pledge to them my house. It didn't seem like such a good idea to me. I mean, at some point, it seems, you need to stop the bleeding. I drove down to their offices in Chicago's Loop several days later and very nervously declined.

I held my breath as the two bankers looked at each other, then, after an excruciating pause, back to me.

"We sort of expected you to say that," they replied. "We'll go ahead with the loan anyway."

I resumed breathing.

I was on my way to the parking garage to drive back to

Lombard and get back to work when something remarkable happened. It occurred to me that there really wasn't anything left for me to do. I mean, I needed to show up whenever a potential buyer was in town to kick the tires, and I needed to keep the company in a reasonably functional state so a new buyer could pick up where I had left off, but there really wasn't any urgent need for me to do, well, *anything* at that point. This was a very new feeling for me. After six years of maniacally building Big Idea and four years of maniacally trying to keep it from falling apart, I now found myself at a point where I could no longer do either. I was done.

Instead of getting in my car and heading west toward Big Idea, I found myself walking out of the LaSalle Bank building and heading east through the Loop. Four blocks later I was staring at the Art Institute of Chicago, a place I had last visited fifteen years earlier, before founding Big Idea and embarking on my "quest." I went in, bought a ticket, and spent the next hour and a half quietly gazing at French Impressionist landscapes. Monets, Pissarros, Seurats. They seemed about as far as you could get from a 363 bankruptcy sale. When I left the museum later that afternoon and headed back to the bank's parking garage, I felt about a hundred pounds lighter. I felt released. Not like someone who has been unexpectedly let out of prison, but more like someone who, having attempted to pull a very heavy weight up a very steep hill for a very long time has suddenly been told he can stop.

The rest of the year, although emotionally difficult, wasn't nearly as difficult as the prior year had been. It was clear that God was allowing a chapter of my life to close and that, regardless of what my continuing role with VeggieTales might be, nothing would be quite the same again.

The remainder of 2003 went something like this: A 363 sale requires something called a "stocking horse bidder," which is a buyer who makes an offer for the company in question that the bank finds acceptable. This offer, then, sets the terms and the starting price for a court-directed public auction to follow. (Throughout the process I was never quite sure if it was "stocking horse bidder" or "stalking horse bidder." Neither made any sense to me, frankly.) Classic Media emerged as the stocking horse bidder, primarily because they were the first interested party to make an offer that included no contingencies. (In other words, no conditions like "subject to signing Phil and Mike into long-term employment agreements" or "subject to successfully renegotiating distribution agreements," etc. Banks hate contingencies.)

Notices now ran in the newspaper announcing a mid-November public auction. Of the forty or so parties that expressed interest in the company, seven showed up in Chicago for the auction, checkbooks in hand. Several Christian companies were there who had expressed great interest in having me continue to guide Big Idea. Another Christian bidder was there who had told me, as a matter of Christian principle, that my role in the failure of Big Idea should preclude me from any future involvement. Several non-Christian companies showed up as well, primarily looking for an opportunity to buy an undervalued media asset. And at least one Christian billionaire was in the running, hoping to ensure Big Idea's survival as an independent ministry. I was familiar with all of the bidders—except one.

A week or two before the auction, several people from a tiny Christian company in Minnesota turned up at our door. "God told us to buy Big Idea," they said. While they were marginally involved in media, their experience was shallow and they lacked even an inkling of a plan for what they would do with Big Idea once they had purchased it. At one point, in fact, they confessed that their plan was to "buy Big Idea, and then wait for God to tell us what to do with it." Given that there were already multiple qualified Christian bidders in the running, this new presence wasn't entirely comforting. I told myself it wasn't an issue, as I doubted they had the wherewithal to last long once the bidding got going. Boy was I wrong.

The public auction was a one-day affair. Show up in the morning, walk home with Bob and Larry that night. By mid-morning, all the bidders were present in a conference room at our law firm in Chicago. Back in Lombard, the remaining staff and I huddled in a conference room with the bidders listed on a white-board. To break the tension we tried guessing the outcome—"handicapping" the horse race, if you will. Much of the day progressed slowly, as various bidders threw out offers, then took long breaks to collect their thoughts and calculate their next moves. By late afternoon the process was still creeping along and no one had yet left the room. Then something happened. In just an hour or so, a bidding war had erupted with two players driving the price up surprisingly high. The bidders? Classic Media, and—you guessed it—the little guys from Minnesota. Opening at Classic's initial bid of $9 million and rising to $14 million over eight painstaking hours, the price had now shot from $14 million to past $19 million in less than sixty minutes. Both parties were clearly determined to walk away with Bob and Larry. All other bidders had now gone silent, several packing up and heading home. The bank and the creditors' representatives were excited but nervous. Who *were* these guys from Minnesota, and did they actually have *that* kind of money?

Fearing the newcomers would win the bid but be unable to finance the deal, the bank stopped the auction and asked both par-ties to substantiate their ability to close the deal at these levels. A representative from Classic Media's backing venture capital fund, present in the room, simply nodded. Not a problem. But the guys from Minnesota protested the move. "That wasn't supposed to be part of the process!" they said. With the Minnesotans' unable—or unwilling—to get anyone on the phone to verify their financial wherewithal, the bank and the creditors halted the auction and declared Classic Media the winner. Final purchase price: $19.6 million. The next day in Chicago bankruptcy court, the judge approved the sale, dismissing the Minnesotans' last-minute offer to bid the assets "well over $20 million" if the auction were to be reopened.

And that was it. Bob and Larry had joined a new family with a whole host of new siblings, including Lassie, the Lone Ranger, Rocky and Bullwinkle, Underdog, Rudolph, Richie Rich, and, more curiously, Casper the Friendly Ghost, Wendy the Witch, and Li'l Hot Stuff, a cute little devil in a diaper. In their divinely ordained but ultimately unsuccessful quest to buy Big Idea, the mysterious late arrivals from Minnesota managed to spark a bidding war that knocked every other Christian bidder out of the race—a curious episode punctuating the curious resolution of a curious tale. As the leader of the Minnesotans left the courtroom that day, he noticed me sitting in the back and whispered, "God's will *will* be done." Looking back on the years following the auction, I believe he was correct. But more about that later.

A year or so after the bankruptcy, I was speaking to a small group of students at a Christian university. I told them stories of Big Idea's rise and fall, and the lessons I had learned from the experience. I gave my thoughts on the state of Christian media and the exciting opportunities I saw for them in the future. Afterward a student said he needed to talk to me. As he walked with me toward my rental car, he said, "I know some guys who used to work at Big Idea." Long pause. "They're still really mad at you." I fumbled vainly for an appropriate response. "I heard you speak last night," he continued. "You didn't apologize for what happened. Whenever you speak, you should apologize." I sat in my car for a few minutes, mulling over his words, amazed at the emotion my dream had generated, not just in me, but in almost everyone who had played a part in my pursuit of it.

A dream is a powerful thing. There is little more thrilling than seeing a dream come to life. And little more heartbreaking than watching it die.

Shortly after *Jonah* hit theaters, I got a letter from a fan in the Midwest with a two-page critique of the film. It hadn't done as well as it could have, he explained, because of serious flaws in its story structure. He went on to explain *Jonah*'s flaws at great length. While some of his points were certainly well taken, what struck me more about the letter was the emotion behind it. He was angry. Really angry. He closed with the interesting statement that if I didn't respond to his criticism, he would send his letter to major Christian magazines and "expose" our creative short-comings to the entire Christian world.

A dream is a powerful thing. Letters like his made me realize just how much emotion people had invested in my dream. Not just the artists, designers, and businesspeople who had moved their families across the country to actively join the effort, but also the fans. This fellow, like many others, was so excited about my dream of a "Christian Disney" that my failure to deliver on that dream struck him much more deeply than I would have expected. Big Idea had become *his* dream, too, and now that his dream was failing, he was angry.

When we lose something, be it a job, a relationship, or a dream, we want to know why. We want to know whose fault it was and who we should be mad at, because we really want to be mad at someone! So it was with Big Idea. If you've read this entire account, it's probably clear that multiple factors brought down Big Idea Productions. The Lyrick lawsuit certainly sealed the deal, but it's unlikely that lawsuit would have happened if our dire cash need hadn't forced us to switch distributors in search of new advances. So *Jonah* is to blame! Well, maybe a little—but certainly not entirely. True, if *Jonah* hadn't been put into production, the cash need would have been less. But what if we'd had the production management in place at the very beginning to produce the film for my $7 million goal and the discipline to see that it was marketed for $7 million as well? And remember, as of April 2000, the company needed $20 million to survive through the *Jonah* production even though *Jonah* was at that point only a $7 million film. The rest of the money was needed to cover our gross overhiring in areas like marketing, human resources, and design. And what led to the overhiring? The wild enthusiasm of 1998 and 1999, inspired partly by exponential sales growth up to that point, partly by the general "irrational exuberance" of that era in business history (think "dot-com"), and partly by the misreading of the VeggieTales business as a packaged goods business rather than an entertainment business.

So the members of that first executive team are the villains! You could probably come to that conclusion, but I don't think you'd be right. I mean, can I really blame packaged goods executives for attempting to use packaged goods marketing techniques to sell films that ultimately show up on store shelves as—packaged goods?

VeggieTales success itself had become a huge challenge. Whenever you have an unprecedented hit, future planning becomes extraordinarily difficult simply because there are no precedents. There were no comparables for VeggieTales. Our sales had skyrocketed 3,300 percent in four years! Against that backdrop, what could we project for the future? More skyrocket-ing? Was our growth almost done or just getting started? Look at another example: Between Christmas 2003 and Christmas 2004, sales of Apple's iPod increased by a staggering 500 percent—a huge success but also a huge challenge. How many iPods do you make for Christmas 2005—500 percent more than 2004? 100 percent more? 10 percent *less*? Unprecedented success is extremely difficult to manage simply because it is unprecedented. Every year is a big ol' guess. Guess wrong one way and you'll choke your success by running out of product or not having enough manpower to support the demand. Guess wrong the other way, and you could crash and burn right in the midst of your success. As wrong as the forecasts my team made in 1999 ended up being, I honestly believe they did the best they could with the informa-tion and the experience they had.

Yeah, I could blame the guy who engineered the distribution moves that sparked the lawsuit, but he wouldn't have had to do that if I hadn't allowed the company to become so huge and indebted. I could blame our production management team for not sticking to my original plan for *Jonah*, but then I have to remind myself that when the film went into production, we didn't *have* a production management team. And I could blame the first bunch of executives for making the company so huge, but then I have to remember that one of the things that attracted them to Big Idea in the first place was a line I put into our mission statement way back in 1997—something about building "a top four family media brand within twenty years." A statement that sounded an awful lot like we were supposed to get really big. A statement that, even at the time, I was pretty sure had emanated suspiciously from my own noggin in response to a business book exercise, as opposed to from God after much prayer and reflection.

So there you have it. The real culprit is Jim Collins, coauthor of the book *Built to Last*. Oh, if only it were that easy. Of course, I could have waited for God to supply *his* twenty-year goal for Big Idea. I could have overruled my executives at any point. I could have stopped the hiring, decreased the forecasts, redirected the strategies. As controlling shareholder, CEO, and sole board member (building a board of directors was something we often discussed but never got around to actually *doing*), I had the final word on everything. So who is ultimately to blame for the collapse of Big Idea? That should be pretty clear by now. I have seen the enemy, and he is me. My strengths built Big Idea, and my weaknesses brought it down.

Throughout Big Idea's history, my business instincts were generally pretty good. But I had no experience managing people or leading teams to accomplish goals. I had, after all, spent my high school years in the basement experimenting with film cameras and computers. I was a shy kid who would rather read *Starlog* magazine or build a rudimentary optical printer out of cannibalized 8mm projectors than show up at the prom or run for student government. As VeggieTales took off, I became terrified that my business inexperience and lack of people skills would result in Big Idea's failure. So, in a panic, I brought in others to help, often spending far too little time getting to know them before or after the hire. I then backed down from my own convictions, assuming that an executive with an impressive resume surely knew better than a Bible college dropout. And I launched projects like *Jonah* before we were really ready to handle them, assuming we'd figure things out on the fly as I had done in my basement and with the very first VeggieTales episode. The results were some amazingly rabid fans and absolute organizational chaos. The result was the rise—and fall—of Big Idea.

For the record, I'm sorry. A lot of wonderful people brought their dreams to Big Idea. And almost all of them were deeply affected both by the persistent organizational chaos and by the trauma of the slow, painful collapse. The ultimate responsibility for both lie with me. And I'm really, really sorry. Just as Big Idea really wasn't ready to tackle the production challenge of *Jonah*, I really wasn't ready to tackle the management challenge of Big Idea.

There. Now I've said it.

The real question to ask in any failure, of course, isn't "Who should we blame?" but rather "What did we learn?" Take a little break—stretch your legs, get a bite to eat. Because now it's time to sing the "What We Have Learned" song.

20

Lessons

"We're over here by Qwerty to talk about what we learned today."

That's what Bob the Tomato says at the end of each VeggieTales episode, and if, by some strange oversight, you were unaware that the story you had just watched contained a valuable lesson, Bob's statement makes it painfully clear. We just experienced something meaningful together, he's saying, and now we're going to talk about what we learned.

Life, like VeggieTales, is filled with learning opportunities. As a kid, I learned that I should not touch a cookie sheet fresh from the oven. I learned that extraordinary care was required when opening my grandfather's pocketknife. I learned that a large dog, a small boy, and a leash are not a great combination, especially on a gravel driveway. I learned that pet turtles and pet dogs should never be left alone together in the backyard. Ever. I learned that if you catch a fish and then run several hundred yards dragging it through the grass to have your mother remove it from the hook, by the time you reach your mother, the problem will have solved itself. Looking back on my life, I have learned so many things I would suspect I

must by now be the smartest person in the world, except I know I
am not, so instead I marvel that others have learned even *more*.

One of the keys to learning, modeled so effectively by a certain
tomato whose voice sounds a great deal like mine, is to always,
after a meaningful experience, pause and ask yourself, "What did I
learn today?" Especially if the experience was painful. So, like a
good little tomato, that is exactly what I did in the months after the
collapse of Big Idea Productions. Not immediately, of course. When
you skin your knee or bump your head, the first thing you need to
do is roll around on the sidewalk and moan for a bit, clutching at
the part that hurts. And that's what I did first. I rolled around on
the sidewalk moaning, clutching at my heart. After I got tired of
moaning and rolling, I got up, looked back at my smashed-up
bike—er, company—and started asking, "How did that happen?"
Which is really another way of saying, "What have I learned?" In
the ensuing months I sorted through many lessons—some practical, relating to business and management, and some spiritual,
relating to dreams and God. I'm going to start with the practical
lessons because, well, I don't know why. Just because.

This is not a business book per se. I am not Jim Collins or
Ken Blanchard or Peter Drucker. I am not Zig Ziglar, though I
think he has a really cool name. I cannot teach you how to "win
friends and influence people" or "manage in one minute." I can't
even teach you how to buy real estate with no money down,
though I think I understand the concept. But there are some
things I learned from the rise and fall of Big Idea that I will diligently apply to whatever it is God has in store for me next.
Perhaps they could help you too.

Thing I Learned #1: Never lose sight of the numbers. This is a
tricky concept, especially when the business I was starting was supposed to be a ministry. I mean, wasn't I supposed to stay focused

on the *ministry* of my enterprise? The message? The audience I was serving? Well, yes, I was. But the numbers showed the financial health of my ministry. And ignoring my ministry's financial health, even for a brief period, was like ignoring my own health. Financial resources are like teeth—ignore them and they'll go away. Ignore your health and you'll go away. Just as dead men make lousy ministers, dead organizations make lousy ministries.

The trick here is that creative people called to ministry—"creative ministers" like myself—are seldom gifted at financial management. And gifted financial managers are seldom effective creative ministers. God equips different people for different roles and, as much as we would like it to be otherwise, none of us can do everything well. So gifted creative ministers need gifted financial managers, and vice versa. The next question is, of course, who should be in charge? Creative ministers like myself, of course, initially believe we should be in charge. After all, we're the ones with the "vision" for the ministry! We're the ones who make it all come to life! Investors and donors, however, often prefer seeing a good financial manager in charge. A "grown-up." Someone who can be trusted to keep an eye on the spending.

So who's right? Neither, I now believe. Give a creative person like myself final authority, and you'll see dramatic, awe-inspiring projects launched. You'll see a flurry of activities and logos and cool T-shirts. Come back in a few years, though, and it probably will all be dead. Why? Because no one is more convinced of an idea's viability than the person who just thought it up. The "idea generator" is quite often the person least capable of assessing an idea's viability and making a final determination on which ideas deserve an organization's attention and resources.

"Oh great—so you're saying the 'bean counters' should be in charge and the creatives should work for them! Traitor!" No, I'm not saying that either. As mature and thoughtful as most gifted financial managers are, I don't believe they should be solely responsible for an organization's direction. Why? Because most gifted finance folks are so heavily influenced by their financial training and focus that they often have a hard time seeing the world in nonfinancial terms. Everything becomes a numbers decision. And nothing kills creativity and ministry faster than viewing everything as a numbers decision.

So who should be in charge? Who should call the shots? Both of them, that's who. The balance between creative inspiration and good stewardship of resources is vital to any successful enterprise. Neither can be subordinated to the other without serious and highly detrimental consequences.

"So how does this work, Mr. Vischer? I mean, really? How can an artistic nut and a strait-laced bean counter *both* have authority for an organization?" Well, rather than attempting to explain this concept, I'm going to show it in the example of perhaps the biggest creative success of the twentieth century, the Walt Disney Company.

When crews started moving dirt in central Florida for the creation of Walt Disney's final dream, they were, in fact, undertaking what was at that point the largest private construction project in the history of the world. It was massive and massively expensive. How did this come to be? I mean, have you ever thought about it? Walt was a dreamer, after all. An inventor. A tinkerer. A storyteller. How did he manage to pull together the financial resources to undertake the world's largest construction project? Or the world's first theme park fifteen years earlier? Or the world's first animated feature film twenty years before that? The answer—he didn't. He didn't pull together the financial resources for any of those projects. Roy did.

Roy Disney, Walt's older brother, is the unsung hero of the Walt Disney Company. As young Walt began to exercise his creativity in his teens, Roy was working as a bank teller. Walt was a dreamer. Roy was practical. When Walt moved to Los Angeles to pursue his filmmaking ambitions, Roy agreed to help out, and the two formed The Disney Brothers Studios. Walt dreamed and drew and filmed. Roy borrowed money from their uncle and labored over distribution contracts and payroll.

Roy didn't work for Walt, and Walt didn't work for Roy, but they clearly understood their roles. Walt dreamed up wild ideas, and Roy tried to make them happen. If the idea didn't seem fundable or viable to Roy, Walt would usually honor Roy's opinion, though not without long and sometimes heated discussion. At one point the two brothers disagreed so bitterly that they didn't speak for months. The company followed suit, drawing lines between "Walt's boys" (the creatives) and "Roy's boys" (the accountants and managers). If either brother had walked away, the company would have failed. There is no question about that. Both brothers were absolutely vital, even though Walt was the one in America's living rooms every Sunday night.

But Roy didn't walk away, and the working out of their conflicts made the partnership even stronger. (Their biggest feud was resolved by Walt literally giving his older brother a peace pipe, which Roy proudly displayed on his office wall until his death in 1971—three months after the opening of Disney World and five years after lung cancer had taken Walt.)

Roy respected Walt and would one day tell a reporter his entire life had been about making his brother's ideas come to life. But Walt also respected Roy and wouldn't proceed with an idea without his brother's approval.

So what made the partnership work? "That's easy—Walt's

ideas were great!" No, they weren't all great. And Walt's personality made even the "great" ideas less than fun to work with at times. Roy didn't love all of Walt's ideas. Roy loved Walt. And Walt loved Roy. Walt felt it was his life's work to use entertainment to improve the lives of the masses. Roy felt it was his life's work to help Walt do what he felt called to do. He wasn't serving Walt, he was serving the ideas. And Walt was so secure in the fact that his big brother really wanted to see him succeed that he would allow Roy to say the one word almost no one else in the world could say to Walt: "No."

The key to the Walt Disney Company was the partnership of Walt and Roy. The key to the partnership of Walt and Roy was mutual submission, based in genuine love for each other. Walt knew he couldn't do what Roy could do, and Roy knew he couldn't do what Walt could do. So they submitted to each other's area of expertise and worked together, ultimately for the benefit of the ideas and the benefit of their audience.

In hindsight, perhaps the simplest explanation for the failure of Big Idea Productions is this: I never found my Roy. I never found the person who could look rationally at my ideas and then, in love, say no. There were numerous people ready to say no to me, but we didn't have the sort of relationship Walt and Roy had, so I was always hesitant to trust them. Some considered themselves "idea people" as well and beneath the surface wanted their ideas inserted ahead of my own. Others just didn't seem to understand what I was trying to accomplish, weren't on the same page. As a result, I didn't trust their "no's." I didn't trust their input. So I barreled ahead, on my own, clutching my ideas like a child clutching a prized stuffed animal in a roomful of strangers whose motives he can't discern.

If God has given you ideas for ministry, look for your Roy. It may not be one person—your Roy may be several people or even a whole board of directors. But the relationship will work only if the people you bring in to perform that role are there because they want to see your ideas succeed—want to see *you* succeed. There can be no other agendas.

If, on the other hand, God has made you a Roy, look for your Walt. Look for someone with creative gifting and calling. That person needs you desperately. This is tricky, of course, because Walts typically hang out with other Walts and Roys typically hang out with other Roys. They don't mingle much—not at work, not at cocktail parties, not at church. Quite often, in fact, they look down on each other.

"Look at those weirdoes with their weird clothes and their crazy ideas. They'll never accomplish anything." Of course they won't! Not without your help, anyway!

"Look at those bean counters in their suits and ties! I bet they've never had a creative idea in their whole lives!" For the record, even accountants have creative ideas. Typically not the type that artists would find interesting, but often wonderful ideas that would help the artists connect their art with their audience more efficiently than they ever imagined. Ignore the ideas of the suits at your own peril, creatives. There is great value—and great creativity—in a clever spreadsheet or financing scheme.

Love. Mutual submission. It all sounds very Christian, and, amazingly, seems to be the key to successful, long-term organizations. Amazing ideas come to life when people with complementary gifting devote themselves selflessly to each other, not for their own success, but for the success of the idea.

Thing I Learned #2: Ignore the voice that says, "You deserve it." "Whenever I travel, I now rent compact cars and stay at the Hampton Inn. Always. I don't care how careful I think I am or how successful my new business might become, I have learned that once

I start upgrading my travel accommodations, I'll start upgrading everything else too. Everything will become more expensive. Once I, as the leader, start spending more money than necessary, everyone else will too. They're watching. And then my entire organization will cost more each day than it should, which will begin to limit the sorts of opportunities I can pursue. "Can't take that job. Not enough money in it." The more I limit my opportunities, the sooner my organization will cease to exist.

It all starts, I think, when a voice shows up inside your head one day and whispers, "You deserve it." I remember the first time I heard that voice. Big Idea was booming, and I was beginning to hire real "executives." Coming from companies like Kraft and GE, they were used to being paid like executives and living like executives. They drove executive cars, lived in executive houses, and ate executive meals. Up until this point, I had always lived modestly, though more out of necessity than deep philosophical conviction. But now I was hanging out with executives, and their lives looked like fun. And then that little voice showed up in my head and said, "You're an executive, too, you know. After all, they all work for you." Good heavens. The voice was right. I was more than just an "executive"—I was the CEO of a successful company! I was the executive of the executives! "Look at all the hard work you've done," the voice continued. "Look what you've built. Don't you *deserve* it?" And suddenly my cars started getting nicer and my meals fancier. I started eying nicer houses in nicer neighborhoods—"executive" neighborhoods. And suddenly everything at Big Idea started costing more. Meals, travel, equipment, everything—because we were successful, and we deserved it.

That little whisper—"You deserve it"—comes, I believe, from the worst part of our sinful natures, the part that always wants another cookie, a bigger house, a nicer TV. I'm pretty sure it's the same voice that told Hitler he "deserved" Poland. Advertisers know the power of that voice, and they use it relentlessly. The new car, the ridiculously high-fat dessert, the fantastically overpriced watch—do you need it? Of course not. But you *deserve* it. I have come to hate that voice. I will avoid any product that tries to influence my purchase decision by telling me I deserve it. Why? First of all, the appeal is insanely selfish. If I deserve it, it must follow that someone else does not. I have achieved more. I am special. As a Christian, of course, it's horrifically bad theology, throwing that whole "the first shall be last and the last shall be first" thing right out the window along with a hundred other verses about self-denial and putting others first. What do I really deserve? Death. That's what I deserve. Death apart from God. I am a selfish dweeb standing before a holy, righteous God. Imagine me trying to explain to God why I "deserve" a nicer car than the guy next to me. "Well, I've worked so hard, and—as I'm sure you can see—I'm *very* successful." Ha. Good one. Seeking our own comfort over the comfort of others is a pretty good definition of the word *sin*. And yet there I was, Mr. Bible College, allowing myself to be coaxed down that path by the fact that my business card now sported the letters "CEO."

In addition to bad theology, though, thinking that I deserve more than others is bad business. Concluding that I deserve a more lavish lifestyle than the people around me fails to consider the fact that the people around me are, more than likely, my customers, the people I'm supposed to be serving with my products. And yet here I am, looking down on them, judging them "less deserving" than myself. I've worked so hard to get where I am. I travel, sacrifice, slave away night after night. Not like these other folks.

Tell me, how easy is it to serve someone you consider less deserving than yourself? Nearly impossible. Want to kill a company quickly? Decide you are "better" than your customers.

Executive pride kills companies. Christian selflessness, on the other hand, is not just biblically sound, it is also good business.

I had an experience years ago that I think of often when I find myself tempted with "executive pride." I was riding home on the subway after putting in one of my killer marathons in postproduction. It was probably 4:00 a.m., and I was half-dead. I felt proud, though—proud of being such a "hard worker." When I got off my train, a thirtysomething Hispanic man got on, headed downtown. From the way he was dressed and the guys just like him I saw in our neighborhood every day, I knew his story almost immediately. He was a family man, married with two or three kids. He was headed downtown at 4:00 a.m. for a menial job in the kitchen of a restaurant or hotel. It was probably one of two or even three jobs he held, all menial, barely above minimum wage. All to feed his family. I watched him sit quietly on the train and felt the air leak out of my puffed-up ego. Who was the "hard worker" on the subway that night? Who "deserved" a nicer car? A nicer house? Yeah, I pulled all-nighters every now and then, but it was work I loved, for which I was well paid. Give me sixteen-hour days filled with thankless, unfulfilling menial labor and see how long I'd last. Who "deserved" a better life? It sure wasn't me.

From now on, I will do whatever I can to eradicate the presumption within any organization I lead that executives "deserve" more than the regular people around them. For me, from here on out, it starts with a Dodge Neon from Dollar Rent-a-Car and a room at the Hampton Inn.

Thing I Learned #3: If you successfully identify a need and create a product that meets it in a unique way, you are the expert. Even if you're a twelve-year-old junior high dropout. Even if the guy next to you has a Harvard MBA and a Fortune 500 pedigree. In the business that was born out of your brain and your instincts, you are the expert. You may find someone who can help you immensely with human resources or finance or marketing. You may find a brilliant consultant who can ask poignant questions that will help further refine your thinking. But when it comes down to your product and the way it meets the needs of your audience, I'll say it one more time, *you are the expert*. Even if you're the youngest guy in the room. If you don't believe this, they never will. If they still don't believe it even after you've made the point, they need to leave the room and keep right on walking out the door. Every good hire brings something vital to an organization. Each new team member, however, needs to recognize what it is you brought that made the organization spring to life in the first place.

Thing I Learned #4: Know yourself. Lesson 3 can get me into all sorts of trouble if I don't have a good grasp of my own strengths and weaknesses. There are areas where I should look to others for help, and there are areas where others should look to me. I need to figure out which areas are which before I start hiring, because hiring people whose strengths complement my own will be the key to my future success. Also, beware of early success. Seeing my first idea turn to gold convinced me that all my ideas would turn to gold, which was not the case. Early success can be a very dangerous thing.

Thing I Learned #5: Bigger is no longer better. In some cases larger organizations do have a competitive advantage, but those cases are becoming fewer and fewer all the time. I wanted my own animation studio. My own design studio. My own sound studio. Why? Because I thought all that creative capability would create more opportunities. I thought a larger staff would mean greater impact. In reality, the opposite was true. A larger staff meant higher permanent overhead, and higher permanent overhead actually *reduced* the range of opportunities we could pursue. Sure, we had people who could do all sorts of amazing things. We could make movies. We could make kids' books. We could make records. But the only opportunities we could pursue were the ones with enough profit potential to cover our huge overhead, which, in our case, pretty much meant "more VeggieTales."

"I have an idea for a children's book."

"Does it have Bob and Larry on the cover?"

"No—it's a new idea."

"Sorry—too risky."

The only thing that was guaranteed to cover our overhead was more VeggieTales, so all other opportunities fell by the wayside. The thing that was supposed to enable me to pursue all sorts of new ideas ultimately sealed me into a tight little box. By the late-1990s, the world was full of great design studios, sound studios, and animation studios all excited to pitch in on great projects. What the world was missing was the stories themselves, which is what I did best. Real impact today comes from building great relationships, not huge organizations. More overhead equals less flexibility to pursue unexpected opportunities. (Boy, do I wish I'd learned that one sooner.) Smaller—and smarter—is better.

Thing I Learned #6: If I had it to do all over again, I would let my business model determine my pay scales. This is a tricky one. We produced our first eight videos with average production salaries in the mid-$30,000s. Our team was happy, though not highly paid. Since VeggieTales had yet to "explode," low salaries were key to our business model. But then sales exploded. As we hired more artists and got to know more about the animation industry, we realized how much Hollywood studios were paying their animators. Disney and Dreamworks were in a battle for animation talent at the time, driving the salaries for good feature film animators into the low- to mid-$100,000s. Compared to the big Hollywood studios, we were grossly underpaying. Since VeggieTales was now booming and we

could afford to pay much more, we came to believe that refraining
from doing so would be morally wrong. We needed to pay our animators "what they were worth." We doubled the average salary
in the studio at the same time we were doubling the size of the
team working on each video. As a result, the cost of each video
quadrupled. No problem, though, since VeggieTales was such a hit.
Besides, it was the "right" thing to do.

Then we attempted to launch our second series, 3-2-1
Penguins. We hired additional artists to build a dedicated team,
keeping pay scales in line with the VeggieTales team, of course. As
a result, 3-2-1 Penguins inherited the cost structure of the "hit"
series VeggieTales. And it never had a chance.

Two years later, a new executive team arrived to save the
bloated, sagging company. What did they immediately realize?
Big Idea's animation studio was just too expensive for our business model. We could cut our production costs by a third, they
estimated, by outsourcing our animation to any of a number of
competent studios in Canada. And so the ax fell, and all those
great animators lost their jobs. Some of them remarked on their
way out that they would gladly work for less money if they could
keep working on the shows they loved with the team they loved.
But it was too late. The damage had been done.

So here's a hypothetical question I wrestle with from time to
time: What if we hadn't raised salaries so high? What if we had will-
fully paid 50 percent or less of the going rate for animators in
Hollywood? Well, some of our animators would have left for higher-
paying jobs on the coast. But not all of them. And others, of course,
wouldn't have come to Big Idea in the first place. But some still
would have. We would have had to settle for the team we could pull
together that valued the work, the environment, and the mission
more than the money. We would have had to grow more slowly.

Would that have been so bad? Looking back at the wreckage of a company partly brought down by frenetic growth, I'd have to say no. A team so motivated by the work and the environment that they were willing to forgo Hollywood compensation would have been a wonderfully tight team—a team that would have been an awful lot of fun to work with.

It almost seems crazy now, but we were comparing our pay scales to those at studios producing $70 million feature films and pursuing the same caliber talent. And yet our business model was entirely based on producing thirty-minute home videos for a niche audience. What made me think we needed to compete for the same talent? A business plan? Or my ego? Did the difference in quality between an early video like *The Toy That Saved Christmas* and a later production like *Lyle, the Kindly Viking* really justify a fourfold increase in production cost? Especially since that increased cost ultimately led to the dismantling of the studio and the loss of all those jobs?

This may be a bit controversial, but I'm not so sure compensation scales are a "moral" issue, at least once you exceed the very bottom of the range. If I create a business model that works only if I pay animators half the going rate in Hollywood, and we find it impossible to hire competent animators at that rate, I know my business model is invalid. It won't work. On the other hand, if enough animators turn up willing to work for that pay scale, the business model may be valid. Turnover will undoubtedly be on the high side, as many of the better animators will move on to higher-paying work, but if we can build turnover into our business model, the business still works.

If we had stuck with our original model, there's a chance Big Idea Productions could still be producing its own animated films with its own team. That team would be a mix of deeply committed people willing to forgo extra money to keep doing the work they love and younger people using Big Idea as a great training ground before a leap to the West Coast. People give up extra money to do all sorts of things they love. Stockbrokers become third-grade teachers. Bankers open coffee shops. Advertising executives wander off to write children's books. Is it that insane to think you could build and maintain an animation studio filled with talented folks jazzed enough about the ministry impact of their work to sacrifice some extra money?

The point is, some things are more important than money. Don't give up on a great idea just because the business model doesn't support "market" pay scales. Give people the opportunity to make that decision for themselves. I sure wish I had.

Thing I Learned #7: Build a team that rows in the same direction. Jim Collins's research was pretty darn conclusive: companies that last do so largely by building their missions and values into their cultures. As I said earlier, if you don't care about customer service, the culture of Nordstrom will spit you out like a bad melon ball. Whether a pro baseball team, a church committee, or a company, a group succeeds when everyone starts on the same page. This doesn't mean everyone needs to think the same, look the same, or talk the same—that sort of conformity leads to groupthink and failure. Diversity is a wonderful thing, as long as the diversity isn't around the purpose and values of the group itself. I was very nervous about this at Big Idea, though, since the page I was starting on was religious. As it turned out, however, being a Christian wasn't necessarily the same as being "on mission." I hired some Christians who didn't fit and some non-Christians who did. The key was that each employee—from the receptionist to the president—was excited about Big Idea's mission and the Christian values we promoted. And it mattered a lot.

My vagueness about Big Idea's true mission and values led to a profoundly confused, dysfunctional workplace. By the time I had figured out the problem, it was too late to do much about it. Even my executive team lacked true understanding of my purpose for Big Idea, as an offsite meeting one day profoundly illustrated.

We had been quarreling about "target audiences" and marketing strategies for weeks. Finally, in frustration, my vice president of human resources brought in an outside consultant to lead the group in some "team building" exercises. Near the end of the day, I stood at the front of the room and tried to explain, as clearly and unflinchingly as I could, my motives for founding Big Idea. "I am a Christian," I said, "and I believe the Bible exclusively holds the truth about our standing before God and the path to restore our relationships with him. I want to share that truth with our culture. That is, at the end of the day, what Big Idea is about."

Most of my executives nodded along appreciatively. Then my president, the ex–Jack Welch fellow who had, by now, been running Big Idea for almost two years, spoke up: "If that's what this is about, I need to opt out."

The room went deathly silent. I felt like a complete idiot. The man I had hired to help me accomplish my mission lacked my motivation entirely. I was mortified to realize that my failure to get to know him before—or after—offering him the most important job in the company had greatly contributed to the organizational mess my ministry had become.

As I build new teams in the future, I will not pursue uniformity in thought process, giftedness, race, or specific religious denomination. In fact, I will pursue diversity in these areas with a vengeance. But I will make sure that each person walking in the door of any organization I lead is a huge fan of our core goals and values. It will make all the difference in the world.

21

Dreams, Part II

I've blabbered on for hours now about Bible college puppet teams and MTV and polygons and pay scales. I hope you're still with me, because it's time for me to ask you one simple question again: Have you ever had a dream?

Boy, I sure have. I wanted God to use me to make a difference in the world. I wanted somehow to single-handedly offset all the lousy messages immature rock stars were packing into their music videos on MTV. My dreams got a bit more specific as I got going, of course. I wanted to make movies and TV shows filled with biblical truth. I wanted to build a theme park. I wanted to create the next Disney. Be the next Disney. And my dreams were all going swimmingly for a while. Everyone loved the shows. Letters poured in from around the world, telling stories of the impact we were having. Kids conquering their fears. Dads deciding Christianity wasn't that "dorky" after all and returning to church with their families for the first time in years. Whole families coming to Christ. All because of VeggieTales.

Inside Big Idea, however, things were not so rosy. My life had become so unpleasant that my Christian background suggested one of two scenarios must be true: (1) I was doing something horribly wrong, or (2) I was doing something horribly right, and, as a result, was coming under withering spiritual attack. My pride insisted it must be the latter, but deep inside I wondered if that were the case. Time and time again I sat down to journal, and invariably I began by writing, "What am I doing wrong?"

And then, finally, it was all over. Finished.

After the bankruptcy sale, Classic Media set up a new company called "Big Idea, Inc." to continue the production of VeggieTales under the direction of Terry Pefanis, the finance executive who had, ironically, tried to buy Big Idea Productions on behalf of Gaylord Entertainment six years earlier. I had brought Terry to Big Idea as a last-ditch effort to avoid bankruptcy after parting company with my second president and CFO in early 2003. For whatever reason, Classic Media decided the "new" Big Idea would be located in Franklin, Tennessee, not far from Terry's home. Both of my positions—chief executive officer and chief creative officer—were eliminated. Classic's executives asked me to continue providing voices for my characters and to write one script per year under the direction of the new company's managers. Lacking any other clear direction from God at that point, and in need of income, I agreed to a two-year creative services contract. I was now a freelance writer for the characters I had created.

God did not kill Big Idea. I never for a second blamed God for the collapse of my dream. I dusted the body for fingerprints, and they were all mine. What I wrestled with, instead, was the fact that God could have saved Big Idea Productions. He could have stepped in, erased my mistakes, and kept Bob and Larry in my hands for the sake of the kingdom. I mean, he's God, right? He can do anything. But he didn't.

He could have stepped in when *Jonah* hit theaters and

doubled our opening weekend box office. He could have done that. But he didn't.

He could have shown up when *Jonah* hit stores on DVD, doubling the sales. That wouldn't have been hard for him to do. It would have saved Big Idea. But he didn't do that either.

And finally, of course, he could have swooped into federal court in Dallas to assure the jury would see the truth in the lawsuit between Big Idea and Lyrick Studios. The case seemed painfully clear to me—it wouldn't have taken much effort. Especially for God. He could have easily done it, and it would have saved Big Idea. But he didn't.

I left the courtroom that day deeply confused. Numb. How could God have let that happen? Why hadn't he shown up? Didn't he care about the work I was doing? The families that were being blessed? How could he just stand back from something that was doing so much good and watch it fall apart?

When I was about five years old, my younger brother fell down our stairs in his walker. They were linoleum-covered stairs with metal edges, and he tumbled down the full flight, head-over-heels in his walker. Amazingly, he came through with only five stitches in his upper lip. My grandmother and my mother both saw it happen, though, which must have been absolutely terrifying. They lunged to try to stop him from falling but couldn't get there in time.

But God can always get there in time. God never arrives "too late." What confused me so deeply is that I knew he saw me fall, and I knew he had the capacity to catch me—to prevent my accident from happening. Yet he didn't. He just stood there, watching me tumble down the stairs.

What kind of God would do that? That is the question this book is ultimately trying to answer. Beyond all the business implications, beyond the interpersonal dramas and the thrill of seeing something wonderful come to life, I'm really chasing the answer to this question: What kind of God would stand back and watch a dream—a good dream, for ministry and impact—fall apart?

It's time to back up again. What we believe about God has a lot to do with how we were raised and the sort of messages we heard when we were kids. As you know by now, I grew up pretty deep in the evangelical Christian subculture. My childhood was filled with potlucks, church picnics, Bible conferences, and missions festivals. Growing up in such surroundings you bump into certain evangelical sayings that stick with you, sayings like, "Only one life, 'twill soon be past—only what's done for Christ will last." As a kid, that phrase really hit me. If the only things that mattered were the things I did for Christ, well, that's what I wanted to do. But there was another saying that stuck with me: "God can't steer a parked car." These phrases may not have been Scripture, but they sure smelled like it. Pithy little sayings like these were so frequently bandied about in my formative years that my personal theology may have been shaped as much by these bumper sticker sentiments as by the Bible itself. As a result, I entered adulthood (1) absolutely committed to spending my life doing things for Christ, and (2) determined not to be a "parked car." I had to get going. I had to get *busy*.

But busy with what?

Mine was not the sort of Christian family accustomed to "hearing from God." Growing up, I don't believe I ever heard an adult in my family or my church begin a sentence with the words "God told me . . ." That sort of talk was for charismatics. We were logical Christians. Intellectual Christians. God had given us brains, and we were supposed to use them. So rather than asking God directly, I spent a lot of time thinking about what my work for Christ might be. Missionary conferences pitched mission fields at us kids like travel agents pitching vacation packages. Watch the slides—make a commitment. But overseas missions didn't seem right for me, so I kept looking. Eventually, I found a place where my storytelling gifts seemed to line up with a need that was tugging at my heart—a need to express God's Word through popular media. And that would be my work for Christ!

That issue resolved, I got busy. I built, and built, and built. Even when I wasn't building, I was thinking about building, dreaming up the things I would build next. And in the midst of it, God showed up, blessing my efforts. *Great!* I thought, *Look at all the good I'm doing!* But I was just getting started. If I could do that much good just by making a few videos, think how much good I could do if I made movies and toys and books and TV shows and theme parks! Think how much good I could do if I built the next Disney!

And so, I got *busier*.

And the good kept piling up, along with awards and accolades for my "goodness." *God must be pleased*, I thought to myself, *because I sure am doing a lot of good now.* I hoped God was pleased, anyway, because all the work was taking a toll on me—on my health, my marriage, and the good people that had joined my chaotically expanding company.

And then, in the midst of my great goodness, everything started to go wrong. Everything. "Ah! My good work!" I screamed. I pedaled and steered furiously to keep my little car on the road—rocks looming on one side, a sheer drop-off on the other—just like in the movies. Good thing I was the *good guy*, I thought, because the good guy never goes over the cliff.

Except that I did. I fell. My dream and I fell all the way to bankruptcy court, where a gaggle of lawyers picked through the wreckage, packed up all the good parts, and mailed them to Franklin, Tennessee, leaving me alone, with nothing. Nothing but my old

Big Idea office chair, my thoughts, and the God who had watched me bounce down the stairs without raising a finger.

For a while, of course, I just lay at the bottom of the stairs and moaned. Then I started asking questions.

"Why, God?"

"Why did you let that happen, because—I mean—wow—that hurt!"

"And I was doing so much good! Didn't you notice? Didn't you see it?"

"Why?"

And then, very quietly, he started whispering to me.

To be honest, God's whispers had started about eighteen months earlier when I received an e-mail from a woman I had never met. She congratulated me on my tremendous success and complimented me on all the impact I was having. But then she closed by advising me to keep an eye on my pride. "That's a little forward," I thought to myself, "considering we've never even met."

The e-mails from the mystery woman kept coming—every month, every other month. For more than a year. "I'm glad things are going—so well for you,"—of course, they weren't, but she didn't know that—"but keep an eye on your pride."

Humph. I filed the messages away as the rantings of an uninformed fan. So God decided to turn up the volume a bit.

Prayer meetings at Big Idea were interesting affairs, because, unlike most churches, the Christians at Big Idea came from many backgrounds—Catholic, Episcopalian, Baptist, and Pentecostal, in addition to a big bunch of generic, white, suburban evangelicals like myself. We white, suburban evangelicals typically organized the prayer meetings and kicked them off with an opening prayer, which, in typical white, suburban, evangelical fashion, were usually short, polite, and pleasantly earnest—heartfelt, without expressing too much passion or expectation of divine response. Given my background, this didn't strike me as anything but typical. Until, that is, one of our Pentecostals stood to pray—an African-American woman from Chicago's southwest side. Suddenly, I was at a different meeting entirely. Words and emotions and heartfelt petitions rolled through the room, surrounding and enveloping and lifting us all about a mile closer to heaven—so close I was sure I felt God's warm breath on the back of my neck. My music major wife learned early on about the difference between singing from your nose and singing from your diaphragm. For the first time, I was learning about the difference between praying from your head and praying from your heart. The generic suburban evangelicals kept organizing the prayer meetings, but the real praying never started until the Pentecostals showed up.

But that last prayer meeting—the one right before the Lyrick trial—was different. There were only thirteen of us, huddled wearily together like the last survivors in a town under siege, and our prayers were marked more by fatigue and desperation than passion. The company had been battered by five rounds of layoffs and was now nervously considering what further horrors the lawsuit could bring. And so we prayed desperately for God to save Big Idea, to keep Big Idea going, to keep the team together. We prayed that God would give me the wisdom to preserve the company we all loved so much.

But not everyone was praying.

One of the women there that night was a good friend of my wife's and an amazing prayer warrior. But she wasn't praying—at least not audibly. She was sitting there silently, as if she wasn't quite comfortable with the tone of the evening—or something. We finished our desperate petitioning, and folks started filing out. She remained in her seat as the others left, then approached me.

"I think God has something for me to tell you," she began. I tensed up a bit, though hoping internally it was good news—perhaps a prophetic word about the court case or the amazing plan God was hatching to restore Big Idea.

"I don't think this is about God and Big Idea," she said. "I think this is about God and Phil."

My throat tightened. This wasn't the word I was looking for. She wasn't done, though.

"Before it's over," she continued, "I think you might need to say good-bye to all of us."

She turned and walked away. I couldn't breathe. Why would she say something like that? What a horrible "word from God"! Besides, it made no sense. How could this crisis not be about Big Idea? Big Idea was my dream—the work I was doing for Christ. Big Idea was so much more important than me—more important to the world, more important to God. No, this crisis had to be about Big Idea. Walking out to my car, I tried to set her statement aside and focus on the work ahead of me.

It was at this point that God apparently got tired of whispering and decided instead to speak plainly. I mentioned my great-grandfather's Bible conference in northwest Iowa. A few years before the bankruptcy, my mother had assumed leadership of the conference. My wife and I hadn't attended in years. We'd just gotten too busy. "You should come this year," my mother implored, "the speakers are going to be great." For a moment I considered it, but then I thought, *Oh, I'm going bankrupt, and that really takes it out of you. No Bible conference for me, thanks. Not right now.* So my mother went, and upon returning, handed me a tape, saying, "I think this was for you."

It was a sermon preached by an old family friend, a pastor named Richard Porter. He opened his talk by saying, "What does it mean when God gives you a dream, and he shows up in it and the dream comes to life, and then, without warning, the dream dies? What does that mean?"

He had my attention.

Rick went on to tell his story. He was, at that time, senior pastor of a large church in suburban Vancouver and had spent eighteen months spearheading an area-wide revival effort. Churches had come together, and a revival service had been staged in a large stadium. The event was a huge success. God had showed up. The Spirit moved. Thrilled to see his hard work paying off, Rick immediately began planning follow-up meetings and couldn't help but wonder if, before long, folks down in the States would start hearing rumors of "something big happening in Vancouver." The revival effort had become his life. His dream.

And then, without warning, 9/11 happened. Everyone got distracted, and the whole thing just died. Dead. Rick was so emotionally and physically exhausted that he couldn't get out of bed. His doctors told him to take twelve months off. His elders told him he could have nine. Day after day, he lay in bed searching for answers, finding himself saying to the God he had served his entire life, "If this is what it's like to work for you, I'm not sure I can do it anymore." After a lifetime of tireless Christian service, the emotion of seeing God bring a dream to life, only to let it die, was more than he could bear.

In the middle of that dark period, he attended his daughter's church one Sunday and listened as the young pastor spoke on the story of the Shunammite woman—a story that, for Rick, would change everything. In case you aren't familiar with the story of the Shunammite woman from 2 Kings 4, it goes something like this. (Yes, I realize most business books or autobiographies or whatever this is don't delve into deep scriptural analysis.

Especially when written by Bible college dropouts. So sue me. It's relevant.)

The Shunammite woman was a wealthy woman in Israel who would prepare a meal for the prophet Elisha whenever he passed through town. Apparently she was a good cook, for soon Elisha was visiting so frequently (here my friend Rick inserted a joke about pastors and "free meals" that I will not repeat), that she went to her husband one day and proposed they build a room on the roof for the prophet. (Which, at the time, was not an insult.) Now when Elisha passed by, he could stop in for a meal and a nap. Well, Elisha was so appreciative of her kindness that he called the woman before him and asked, "What can I do for you? What do you need?" "I don't need anything," the woman demurred. "I have a home among my people."

But Elisha's servant approached him later and said, "Sir, her husband is very old, and she has no son." Meaning, in that day, before long she would have no one to provide for her. She would be destitute. Elisha called the woman back and proclaimed, "A year from now you will hold a son."

Her response to Elisha's promise shows how deep this longing must have been. "No, my Lord," she said, "Do not lie to me." She wasn't calling Elisha a liar, of course. What she was really saying was, *Don't go there. Don't touch that. Don't play with my emotions. It has taken me years to put that dream to sleep. Don't wake it up.*

But true to Elisha's word, the next year finds her holding a baby.

Even if you have never struggled with the unfulfilled desire to have a child, you still can imagine how much she loves this baby. Not only is he her son, he's also her dream! Her future! Her promise from God! He's everything!

The boy grows and one day walks out to his father in the fields, complaining of a headache. "Go to your mother," his father says. And the young boy goes to his mother, curls up in her lap, and dies.

And there she is, holding the dream God gave her, dead in her arms.

If anyone tells you the Bible is "dry," they aren't reading it.

The woman takes her dead son up to Elisha's room and lays him on the prophet's bed. Then she takes a donkey and heads quickly for Elisha. When Elisha sees her in the distance, he calls out, "Is everything all right? Is your husband all right? Is your son all right?"

"Everything is well," she replies. She explains what has happened, though, and Elisha immediately springs into action. "Take my staff and my servant," he says, "Go and lay my staff on the boy."

But the woman refuses. "As surely as the Lord lives and you live, I will not leave you."

So Elisha returns with her. Upon arriving at the woman's home, Elisha enters the upper room alone and prays. He then lays down on the lifeless child, hand to hand, foot to foot, nose to nose. The boy sneezes and opens his eyes. Elisha brings him downstairs and hands him back to his mother.

That is the story of the Shunammite woman.

I know what you're thinking because I thought the same thing myself: *What is the point of all that? I mean, why put the poor woman through that exercise?*

The young pastor concluded his sermon by saying, "If God gives you a dream, and the dream comes to life and God shows up in it, and then the dream dies, it may be that God wants to see what is more important to you—the dream or him."

The Shunammite woman's response is clear. What does she do when her dream dies? She heads straight for the man of God. When he sees her coming and asks, "Is your husband all right? Is your son all right?" she says, "Everything is well." When he asks her to return home with his servant, she says, "As surely as the Lord lives and you live, I will not leave without you." She doesn't understand what is happening, but she is going to hang on to God no matter what.

C. S. Lewis said, "He who has God plus many things has nothing more than he who has God alone." Now, I have no problem with that statement when I think of it like this: "He who has God plus a big, shiny car has nothing more than he who has God alone." Sure. I'm fine with that. Or "He who has God plus a fancy house has nothing more than he who has God alone." No problem. But if God is *infinite*, we can't add anything to him. Nothing, added to God, can meet our needs any more than God alone. So we need to put *everything* in that blank.

"He who has God plus a wonderful, healthy marriage has nothing more than he who has God alone."

Hmm. Gee.

And the one that really got to me: "He who has God plus an amazing ministry impacting millions of lives around the world has nothing more than he who has God alone." Nothing more. As I came to the end of the tape, sitting in my car in my garage, Rick said this: "If God gives you a dream, and the dream comes to life and God shows up in it, and then the dream dies, it may be that God wants to see what is more important to you—the dream or him. And once he's seen that, you may get your dream back. Or you may not, and you may live the rest of your life without it. But that will be okay, because you'll have God."

I couldn't get out of the car. I couldn't speak. God was enough? Just God? Even without all the work—all the crazy pedaling and accomplishing? Just God?

I started thinking about Abraham. He, too, had a "dream." God had given him a promise, in fact. "From you I will bring a great nation—your descendants will be as numerous as the stars in the heavens." Whoa. Cool. But somewhere down deep, a little voice in Abraham's head was saying, "Well, that's great, God . . . but I don't even have a *son*!"

"Okay," God replied, "first I'll give you a son."

Fifteen years later, here comes Isaac. Like the Shunammite woman, we can only imagine how much Abraham loves Isaac—after all, not only is Isaac his son, he's his dream! His promise! And then one day God shows up and says, "What do you love more, your dream or me?"

Abraham replies, "Sure, God, that's easy. You!"

"Okay then—put him on the altar. Kill him."

Long pause. Abraham's stomach drops. His eyes dart frantically around the room.

"But God—he's my son. He's my dream! The promise you gave me! He's how you're going to impact the world through me! He's *everything*!"

"Put him on the altar. Kill him."

And what God learned about Abraham that day was that he would let go of *everything* before he would let go of God.

And God said, "Okay, now I can use you."

As this truth sunk in, I found myself facing a God I had never heard about in Sunday school—a God who, it appeared, wanted me to let go of my dreams.

But why? Why would God want us to let go of our dreams? Because *anything* I am unwilling to let go of is an idol, and I am in sin. The more I thought about my intense drive to build Big Idea and change the world, the more I realized I had let my "good work" become an idol that defined me. Rather than finding my identity in my relationship with God, I was finding it in my drive to do "good work."

The more I dove into Scripture, the more I realized I had been deluded. I had grown up drinking a dangerous cocktail—a mix of the gospel, the Protestant work ethic, and the American dream. My eternal value was rooted in what I could accomplish. My role here on earth was to dream up amazing things to do for God. If my dreams were selfless, God would make them all come true. My impact would be huge. The world would change. Children would rise up and call me blessed, and I would receive a hero's welcome into heaven. The most important thing, though, was to be busy. Industrious. Hardworking. A self-made man—er, Christian. The Savior I was following seemed, in hindsight, equal parts Jesus, Ben Franklin, and Henry Ford. The Christians my grandparents admired—D. L. Moody, R. G. LeTourneau, Bill Bright—were fantastically enterprising. The Rockefellers of the Christian world. Occasionally I would read about different sorts of Christians that would confuse me, like, say, Mother Teresa. Mother Teresa seemed like a great woman, but her approach struck me as highly inefficient. I mean, she was literally feeding the poor. One at a time. Didn't she see that her impact would be much greater if she developed some sort of system for feeding the poor that could be franchised around the world? She could be the Ray Kroc of world hunger! Wouldn't that be better?

And then there was Henri Nouwen. A Catholic priest with a brilliant mind, Henri was invited to teach at Harvard. (Yes, *that* Harvard.) As a teacher, could you possibly have any more impact than that? God was clearly positioning Henri for some major impact. And then in 1985, after just three years at Harvard, Henri walked away to spend the rest of his life living in a community for the disabled, devoting a significant portion of his time every day to the care and feeding of a severely disabled young man named Adam. Why? Because he was convinced that is what God wanted him to do.

When I read Henri's story for the first time, I thought he was a loon. How could he think God was calling him from his high-impact position at Harvard to a low-impact life quietly writing and caring for one handicapped man? God would never call us from greater impact to lesser impact! Impact is everything! How many kids did you invite to Sunday school? How many souls have you won? How big is your church? How many videos/records/books have you sold? How many people will be in heaven because of your efforts? Impact, man! Clearly, Henri was a loon. Mother Teresa—she was pretty good—but think what she could have done with an MBA and a business plan.

That's what I thought anyway, until I watched God stand back and allow my "world-changing good work" to fall apart. And now my friend Rick and C. S. Lewis and the Shunammite woman and Abraham were telling me that I was off track. Out to lunch. It was like a recess pile-on, and I was at the bottom. But God wasn't done yet. He was about to throw Henry Blackaby on the pile.

Henry Blackaby is a lifelong Baptist pastor and church planter who unexpectedly became a successful author in his late sixties after penning the devotional study *Experiencing God*, based on his own life experiences. My wife had enjoyed the book immensely, though I was too busy with my world-changing to pay much attention. Still, I was aware of Henry Blackaby and his book, enough so that it surprised me to see his name on the spine of another book tucked casually into a stack of books in our bedroom. It was a study of the life of Samuel. I would later learn my wife had purchased this second book—a devotional about Christian leadership—as a gift for me, then, mindful of prior failed attempts to play the role of the Holy Spirit in my life, had set it aside for a later date. And so here I was, minding my own business, sitting quietly and somewhat lackadaisically on the bench at the foot of our bed, when God decided it was time for Henry to jump on the pile.

"Hmm—didn't know Blackaby had written another book," I said.

I picked it up and opened it to week one, day one. A few paragraphs down I read these words: "If you start something and it does not seem to go well, consider carefully that God, on purpose, may not be authenticating what you told the people because it did not come from Him, but from your own head. You may have wanted to do something outstanding for God and forgot that God does not want that. He wants you to be available to Him, and more important, to be obedient to Him."

Dang. I glanced around to see if Henry was sitting in the room somewhere, chuckling at me. Over the next few weeks, I dug into Henry's study of the life of Samuel with a zeal previously reserved only for my own "big ideas."

Day four: "It is not more head knowledge we need; it is a heart relationship we must develop."

If he sounded a bit like Yoda, the analogy was fitting. My friend Dick Staub recently wrote a book called *Christian Wisdom of the Jedi Masters,* inspired by a conversation he had with a frustrated young Christian friend in Seattle. After hearing the young man describe his longing for an older Christian mentor, Dick adroitly responded, "So you're saying you long to be a Christian Jedi, but my generation failed to produce a Yoda." Yep, the young man nodded. That was it exactly.

Suddenly I felt as if I were Luke Skywalker, running through the swamps of Dagobah with a seventy-year-old Baptist church planter on my shoulders. I had found my Yoda.

Day five: "It is not what is in your heart, nor what you want to accomplish for God, nor what you want to see in your church, nor even what you want to see in your group of churches. The key is not what you want to see (your vision), but what is in God's heart and what is in His mind."

Ow. Now he was hitting close to home. My life had been all about vision. I was, after all, a visionary, chasing a long line of visionaries like Walt Disney, Henry Ford, and Steve Jobs. I had grown up in a culture where church leaders were starting to look more and more like visionary CEOs, reading books like *Built to Last* and crafting far-reaching BHAGs for their ministries. "To evangelize the world by the year 2000." That was a good one. And yet here was little Yoda Henry Blackaby, standing alone in the corner of his swamp making such radical statements as, "We have no business telling God what we want to accomplish for him or dreaming up what we want to do for him." And "The people of God are not to be a people of vision; they are to be a people of revelation."

What? That's blasphemy! Or at the very least, highly un-American! Of *course* we're supposed to be people of vision! There's that verse—Proverbs 29:18—"For lack of vision, the people perish." Ha!

I was big on that verse. I'd even been introduced with that verse. "'Where there is no revelation, people cast off restraint!' Here's Phil Vischer!" Yet Yoda Henry was ready to skewer that one with his little green light saber, quickly pointing out that when we quote Proverbs 29:18, we always quote the King James Version. Check a modern translation like the New International Version, he advised, and you'll find the verse reads, "Where there is no revelation, the people cast off restraint."

What? Why so different? Because the King James Version was completed in the sixteenth century, long before the word *vision* had become a descriptor of creative brainstorming. Think about it.

Who in the Bible had a vision? Well . . . Peter. Peter had a vision for taking the gospel to the Gentiles. What was his vision? He saw a sheet come down from heaven filled with every kind of animal, and a voice said, "Get up, kill, and eat." That was Peter's vision for taking the gospel to the Gentiles.

I know what you're saying "That's not a 'vision' like we mean today! That's more of a, well, a divine revelation!" Exactly. What we have here is a linguistic issue. Proverbs 29:18 has nothing to do with the children of God being "visionary thinkers" and everything to do with the children of God falling into chaos and sin when they ignore what God has revealed to them through his Word.

Yoda Henry was rocking my world. But I didn't seem to be alone in my delusion. Megachurches, megaministries, mega-Christian celebrities—we all seemed to be drinking the same cocktail. We were all casting our visions, emblazoning our BHAGs on banners, lapel pins and PowerPoint presentations. And quite often, as the crowds cheered, we were standing behind entirely inaccurate interpretations of one little verse in Proverbs.

"So what are you saying, Phil? That we aren't supposed to do good works? We aren't supposed to strive to help others?"

Of course we're supposed to do good works. Good works are the fruit of our faith. As the apostle Paul put it to the church at Ephesus, "We are God's workmanship, created in Christ Jesus to do good works" (Ephesians 2:10). There you go. Gas up the car! Let's get busy!

Wait a minute, Paul wasn't finished: ". . . which God prepared in advance for us to do" (Ephesians 2:10).

That second part of the verse is kind of interesting. According to Paul, God had in mind even before I was born the "good work" he wanted me to do. I don't have to dream it up, I don't have to read a hundred business books and craft a "vision paper," I don't have to try a bunch of stuff and see what works. I just have to stop and listen.

The problem with the saying "God can't steer a parked car" is that, while it's *cute*, it isn't *biblical*. When people of great faith in the Bible don't know what God wants them to do, they don't just run off and make stuff up. They wait on him.

"Wait." Wow. You can't get much more un-American than that. Now. Bigger. Faster. More. Very American. "Wait." Hmm. The word brings to mind Russians shuffling in line for toilet paper and meat. Is it any wonder young Christian kids can't wait to do something big? I've met hundreds of them, fresh from Bible college or film school or art school, eager to get busy and write that one hit Christian song or make that one hit Christian movie or start that one hit Christian ministry that will change everything. That will save the world. You know, like Noah. He *actually* got to "save the world"!

"Where's my ark? I wanna save the world too!"

Yes, Noah was given "a vision." Or more accurately, a revelation. It came with blueprints and everything. But how old was Noah when God tapped him on the shoulder and gave him something big and dramatic to do?

He was nearly five hundred. Five hundred years old.

I think we need to focus our attention a little more on what Noah did with the *first* five hundred years of his life. "Well, wait—we don't know what he did!" No, we know *exactly* what he did. Genesis 6:9 says, "Noah was a righteous man, blameless among the people of his time, and he walked with God." What did Noah do for the first five hundred years of his life? He walked with God.

"That's it?" Yes. That's it. That's it exactly. There at the bottom of my Yoda Henry Blackaby, Abraham, the Shunammite woman, C. S. Lewis, my friend Rick pile, I started to get it. The Christian life wasn't about running like a maniac; it was about walking with God. It wasn't about impact; it was about obedience. It wasn't about making stuff up; it was about listening. Noah didn't hit the ground running and get "busy," sketching out visionary ideas on his whiteboard. He didn't spend five hundred years randomly building things—whacking pieces of gopher wood together and saying, "It's kind of a . . . rowboat. And look! I made sort of a helicopter-ish thing. . . . Need one of *those*, God?"

No. Noah walked with God. He waited on God. He shared the love of God with every single person who crossed his path. He lived righteously, following God's commands. Even the little ones. *Especially* the little ones. And when God needed someone at a specific time in history to advance his will in a specific and dramatic way, he knew who to call, because he knew who was listening.

As I write this, I am growing increasingly convinced that if every one of these kids burning with passion to write that hit Christian song or make that hit Christian movie or start that hit Christian ministry to change the world would instead focus their passion on walking with God on a daily basis, the world would change. What is "walking with God?" Simple. Doing what he asks you to do each and every day. Living in active relationship with him. Filling your mind with his Word, and letting that Word penetrate every waking moment.

So why do I believe a thousand kids walking with God will have more impact on the world than one kid making a hit movie? Because the world learns about God not by watching Christian movies, but by watching *Christians*. We are God's representatives on earth—his "royal priesthood." We are his hands and feet. What I put in my movies is more or less irrelevant if it isn't coming out in my life. I realized I had become so busy trying to "save the world" with my visionary ministry that I was often too stressed and preoccupied to make eye contact with the girl bagging my groceries at the supermarket. And where does Christianity actually happen? Where does the "rubber meet the road," as it were? Up on the big screen in a movie theater? On TV? No. Across the checkout line at the grocery store, between me and a girl who makes a fraction of what I make and assumes I don't give a rip about her life. That's where it matters. And that's where, I realized, I was blowing it every day.

Week two, day four: "When God encounters His people . . . sin is exposed immediately. People cry out to God, 'Oh God, forgive me!'"

Yoda Henry struck again. In the quiet of our attic, as the remains of my company were being packed up and carted away, I realized my total preoccupation with my own dreams and ideas had rendered me virtually useless to the people around me. Useless. I was failing to demonstrate God's love. I was failing to walk with God. "Oh God, forgive me," I said, falling to my knees. On my next trip to the grocery store, I made a point to smile at the checkout clerk and ask how she was doing. I meant it too.

And then I decided it was time I learned how to wait on God. How did that go, you ask? For a while, very poorly. Unaccustomed to waiting on anything, my first thoughts after the bankruptcy involved elaborate plans to get it all back—to get back in the game. But then God buried me under that pile of spiritual giants and just left me there, unable to move. I kept going through Henry Blackaby's study of Samuel and reading the Bible more voraciously than ever before. I went through all of Paul's letters, writing down every instructive or directive statement. After the bankruptcy, I had taken a small office a couple of blocks from my house in the Chicago area, just for me. And every day I would walk to my office and spend the morning reading the Bible and praying. No agenda. No video to write, no sermon to compose, no strategy for global evangelism to craft. Just reading and praying.

This went on for weeks. At first I was anxiously expecting God to reveal the next "big thing"—the next mountain he wanted me to climb—the next life-changing story he wanted me to write. But after a few weeks stretched into a few months, I didn't care so much anymore. Eventually it struck me that I no longer felt the *need* to write *anything*. I didn't *need* to have any impact at all. Whatever needs I had were being met by the Scripture I was reading and by the life of prayer I was developing. My passion was shifting from impact to God.

It took several months, but what I was starting to feel I can only describe as a sense of "giving up"—of "dying." It actually frightened me at first, because I wasn't sure exactly *what* was dying in me. And then one day it was clear. It was my ambition. It was my will. It was my hopes, my dreams. My life.

There is a scene in C. S. Lewis's *Voyage of the Dawn Treader* involving Eustace, a boy so selfish, prideful, and greedy that he wakes up one day to find he has literally turned into a dragon. Life as a dragon proves so lonely and the dragon skin so uncomfortable that he soon longs to return to his friends, longs to be human again. In this scene, Aslan the lion leads Eustace the dragon to a pool. Eustace enters the pool and tries unsuccessfully to scratch off the aching dragon skin. Then Aslan says, "Lie down. This is going to hurt." And with a long, terrible claw, Aslan digs deep into Eustace's skin, ripping it wide open. It is the most painful thing Eustace has ever experienced, but when it is over, he stands up, a boy again. Reborn.

God could have spared me from the pain of Big Idea's collapse. He could have spared me from the consequences of my own mistakes and missteps. But he didn't. And it *wasn't* about "God and Big Idea." It was about "God and Phil." My ambition, my dreams, my misplaced sense of identity and value were dragged kicking and screaming up onto the altar. And now they were dead. Ripped apart like dragon skin.

I realized this when I heard myself say to my wife one night, "I don't want to write anything." I was ready to be done, if that's what God wanted. To just rest in him and let everything else fall away. At long last, after a lifetime of striving, God was enough. Not God and impact or God and ministry. Just God.

And then, a few weeks later, something interesting happened. I was lying in bed, pondering a spiritual truth that God had impressed upon me. *Hmm*, I thought, *I should write that down and save it for a speaking opportunity*. But then suddenly the lesson sprang to life in my head, not as a sermon, but as a story about two pigs in business suits who, though they live right next door, don't know each other's names. Within an hour the whole story was clear in my head. I walked to my office the next day and, a few hours later, had the finished text for a picture book based on a story so simple, yet capturing such a deep spiritual truth that the first time I read it to my wife, she cried. And I thought, "Oh . . . is *this* how it's going to work now?"

And the next week, another idea came. And then another, and another. And before long, I had more ideas than I knew what to do with. Some ideas so small I could lose them in the cushions of the couch and others so big they took my breath away.

But what astonished me is that each one was either derived *from* or confirmed *during* a time of waiting on God. Each one came without a hint of anxiety about what it should be, how far it should go, how many lives it should touch. If Big Idea felt like rolling a giant boulder up a hill, this new life—this "abundant life"—felt like gliding on ice.

I took a couple of my new stories to a Christian agent to see if they should become children's books. The agent suggested I spend a day with his staff at a whiteboard talking things through. The first question they asked was "Where do you want to be in five years?" I almost choked. They were asking me for my "vision" for my *new* ministry. After a long pause, I gave the only answer I could think of: "In the center of God's will." The guy at the whiteboard didn't quite know what to do with that one. I insisted that he write it down at the top of the whiteboard so that it would frame the rest of our discussion.

Like Eustace, I have a new life. It is a wonderful life marked in ever-increasing measure by love, joy, peace, patience, kindness, goodness, faithfulness, gentleness, and self-control. It is a life almost entirely free from anxiety and stress, except on the days when I let my focus shift from God to the "impact potential" of my new projects. Then I feel the dragon skin slowly creeping back up my legs. But even at those moments, I know that a half hour to an hour spent meditating on God's Word and waiting on him is all it will take to set me free again.

God doesn't love me because of what I can do for him. He just loves me—even when I've done nothing at all. "While we were still sinners, Christ died for us" (Romans 5:8). That's wild, wild stuff.

I started a new company in 2005 called Jellyfish. Why the name? Well, jellyfish are cute and sort of silly, but there's a deeper meaning. Jellyfish can't locomote. They can't choose their own course. They can go up a little, and they can go down a little, but to get anywhere laterally—to go from point A to point B—they have to trust the current. For a jellyfish, long-range planning is an act of extreme hubris. Lunacy, really. And so it is for me. I believed I could change the world, and the weight of that belief almost crushed me. But guess what—apart from God, I can do nothing. I can't get anywhere. I'm useless. Spineless. Without form. My ability to accomplish anything good is dependent on my willingness to dwell in the current of God's will. To wait on God and let him supply my form and my direction. Like a jellyfish.

Here's the deal, and this is important, so listen closely: If I am a Christian—if I have given Christ lordship of my life—where I am in five years is none of my business. Where I am in twenty years is none of my business. Where I am tomorrow is none of my business. So our plan at Jellyfish—and it's an odd one, I'll admit—is to make no long-range plans unless God gives them explicitly. No "BHAGs," no inspiring PowerPoint vision statements. Just a group of people on their knees, trusting God for guidance each day. Holding everything loosely but God himself.

This was my message as I stood to deliver the commencement address at a large Christian university just a few weeks after the bankruptcy sale. It seemed to me a good candidate for "worst commencement speech ever," but I was convinced it was what God wanted me to say. I was to stand in front of a thousand Christian graduates, eager to make their mark on the world, and tell them to give it up. To take their dreams and aspirations and let them go. Kill them. To find their peace in God alone. I was terrified—half convinced that the school president would pull me behind the curtain and chastise me for undoing four years of hard work in one twenty-minute talk. Nervously, I gave my speech, then returned to my seat on the platform, bracing for the fallout. But no one grimaced. No one yanked me behind the curtain. Instead, there was applause. And then one student near the front stood to his feet, and then another and another, until 2,500 students and family members stood together, applauding. A line of students and parents met me afterward, thanking me for the message. Several middle-aged men thanked me profusely, fighting back tears as they told stories of their own failed endeavors and the waves of self-doubt and confusion that had ensued. An older faculty member remarked that it was the first standing ovation he could remember in his long tenure at the university. The head of the business school vowed to make my talk required listening for all future business students. "You should write a book!" several said.

I was flabbergasted. I was the VeggieTales guy—the guy who makes silly Bible stories for kids—and now middle-aged businessmen were fighting back tears as they listened to my story, a story not about talking vegetables, but about me. A story not about my inspiring success, but about my failure. Within weeks, my speech was being passed around on CD and circulating on the Internet. *Christianity Today* asked for a copy for an upcoming story, then several Christian publishers called to talk about a book. "No, thank you," I said, "I write fiction for children, not nonfiction for adults." But the story kept resonating.

A few months later, I was asked to speak to a crowd of 3,500 children's pastors, so I spent a day or two expanding the commencement address to a forty-five minute talk about "dreams" and "vision." Again, the response was overwhelming, and within two months I was getting letters from as far away as England, from people wanting to tell me they had heard my talk and it had changed their lives. "And by the way," they'd say, "you should write a book."

Finally, I could take no more. "Okay, God," I said in frustration, "What are you trying to pull, here? My ministry is to kids! Through funny stories!" But God was clearly working, and, as Henry Blackaby says, one of the easiest and best ways to experience God is to identify where he is working and join him there. "But I don't know how to write a book for grown-ups!" I griped. Then I thought of a story about my father, a hot air balloon, and the mayor of Muscatine—a story that might be a good way to start a book. And I thought of the first line: "Evelyn Schauland was a fancy woman." And I thought, *Okay, that wasn't too hard— maybe I can do this.* Eighty thousand words later, you may be convinced I was wrong. But that would be okay, because God has taught me to focus not on results, but on obedience. Not on the destination, but on the journey.

So what's the point? What should you take away from my first attempt at adult nonfiction, other than, perhaps, an inkling that I should return to my day job?

Simple. First, God loves you. Not because of what you can do, or even because of what you can become if you work really, really hard. He loves you because he made you. He loves you just the way you are. He loves you even when you aren't doing anything at all. We really shouldn't attempt to do anything for God until we have learned to find our worth in him alone.

Second, when it is time to do something for God, and that time will come quickly if you're listening, don't worry about the outcome. Don't worry about "10 percent more" or "30 percent less." That's his job. Your responsibility is simply to do what he asks.

Finally, and I am very serious when I say this, beware of your dreams, for dreams make dangerous friends. We all have them— longings for a better life, a healthy child, a happy marriage, rewarding work. But dreams are, I have come to believe, misplaced longings. False lovers. Why? Because God is enough. Just God. And he isn't "enough" because he can make our dreams come true—no, you've got him confused with Santa or Merlin or Oprah. The God who created the universe is enough for us—even without our dreams. Without the better life, the healthy child, the happy marriage, the rewarding work.

God was enough for the martyrs facing lions and fire—even when the lions and the fire won. And God is enough for you. But you can't discover the truth of that statement while you're clutching at your dreams. You need to let them go. Let yourself fall. Give up. As terrifying as it sounds, you'll discover that falling feels a lot like floating. And falling into God's arms—relying solely on his power and his will for your life—that's where the fun starts. That's where you'll find the "abundant life" Jesus promised—the abundant life that doesn't look anything like evangelical overload.

The impact God has planned for us doesn't occur when we're pursuing impact. It occurs when we're pursuing God.

In 2003, my dream died. And I discovered, once all the noise had faded away, what I had been missing all along.

"As the deer pants for streams of water, so my soul pants for you, O God" (Psalm 42:1).

My soul is no longer longing for the impact I can have, nor for the megachurch I could build, nor for the mark I could make on the world. Nor for the happy wife, the healthy child, the meaningful work.

"As the deer pants for streams of water, so my soul pants for *you*, O God."

Let it go. Give it up. Let it die. Let Christ shred your dragon skin and lead you into a whole new life. Trust me. It's worth it.

22

Me and Walt

Before I get back to making silly films for children, I need to tell you one last story. I'm not quite sure how Walter Elias Disney came to be such a central figure in my life. It may be because the films produced by his studio were the only films targeting kids my age in the years I was deciding to become a filmmaker myself. It may be due to the profound impact the creativity of Disneyland had on me when I first visited at age eight. That trip from Iowa to California was the last trip my family made together. From that point forward, I traveled with my mom or with my dad. But never again with my family. So perhaps part of my fondness thereafter for all things Disney came from a deep longing for the innocence and wholeness represented in Walt's work and my first interaction with his park. The way things were before we were broken.

On top of all that, I was so quiet and detached in junior high and high school that I didn't feel I had any real identity at all. I loved what Walt was about, though—goodness, wholeness, creativity. I wanted to be good, like Walt was. I wanted to be loved, like Walt was. I wanted to be loved for being good. Like Walt was. I had no idea how deep this "Walt longing" had become until I was eating dinner one evening with my wife at our favorite Thai restaurant near Big Idea's Lombard offices. I was deeply upset by the conflict raging between myself and my second president and CFO. "They want to shut down the studio," I told my wife, "let everyone go. Send the animation work to Canada." I explained their reasoning, which, unfortunately, made a lot of sense. If I really wanted to save the company, the move was probably necessary. But I was adamantly, vehemently against it.

"Why are you so against it?" my wife finally asked.

There was the obvious answer, the loss of jobs, the disruption of people's lives. But, of course, the collapse of the company would eliminate even more jobs and disrupt even more lives. There had to be something deeper. Something fundamental. And then suddenly I knew exactly why I couldn't stomach the loss of my animation studio.

"Because if I don't have an animation studio," I responded, tears suddenly welling in my eyes, "how can I be Walt?"

It seemed ridiculous. A grown man crying in his pad thai because he can't be Walt Disney. But that is how intense this longing had become in me.

Of course, God knew that. And so, in his infinite wisdom, he went to work on that issue, too. Since I was lousy at hearing his voice directly, he again chose to speak through someone near me. Someone who *was* listening.

As I've mentioned, Big Idea was a collection of Christians from wildly diverse backgrounds and traditions. Another key Big Idea prayer warrior, the wife of an artist and another close friend of Lisa's, often received mental pictures during times of prayer. I had never interacted with her much and had certainly never confessed to her my deep "Walt longing," but one day, quite unexpectedly, she sent me an e-mail.

"I was praying this morning," she said, "and God gave me a picture for you."

Oh my. This was a new experience. She described the image.

"It was a picture of you as a little boy. You were at Disneyland, and you were looking for your father."

That was it. That was the picture.

They say God's Word is "sharper than a two-edged sword," and a picture is "worth a thousand words." Both of these statements must be true, because this simple picture from God split me right down the middle. I was undone. Since age nine I had been unsuccessfully looking for my father in one way or another—in youth group leaders, in the older men I'd hired. . . . In Walt? I loved Disney, but even while walking through his most amazing creations, even in the midst of my reckless pursuit of his legacy, I still felt lost. Like a little boy who couldn't find his dad. My life had been summed up by one picture—one image from God.

Great, I thought, *how depressing. Got anything else?* But that was all she had for me. I carried that image in my head for several months as Big Idea lumbered toward bankruptcy. Then one day another e-mail arrived.

"I was praying this morning, and God gave me another picture."

Oh boy. I wasn't sure I was ready for this.

"You're a little boy at Disneyland again."

Great. Here we go.

"But now you're on Jesus' shoulders. The two of you are walking around Disneyland, and you're having the time of your life."

End of transmission. I sat at my computer, stunned. I wanted to be thrilled. I wanted to be happy. I wanted to feel like I was on Jesus' shoulders having the time of my life. But at the time, I was still desperately clinging to my sand-castle dream, even as the surf was sweeping it out to sea. It was a pretty picture, but it didn't feel true. Because it confused me more than helped me, I temporarily filed this second picture away. Maybe someday it would be true—somehow. I hadn't really ever felt any closer to Jesus than I had felt to my own mother and father, so this "time of my life at Disneyland" scenario seemed little more than a pipe dream. *Nice try,* I thought. *Better luck next time.* The "lost boy" still rang truer than "happy Jesus kid."

Then I bumped into my friend Rick's sermon. And the Shunammite woman. And Abraham. And Henry Blackaby. I started trusting God more and my dreams less. I realized that I wasn't the sum of my achievements. I realized God had let my dream die, not because he didn't love me, but rather because he loved me so much—because I was actually more important to him than any "good work" I could possibly accomplish. I summed up everything I'd learned in a commencement address, and I felt a new wholeness settling around me. I had died, it seemed, and then come back to life. Or, perhaps, come to life for the very first time.

A year later I was invited again to speak in the Los Angeles area, and I knew there was something else I needed to do while I was there. My talk wasn't until the afternoon, but I booked a 6:00 a.m. flight out of O'Hare that had me, by 10:00 a.m. Pacific time, at the front gates of Disneyland. It was time to make my peace with Walt.

For the next two hours I walked the park, looking at Walt's handiwork and the smiles on the faces of his "guests." The only ride I rode was The Pirates of the Caribbean, because it was the ride that had ignited my love affair with all things Disney in the first place. I passed a young boy, maybe five years old, sobbing in his stroller as his mother berated him for some unknown offense. *Oh no,* my heart cried out, *not at Disneyland. Please don't yell at him here.*

I had lunch by Tom Sawyer Island, then headed to the place I knew would be the end of my journey—the very center of the park "hub" in front of the castle where stands the bronze statue of Walt and Mickey created by fabled Disney sculptor Blaine Gibson. Now an official "Disney legend," Gibson is the man responsible for every American president in The Hall of Presidents and most of the pirates in The Pirates of the Caribbean. He had come out of retirement in the mid-1990s to execute this tribute to his longtime boss and friend, overseeing the casting of the two full-size copies that now reside at the center of Disneyland and its sister park in Orlando, surrounded in each location by a circle of park benches. For Disneyphiles, this spot in Disneyland is the "Holy of Holies." I took a seat on one of the benches, just in front and to the right of Walt and the mouse that had made him famous. Then I thought.

I thought about the prior fourteen years of my life—my breathless pursuit of—of something. Impact? Creativity? Legacy? Identity? I wasn't exactly sure. I thought about Chris Olsen helping me drywall that very first storefront office on Foster Avenue. I thought about Robert Ellis animating through the night in his parka. I thought about artists like Tom Danen, Ron Smith, Dan Lopez, and Joe Sapulich, who had blown me away with their skill and dedication. I thought about staff meetings with Krispy Kreme donuts and orange juice—me up in front energizing the crowd, making them feel like they were part of something big. Something special. I thought about Bill Haljun's pants, his warm smile, and his open door. I thought about the kids who lined up at bookstores for pictures with Bob and Larry. The half-million people who turned out at premier parties for one of our videos in 2000. I thought about Marie, the sixty-five-year-old African-American woman who worked our reception desk—the woman who, on the day I had to clean out my office, had looked deep into my eyes and said, "God is about to explode in your life." I smiled as I realized how right she had been. I thought about how things had ended—angry words with men I admired. The laying off of good friends. Bill Haljun. Ron Smith. Robert Ellis standing before me, tears falling onto his raggedy, overworn Big Idea third anniversary sweatshirt. "But this is what I do," he said to me, "I bounce veggies."

I looked up at Walt. He seemed so happy—so calm. Like everything had been a breeze. A walk in the park. Then something caught my attention. It was a woman and her adolescent daughter, camera in hand, walking toward me with big smiles.

Uh oh, I thought, *I've been spotted*. It happens a lot. Fans will spot me somewhere and ask for a picture or an autograph. I've gotten used to it in the years since I first put myself at the front of a VeggieTales video. Some want to tell me stories or introduce me to their kids. Others simply want to say "thanks." Watching the smiling mother and daughter approach, I quickly switched into "gracious fan reception mode" and smiled back. I was, after all, the creator of VeggieTales. It was part of my job.

"Excuse me," the woman said, "would you take a picture of us? With Walt?"

I almost choked. They weren't there for me. They didn't know me from Adam. I was just a stranger on a bench—a stranger who could take a picture of them with their real hero—Walt Disney. I cheerfully obliged, snapping their picture as they stood beaming in front of the bronze likeness of the man who had inspired them.

"Thank you so much!" they said, and hurried away. Chuckling at the irony, I turned back to continue my thinking—only to find someone else sitting in my spot. I scanned the circle of benches. Not a single open space. I couldn't help but smile as I looked up at Walt.

"Well, I guess it's time to go," I said with a chuckle, then turned and headed toward the front gate.

Walt would be Walt, and I would not. Not even "the *next* Walt" or "the *Christian* Walt."

And that was, for the first time in my life, fine with me.

Phil. That's who I was. But who is Phil? I mean, *exactly*? What does he do? How far will he go? Where will he be in five years? Ten years? Twenty?

That, of course, is none of my business.

As I strode down Main Street, heading for the parking lot and my new life beyond, it didn't really feel like I was walking at all. It felt like I was riding—on someone's shoulders.

And I was having the time of my life.

Irony

On August 5, 2005, almost two years after the bankruptcy and in the midst of the writing of this book, a federal appeals court overturned the verdict in the Lyrick lawsuit. That's right, overturned it. Threw it out.

I couldn't stop laughing.

The court decision that had pulled my characters, my company, and my dreams from my arms had been overturned. Did it change anything for me and Lisa or Big Idea's four other shareholders? Of course not. The bankruptcy sale had taken place, the assets had been sold to cover the debt. None of that could be reversed. But it was good for Big Idea's creditors, who would no longer have to split the proceeds of the sale with Lyrick Studios' new parent company. And it was good for Big Idea's fans and former employees, who could rest easier knowing the company they loved so much had been cleared of any moral or ethical wrongdoing. So that felt good.

But mostly, I just laughed. I laughed at the ease with which the appeals court judges had seen through Lyrick's arguments. Back in Dallas I had prayed for divine intervention to make sure the judge and jury would see the truth. In hindsight, it may have taken divine intervention to *prevent* them from seeing the truth, as painfully obvious as the case appeared to the appeals court judges. Had God actually shown up to make sure we *lost*? To force me to put down the weight I had hefted, Prometheus-like, for so long? Had God walked into a Dallas courtroom and blinded the jurors and judge to save me from myself? To restore me to the life he intended and put me in a position to, among other things, share all this with you?

"Are *you* responsible for this?" I asked, looking to heaven and still laughing at the news. I'm not sure I heard his answer—but I'm pretty sure I saw him wink.

Oh, man. What a trip.

Learn more about Phil and his new creative shop Jellyfish at **philvischer.com**

While you are there, type in this code: **philbook** to read more of Phil's story in an additional unpublished chapter of his book!

Hope to see you there!